THE AUTHOR AND THE BOOK

Dr. Arnold A. Hutschnecker was graduated in 1925 from Friedrich Wilhelm University, Berlin, and has practiced internal medicine in New York since 1936. He is a member of the Medical Society of New York, and four other leading medical and psychiatric societies.

In his over thirty years experience as a doctor, he has allied himself with every aspect of modern preventive medicine. Dr. Hutschnecker believes firmly that the mind and the body are one. In his observation of the sick and the bewildered going to and from his office, he saw a clear need for an authoritative guide for people—to help allay the daily anxieties and stresses that cause serious illness.

To the question of what he calls "the enigma of health"—the ability to meet life confidently and successfully—here is his answer—THE WILL TO LIVE.

Its popularity with doctors and laymen created a demand for nine printings, and it has been translated into German, French, Italian, Dutch and Spanish. Millions read a condensed version of THE WILL TO LIVE in the *Reader's Digest,* and its foreign editions. Dr. Hutschnecker is also the author of LOVE AND HATE IN HUMAN NATURE.

THE WILL TO LIVE

by

Arnold A. Hutschnecker, M.D.

Perfect Health Through Emotional Stability Is This Book's Goal . . .

IF YOU WANT IT, IT *WILL* BE YOURS!

Here, Dr. Hutschnecker shows you how to avoid illness by understanding the emotional disturbances that produce them. *The Will to Live* reveals an astonishingly simple and effective plan for healthier, more secure living. This new, revised edition brings you the author's professional opinion of tranquilizers . . . and what they can do for you.

From the first part, *To Live Or Not To Live,* you become aware of the "hidden" aspects of health that greatly affect your well-being. Dramatic case histories help answer the vital question, "What *is* health and what emotional attitudes are necessary to maintain it?"

After proving how your physical well-being depends on your emotional health, you are introduced to the force of the death wish. You will learn to harness the devastating power of this destructive drive

WHY WE HAD TO
REVISE AND ENLARGE THIS
UNUSUAL BOOK

The unprecedented popularity of *The Will To Live* made another edition imperative. We took the opportunity however, of enlarging and revising this new edition to bring you the new medical developments, to tell you even more about your mind-body health.

We introduced information on tranquilizers to show how they help you . . . added a new chapter to the discussion of psychosomatics, and summaries that give you at a glance the gist of each fascinating chapter.

It is a privilege to publish this improved, expanded version of a most important and helpful book.

The Publishers

—and use it creatively. You will discover why two people faced with the same problem may take completely opposite paths . . . and which road is best for *you*.

You will be intrigued as Dr. Hutschnecker proves that "Love is as healing as potent drugs."

At this point in the book, Dr. Hutschnecker shows you warning signals of emotional disorder . . . and how you can avoid the pitfalls they may reveal. The author-physician guides you in the analyses of *your* individual problems. With the aid of *The Will to Live,* you will be able to alter your emotional response to crises—and avoid serious or fatal illness that may occur.

All of Dr. Hutschnecker's views and instructions are documented by informative case histories—from the doctor's practice and the experience of other top men in the field. Summations at the end of each chapter review every one of his powerful concepts.

The complete program for physical and mental health *is at hand*. Grasp it, and you will be capable of overcoming the stress of everyday living *and* be able to meet the demands of any crisis.

Also by Dr. Arnold A. Hutschnecker

LOVE AND HATE IN HUMAN NATURE

Arnold A. Hutschnecker, M.D.

THE

WILL TO LIVE

NEW REVISED EDITION

PRENTICE-HALL, INC.

Englewood Cliffs, N.J.

LIBRARY OF CONGRESS CATALOG CARD No. 58–9389

First printing . . . . *April, 1958*
Second printing . . . . *January, 1960*
Third printing . . . . *November, 1960*

PRINTED IN THE UNITED STATES OF AMERICA

95971–T

To
the memory of
MY MOTHER

Acknowledgments

The Will to Live has had a somewhat unusual history. As a first book of an unknown author it has seen nine printings, two large paper-bound editions, translation into almost all major European languages (French, German, Italian, Spanish, Dutch), publication in Great Britain, condensation in the domestic and all foreign editions of *Reader's Digest,* and now this completely revised new edition by a new publisher. Approval by the medical profession, psychologists, the clergy and scores of people everywhere and in all walks of life is most gratifying to the author.

Our often fallacious knowledge of anguish and pain, our own and that of people one as a doctor sees professionally, convinced me a long time ago that the sharply drawn orthodox lines of medical thought are in dire need of revision if our first criterion of science, the search for truth, is to remain a principal objective. Mind and Body are one. Their dynamic interaction can be understood if we are willing to approach psychological principles with the same objectivity that we have learned to apply to physiological processes.

Psychosomatic medicine deals with that interrelationship in accordance with scientific standards.

The growing literature on this subject opens immense new vistas in the understanding and treatment of physical illness and also of wider concepts of healthier and happier ways of living.

The gains must become not merely another specialty, but

must be an integrated part of all medicine, for the benefit of the individual and of mankind as a whole.

I acknowledge gratefully the works of all men and women who have contributed to the new medical concept. Dr. Carl Binger was the first authority to read the original manuscript. I wish to thank him for his encouragement and criticism. I acknowledge the permission of W. W. Norton & Company to use some quotations from Dr. Binger's book, *The Doctor's Job.* I am grateful to the same publisher for allowing me to reprint some passages of Dr. Franz Alexander's book, *Psychosomatic Medicine, Its Principles and Applications.*

I wish to thank Dr. George Draper, one of the medical pioneers of the psychosomatic concept, for reading the original galley proofs and for his heartening readiness to find in this book his own scientific ideas confirmed.

Dr. Flanders Dunbar's book, *Emotions and Bodily Changes,* was a copious spring of case and reference material. I wish to thank her publisher, Columbia University Press, for allowing me to reprint some passages.

Psychosomatic Medicine, by Drs. E. Weiss and S. O. English, published by W. B. Saunders Company, was another source of valuable information. I am indebted to this publisher for permitting me to use quotations from the book.

Dr. Karl Menninger's book, *Man Against Himself* (Harcourt, Brace & Company), was inspirational and reassuring in its enlightening, forward ideas.

The limited space does not permit me to state the various other sources of facts. Because of their importance I feel obliged to name Freud's *Collected First Papers* (Hogarth Press, London, and the Institute of Psycho-Analysis), as well as *The Outline of Psychoanalysis, The Problem of Anxiety,* and *The Question of Lay Analysis,* published by W. W. Norton & Company.

I wish to give credit to the *Journal of the American Medical Association,* to Dr. Hans Selye's book, *Stress,* and to *Psychosomatic Medicine, Journal of the American Psychosomatic Society.*

I am indebted to various specialists, the late Dr. Franz Groedel, and the late Dr. Ernst Graefenberg, and Drs. Ralph Jacoby and Francis P. Corrigan for reading my manuscript and for their reassuring comments.

To Ruth Goode I am greatly indebted for her assistance, her enthusiasm and her steadfastness, with which she helped me in preparing and organizing this book.

Others who deserve credit are Jean Dalrymple, Harold H. Corbin, Lillie Schultz, and my wife, who was my first reader and critic.

Yet my greatest debt I owe to my patients. Their physical and emotional suffering made every single one a teacher. No better words were spoken to describe their contribution than those by Sir William Osler: "To study the phenomena of disease without books is to sail an uncharted sea, while to study books without patients is not to go to sea at all."

Preface

We know that a man who puts a bullet into his brain does so with the full intention of killing himself.

It is not so obvious that another man may be killing himself just as surely—even though unconsciously—by way of illness.

Daily observation of men and women in distress led me long ago to an inescapable conviction: human beings experience health or illness, a joyful life or a rejection of it, according to how well the elementary *will to live* meets the challenge of an ever-present, unconscious drive to self-destruction.

True understanding of this concept of two opposing forces in everyone has halted many a patient's drift toward disaster and has helped him to take his first steps on the road to recovery.

Everywhere in the civilized world the doctor does his best to live up to his Hippocratic oath "to help the sick." Yet, however devoted he may be in attending to his practice, he can help only the people who come to him. The wish to break through this limitation, to carry an understanding of this concept to as many people as possible, led me, inevitably, to the writing of *The Will to Live*.

A large volume of correspondence assures me that the book indeed has not only brought help to the sick, but that it has lifted the depressed spirits of many. One woman, who had lost both parents within a short time and felt she must soon follow them, volunteered the truly gratifying comment that the book clarified for her the full impact that people feel on the death of someone dear. She said the chapter "Man Dies When He Wants to Die" shook her back into a fuller acceptance of life and a sense of purpose in living.

Many who were well and wished to remain well learned how to safeguard health in an emergency. There was a businessman who wrote to say that he was sipping warm milk and rice at his desk to protect his digestion during a period of intense stress.

Some saw for the first time that they could live joyously despite lifelong frustration. There was a New England spinster, for example, who had been watching her years go by in dutiful devotion to an aging mother . . .

There were those who found the answer to perpetual fatigue, and others who freed themselves from chronic pain, when a story in these pages reached into their own experiences.

A minister expressed his wish that the book could be placed in the hands of hundreds of the clergy, so that they in turn could make it known to their parishioners. A woman who was about to leave a state mental hospital wrote that she found new hope for a future she knew was not going to be easy.

These are only a few of many who have felt inspired to reveal their own experiences. Never are we so moved to a reverence for life as when we see the quiet heroism of these average men and women.

From the first, this book aimed to present a physician's view of the interrelationship of mind and body. The part played by the emotions in physical health and illness has become considerably clearer since its original publication, and much that was only indicated before can now be stated firmly with the support of additional clinical evidence.

With this new and revised edition, *The Will to Live* is brought once more abreast of the latest advances in medicine. There is a new chapter dealing with anxiety and touching upon the hopes and subsequent doubts raised by the tranquilizer drugs. The chapters setting forth the practical application of the underlying principles have been expanded.

There are moments of crisis in the struggle for existence when all outward entanglements fall away and the essential human being stands forth clear and recognizable. At such moments there is revealed the true dignity of man, who has triumphantly lifted himself out of chaos and darkness.

In times of crisis in our lives, we feel the need to communicate. Then a simple word of understanding is more powerful than the most potent drug. And it is then that the drama of other men and women who have met and conquered the same destructive forces becomes meaningful to us, a source of new strength for our own will to live.

A. A. H.

Contents

PART I
To Live or Not to Live

*bolic Three Score and Ten—Emotion Defeats Rea-
son—How Not to Shorten Life*

PART II
The Pathways of Illness

PART IV
The Doctor as Teacher

The Will to Live

I

To Live or
Not to Live

*Two souls alas! are lodg'd
within my breast,
which struggle there for
undivided reign.*
                    GOETHE

1

Many Die a Thousand Deaths

They are afraid, and they take great care to conceal it.

A LAWYER, a man trained to deal with other people's troubles and most capable at it, sat in my office. His hand stroked the polished surface of my desk, back and forth, back and forth, with an unconscious gesture as he told me of the nightmare that went with him day by day.

"In the subway, on the way to my office in the morning, I've had the sensation that I was about to have a heart attack. Once I even rushed out of the subway and went through the streets of a strange neighborhood, looking for a doctor. When I found one I walked up and down in front of his office. I didn't want to go in. I just wanted to be near a doctor in case it happened. I had the frightening thought that the doctor might not be in, and then I remembered that his nurse would be there. She would know what to do.

"After a while I felt better and went back to the subway and on to my office."

Repeated thorough examinations showed his heart to be sound, his cardio-vascular system in good order.

"But why, Doctor? Why do I have these alarming thoughts? What's wrong with me?"

A young woman came for examination: twenty-nine, attractive, poised, intelligent, a private secretary and from all outward signs a competent one.

"It's hard to describe," she said, "this sensation in my ear, more like an annoyance than a pain. And a persistent twitching in my right arm, for about the past month. When I wake up both arms are stiff; they loosen up gradually during the morning. Lately the stiffness has been creeping into my wrists and fingers.

"Doctor, my mother has been crippled with arthritis for years."

Was there anything else?

"Not really. Only that—well, when I get out of bed in the morning I feel light-headed, almost dizzy. Sometimes it comes over me when I'm walking in the street. Twice lately I've walked so absent-mindedly that I've almost been hit by a car. It frightened me—

"But I'm afraid I'm taking too much of your time." Here was the familiar withdrawal, the realization that she had said more of what really troubled her than she had intended.

The competent private secretary had no arthritis. She had no sign or symptom of any physical disorder whatever. Yet she lived in terror of a crippling disease, even to the point of unconsciously courting death by her absent-mindedness in the city's traffic.

There was the engineer, ruddy-faced, with a bristling crew cut and an erect military posture. He was forty-two. Everything, he said, was fine—at home, on the job, in his relationships with his superior and the people with whom he worked. It was painful for him to say what he had come for, but at last he put it into words: he believed he was becoming impotent.

"I had no trouble like this overseas during the war. Perhaps it's normal, at my age?" he asked. "I suppose I should expect it—waning powers and all that?"

There was no organic cause for impotence, nor any sign of waning powers. He was a man in his vigorous prime.

A young businessman, thirty-two, vice-president in a manu-
facturing firm, opened the consultation in a businesslike manner.

"My wife thinks I ought to have a check-up. This cough has
been hanging on for four weeks. Perhaps I'm smoking too
much."

Everything about this patient fitted the pattern of the rising young executive with no doubts about himself or his future.
But he had one betraying mannerism. Repeatedly, and unknowingly, he drew his handkerchief out of his pocket and
dried the palms of his hands.

"Have you any other complaints? How are you sleeping?"

"Fine," he answered readily. Then he shifted in his chair. "To
tell the truth I'm not sleeping so well." He leaned forward.
"Doctor, I don't seem to be able to throw things off the way I
used to. I have the feeling that I'm aging, that I've passed my
peak."

Out came the handkerchief again. "Just as I'm falling asleep,
the thought of dying comes into my mind. It snaps me awake,
my heart begins to pound—and that's the end of sleep.

"But I didn't really mean to go into all that," he interrupted himself, and sat silent. Apparently he had said all he
meant to say, for the moment. We proceeded to the examination.

There was no sign of disease in this young businessman, beyond a slight bronchial catarrh that might have been the end
of a cold. He was in perfect physical condition and in the full
vigor of youth. Yet he was haunted by the thought of aging
and death.

Peace of Mind in a Pill

What is wrong with the young businessman, the brisk engineer, the capable secretary, the distinguished lawyer who
rides to his office each morning hiding his terror behind his
open newspaper? All are in perfect physical health. Yet they
are haunted by thoughts of aging, of declining powers, of crippling disease or of sudden extinction.

These troubled people, chosen at random out of a doctor's file, are only a few of many who live with a perpetual threat of some imminent disaster although they are apparently in full health and in possession of all their powers. Behind their brave façade they die a thousand deaths. They are suffering from the most common affliction of our time: anxiety.

Their symptoms vary but they are alike in two respects: they are afraid; and they take great care to conceal it. They go to the doctor with many a small ache or pain but without consciously intending to reveal their apprehension. Sometimes, in the presence of a sympathetic doctor, a sign of that inner terror escapes them. When they hear themselves daring to reveal what they have kept hidden with such great effort, they retreat and quietly close the door of the dark room they had entered by mistake.

Sometimes they confide in the doctor by indirection. A young professional woman, smart and crisp, shows a discoloration on the skin of her leg.

"A friend of mine has the ridiculous idea that anyone can pick up a venereal disease without knowing it, or that a cancer can begin with a pimple. I know it's silly but I'd like to be able to tell her how wrong she is. Some people are afraid of their own shadows!" she exclaims, and laughs charmingly. And who is this frightened friend, supposing that the friend exists at all, if not her own inner quivering self?

Anxiety may produce no obvious physical symptoms or a great variety of them. One man suffers the sensations of a heart attack and another is impotent without organic cause. Some have moist palms, ringing ears, a sense of pressure in the throat, a headache, a throbbing at the back of head and neck, or dizziness. They make unconscious gestures of restlessness, or their muscles twitch when the gestures themselves are suppressed.

A schoolteacher, unmarried, had no complaint except that she seemed to be gaining weight and wanted a sensible diet. "I'm getting to feel so huge and fat and ugly—" she began, and burst into tears.

A consulting economist suffered cold sweats, sleepless nights, blankness of mind each time he had to write a report. He was sure he would lose his clients because his reports were late, and yet he had never once failed to deliver them on time.

"Doctor, would a tranquilizer do me any good?"

News of the tranquilizers has spread like a brush fire among the anxious. In the first three years after these drugs became available, it is estimated that nearly fifty million prescriptions for them were filled. In another estimate the number of tablets consumed in the same period is eight times the population of the United States—as though every man, woman, and child down to the tiniest infant had already taken eight doses of one or another tranquilizer.

Before Serpasil, Thorazine, Miltown, Equanil, Atarax and the rest, there were, of course, sedatives of many kinds, especially the barbiturates, the sleeping pills. Now we have the tranquilizers. They are remarkable drugs. They do more for a patient in an acute state of stress than anything we have had before. But they, too, leave untouched the deeper sources of anxiety.

Why this frantic need for medicines to calm us, to give us a serenity we somehow cannot achieve when, according to the most sensitive medical tests, we are in perfect physical health? Why should we need millions upon millions of "peace of mind pills?"

Anxiety is not an invention of the twentieth century. Our ancestors made signs against the Evil Eye and went to the witch doctor for amulets and incantations against an enemy they dreaded but could not see. Anxiety is one of the many responses to the stress of living. The public speaker, the concert artist, the actor waiting in the wings for his cue, is anxious. His tensed muscles, rapid pulse, the many sensations of what we call stage fright, are part of that readiness without which he perhaps may not give a good performance.

When we are preparing for a crucial interview, anticipating a piece of news, or embarking on a venture, to be anxious is normal. When the critical moment is over, if the news is good or the venture a success we slip back from the peak of readiness to the level of comfortable daily activity. Some rest, some food or drink, a little recreation, and we are ourselves again, with perhaps a heightened sense of satisfaction because we have won a victory.

If the outcome was not good our response is more complex. We must absorb the defeat, learn from it what we can, and try again. Life is a series of such trials; to live is to struggle. We must take account of the anxiety that hampers us, as well as of our resilience in accepting both victories and defeats.

But when people are driven and haunted and perpetually mobilized for a crisis that is not there, for a danger they do not see or hear, then theirs is an anxiety that has no basis in reality. It is spectral.

This anxiety deprives us of our joy in living. It constricts our productive powers. It is a threat to health.

What Is Health?

Health is not a stable condition of soundness throughout, like a steel building on a concrete foundation. Health is a state of balance maintained by perpetual adjustments to forces from within and without. Through the years, the days, the hours both waking and sleeping, we are steadily responding to the conditions of life, to hunger and food, to cold and heat, to fatigue and rest, to anger and pleasure. We must also deal with our ambitions and our fears, with jealousy, with grief, with feelings of inferiority, with defeats as well as victories, and with the inevitable acceptance of aging. Health depends on how well the individual as a whole can maintain balance through all these changes.

The extraordinary power of a healthy individual to protect his state of health was demonstrated in a remarkable experiment. Cancer is considered a most deadly disease. Yet when live cancer tissue was implanted in human volunteers their healthy bodies responded with a "most vigorous inflammatory reaction." The invader was intensely fought off. The transplants were "promptly rejected and disappeared." This experiment was reported in October, 1956, by Dr. Cornelius Rhoads, the scientific director of the Sloan-Kettering Institute for Cancer Research.

Health is thus not a static but a fluid state, with the individual constantly seeking and battling to maintain equilibrium through a wide range of reactions, some hardly noticeable, others intense and violent.

While illness appears to us as a temporary and sometimes serious disturbance of this equilibrium, it is also a sign of the struggle to regain the wholesome state of balance. Fever, for example, is a symptom of illness. But it arises from the positive effort to fight against infection, wounds, and the manifold ills to which life exposes us. Doctors long ago expressed the belief that if they knew how to make fever they would know how to heal, and more recently fever has been artificially induced in the treatment of some diseases.

Hippocrates, the ancient father of medicine, described illness as a combination of suffering and toil. The child in fever moans and tosses. The sick man suppresses his moans as best he can but his suffering is evident, and he shifts and turns restlessly in his bed. The body suffers and toils, striving to overcome the stressful elements whatever their nature, laboring to regain the equilibrium of health.

Suffering and toil, the evidences of illness, are also what we see in these many who suffer no physical disease, the people in anxiety. We see suffering in the drawn face, in the eyes. We see the restlessness of the body, the shifting and turning in the chair, the unconscious gesture of hand to hair, to cheek, the twisting of fingers and plucking at fingernails, the moist palms and sometimes the beads of moisture on lip or forehead. Suffering and toil trace their silent record in the labored breathing, the rapid pulse, the rise in blood pressure.

And they do suffer pain of the body: headaches, muscle spasms, the thousand manifestations of a system that is not in the equilibrium of health. We cannot doubt that they are ill. Is this illness imaginary?

A study of a thousand out-patients of a leading hospital in
New York was reported in the *Journal of the American Medical
Association* in January, 1957. These patients complained of a
variety of physical symptoms, but their illnesses were not
readily diagnosed. They were given the extensive examination
of which modern medicine is capable. Only one in every six revealed actual physical illness. About five out of six, more than
eighty per cent, showed no physical illness whatever.

But the doctors did not dismiss their illness. They concluded that the mere absence of physical illness *is not health,*
and that these five patients out of six were suffering from
"emotional illness" which should be recognized in its own
right. Although their examinations revealed no physical illness,
they were nevertheless unmistakably ill.

The World Health Organization in its constitution defines
health as a state of physical, mental, and social well-being and
not merely the absence of disease or infirmity.

Is All the World Sick?

We often say, as an excuse for man's confusions and his foolish behavior, that the world is sick. But it is literally true. A
study of world health not long ago revealed that half the human race is physically ill: one and three-quarter *billions* of
people, suffering in the grip of bodily disease.

Of course that figure includes lands remote from ours where
the wonders of modern science and technology have not penetrated. In those lands, people still live their lives in near-
starvation and are swept by plagues following in the wake of
famine, flood, drought, earthquake, and other natural disasters.
If good food, good sanitation, good medical care were to reach
those lands, the tragically high toll of illness should soon decline.

Can we be sure of that? What of ourselves who live amid
these blessings? We are hardly surprised when we read in the
daily newspaper that another miraculous drug has been discovered, another infectious disease conquered, a new surgical

technique developed. Yet for all its heroic striving the science of medicine never seems to catch up in the race against illness. As bacteria are overcome, viruses arise. As tuberculosis and pneumonia decline, heart disease and cancer become the new killers. Typhoid and other fevers vanish with improved sanitation, and the World Health Organization reports that paralytic polio takes its highest tolls in regions of good sanitation; meanwhile the researchers labor and bring forth a new weapon, the Salk vaccine.

Each time a new defense is discovered against some old enemy of man, a new enemy springs up. Despite the vast sums we spend for health, the number of physically ill does not diminish, and the number of mentally ill increases. Half our hospital beds are occupied by mental patients. A psychiatrist, analyzing industrial and Army records, estimates that eighty per cent of Americans walking the streets, going about their business, are in need of psychiatric care.

More troubling still is another estimate, a conservative one, that fifty per cent of all patients passing through doctors' offices complain of symptoms for which little or no physical causes can be found. In the hospital study of a thousand patients the number was eighty per cent; five out of six were ill but showed no physical illness.

For all our streamlined machinery, our miracle drugs, our surgical skills, the doctor can find no medical help for perhaps half or more than half of the sufferers who come to him for help. By the physical means available to him he can scarcely discover what is wrong with them.

We must ask ourselves some still more puzzling questions. Why do some people become ill while others stay well? Why does one man's heart give out at fifty while another's continues to beat strongly, long past the allotted three score and ten? Why, when many suffer the same exposure, do some catch cold while others do not?

Medical science has had its ready answers in the past: susceptibility, inherited tendency, constitutional weakness, environmental factors. These and many others have been offered to explain the point of lowest resistance. All are merely different ways of saying the same thing: we don't know. For none holds up under persistent examination. They are explanations which do not explain, answers which lead only to more questions.

When clinical medicine stood on the threshold of its great century of progress, its leaders drew a line between the mental and the physical. They mapped the body of man as the physician's only proper concern. A professor in the university where I earned my degree warned his students against crossing the boundary.

"I have sliced the human brain into thousands of slides. I have stained them, I have microscoped them," he would say, and add thunderously, "and never have I found any trace of a soul!"

Scientifically, methodically, as medical knowledge grew too vast for one mind to encompass, modern medicine divided man into segments, with each segment presided over by a specialist. I remember a case reported at a medical meeting. A battery of physicians had been assigned to examine a man who had applied for an extraordinarily large life insurance policy. Everything was normal, including the electrocardiogram. A few days after the policy was issued the man dropped dead.

It is like the story told of Forain, the French painter, who became ill and was examined by half a dozen specialists. The heart specialist pronounced his heart in good shape, the lung specialist declared his lungs to be fine, the kidney specialist reported that his kidneys were functioning properly, and so on until Forain broke in: "Then, gentlemen, it seems that I am dying in perfect health!"

Not often do physicians suffer so dramatic an affront as the death of a man whom they have just pronounced perfectly well. But what of the fifty per cent or more, those in whom the doctor can find no organic cause of illness, neither by examination, X-ray, laboratory tests, nor exploratory surgery? These are a daily embarrassment to the doctor, a plague and a cross to the profession.

Some, mindful of the physically sick whom they can help,

tend to be impatient with these "imaginary" illnesses. They say with blunt honesty, "Forget it, pull yourself together, there's nothing wrong with you." Or, a little more conciliatory, they offer a sedative or a tranquilizer.

And the patient? The doctor has told him there is nothing wrong. Why, then, does he not rejoice? Why, instead, does he go from doctor to doctor, seeking recognition for his suffering, begging for understanding and help? When at last the tortured body produces an ulcer or gallstone that the X-ray can photograph, or a change in the blood chemistry, why does he greet the dire news with relief, and willingly sacrifice one organ after another to the surgeon's knife?

Some patients can exhibit at least a spastic colon, a rapid pulse, an excess of gastric acidity. Doctors call these disorders functional, as opposed to organic illness. Asked what "functional" means, the doctor explains: the organ is not diseased; it is only a nervous condition, tension, a state of stress, too much worry. He prescribes vitamins, antibiotics, diathermy, a change in diet, a vacation in Florida—and now, a tranquilizer. But he knows, and in time the patient knows to his sorrow, that relief is temporary, and that sooner or later the same patient will sit in the same or another office with the same or a new set of symptoms.

We used to call these patients hypochondriacs, hysterics, neurotics and psychoneurotics. Recently a new word has come into the layman's vocabulary. A patient will say of his headache, "It's purely psychosomatic," as once he would have said, "It's just nerves."

Mistakenly, many people still identify "psychosomatic" with "mental" and "mental" with "imaginary." For many, to call an illness psychosomatic is to regard it with moral disapproval, to stamp it as a morbid fancy, a sign of weakness. Tell a man his symptoms are psychosomatic and, unless he really understands the term, he will shamefacedly try to ignore his illness.

As one youthful bystander observed:

> *Stomach or headache, a back that's sciatic,*
> *There's no pain that can't be psychosomatic.*

Why, soon all our doctors won't recognize death.
They'll claim that the patient is holding his breath.

Although our understanding is growing, the division between body and mind still persists. Suffering man is still tossed
between Scylla and Charybdis. On the one side medicine either
rejects his illness—"Pull yourself together, man, there's nothing
wrong with you"—or sends him from specialist to specialist. On
the other side are the dreaded, the mysterious psychiatrists.
The ordinary man hugs his physical symptoms closer, frightened at the implication that he may be *mentally* ill.

But slowly, painfully, we are relearning in new ways the
Hippocratic truth: if a part is ill, the whole is ill. Illness is
more than a malfunctioning system or a diseased organ. Illness
is the outer expression of a deep and possibly dangerous struggle going on within.

We are moving toward the recognition that in illness of any
kind, from the common cold to cancer, emotional stress plays a
part. The cold germ or the malignant cell is like the shot at
Sarajevo as the cause of World War I, when all the powers of
Europe were poised to leap at each other and needed only the
excuse of an archduke's assassination.

Illness may be a group of physical symptoms with an identi-
fiable physical cause, or it may show no physical evidence that
we can trace. But it is equally, in both instances, a sign of a
struggle of the whole individual to survive.

The "will to live" is a familiar enough phrase. Intuitively we
recognize this powerful drive within us to stay alive. Doctors
bow to it when they say, in a crisis of illness, "We have done all
we can—now it is up to the patient," and summon a wife or
child or mother to the dying man's bedside to rouse him to a
last effort. Miracles of healing have been done by faith. In every
physician's experience there are extraordinary recoveries—and
heartbreaking, inexplicable failures—that cannot be accounted
for by purely biological science.

Anxiety is one of the signs that the will to live is under direct
attack.

The Half-Heard Whisper
of Anxiety

To the man or woman in the grip of anxiety the pounding heart, the quivering stomach, the throbbing head are like a half-heard whisper of alarm; the listener is aware of the fear of which it speaks, but not of its cause. Sometimes the whisper seems so frenzied, so immediate, that a man rushes out of the subway in search of a doctor. Sometimes it is so muted that a young woman walks into the path of an automobile, unaware of her real danger in her absorption with the danger she cannot quite hear or see.

Anxiety can first make us unaware that we have hurried up the stairs, and then transfix us at the top, magnifying the normal acceleration of the heart into a racing hammering tumult. Anxiety can exaggerate an ordinary gas pain into an agony like that of a bursting appendix. It makes us tremble on the verge of tears at the signal or a certain word, a certain person, a certain task. Or it holds us frozen, paralyzed, before a particular situation or decision so that we cannot act.

Anxiety sows in the mind thoughts that our life is threatened, that the plane will crash, the car skid, the train go off the rails. It keeps us awake with the fear that the alarm clock will not go off to wake us for an important engagement, and it drives us to make lists and memoranda for ourselves lest we forget an important name or date or address. Anxiety can be so intense as to make us forget our own phone number or one that we know as well as our own.

In reality any of these events that we fear can come true. An acute appendicitis, a plane or train or car wreck, a faulty alarm clock are real possibilities in anyone's life. But anxiety turns all these dire possibilities against oneself. A remote possibility, to the anxious mind, becomes a certainty.

And anxiety does disrupt our body's normal functioning. Any part may show its effects, from a skin rash to a change in blood chemistry. Heart and arteries, stomach and digestive functions may become the focus. A man may be rendered impotent and a woman frigid by anxiety.

Shall we dismiss these warnings? Shall we say they are all imaginary and try to ignore them?

Or shall we rather heed the whisper of anxiety for what it is, a signal that the will to live is threatened and in need of support?

We cannot always avoid anxiety, but we need not remain its defenseless victims. There are steps we can take. One is to tackle the fears themselves and see whether they have any basis in reality. At the onslaught of anxiety the most capable adult may be thrown backward in time, into the state of panic of a frightened child. But he can stop and remember: he is no longer a child, and helpless. He is an adult with power and judgment to act in his own behalf.

Whatever the causes of our anxious state, body and mind are meanwhile struggling to maintain the equilibrium of health and they need support in the struggle. Many of us have found our own ways to bridge a stressful hour. One walks in the park, another spends a vigorous forty minutes in the gymnasium; others turn to the healing power of books or of music or find comfort in the words of a friend or a respected counselor. Some seek spiritual solace. Some look for diversion.

Nor do we need to be heroes and manage all this by ourselves. It is not an act of weakness to accept the doctor's help, and take the sedative or sleeping pill that he prescribes. Sleep and rest restore the energies to cope with stress. The tranquilizers help to calm the frantic, driven feeling of anxiety, and to relax tensions so that one can carry on one's everyday life at less cost (although we must remember that these drugs must be used with caution, since they may also deepen a depression and thus hinder rather than support the will to live).

There are other medications the doctor can give to allay the sharpest discomforts. There are also changes he can suggest in a way of living, an alteration in diet, a trip or visit away from home.

Such measures can be looked upon as cures—which they are not—and the patient may be disappointed. But we can also see these measures as first aid to body and mind in the struggle for health in which the whole human being is involved. Then a drug that allays distress, a regime of diet or exercise, a vacation or a new use of leisure time, is a support and a spur to the will to live.

By themselves these aids of medicine will not silence altogether the troubling whispers from within. But they do enable us to face a painful dilemma. They buy us time so that we can gain some objectivity toward a troubling situation. They grant a person a respite during which he can consolidate his physical and emotional resources. With such aids we come to manage our anxiety, and turn its essential destructiveness to positive purpose in the cause of health.

For this positive purpose we need to look more closely at that destructive force, of which our anxiety warns us.

—————————— SUMMING UP——————————

Health is not merely the absence of physical illness.

❉ ❉ ❉

Emotional illness is illness in its own right.

❉ ❉ ❉

Anxiety is a whisper of danger from the unconscious; whether the danger is real or imagined, the threat to health is real.

❉ ❉ ❉

Anxiety is not only a disturber of the peace but a positive warning that we must bring order into our dealings with life.

❉ ❉ ❉

Tranquilizers and other medications buy us no more than a rest from anxiety, but we do well to use that respite in the cause of health.

❋   ❋   ❋

"A tranquil mind is a mind well ordered," said Marcus Aurelius.

2

The Legion of the Tired

For each man has within himself the power
to destroy as well as preserve himself.

THE PATIENT sat on the edge of her chair, ready to run away. "Probably I shouldn't have come at all," she said. "I've been to so many doctors. Maybe there's no help for me."

After a hesitant pause, she went on. "First I was treated by our family physician. After two years of trying, he gave up. He said he had given me 'everything in the book.' He sent me to a specialist."

Then the patient named specialist after specialist: gynecologists, cardiologists, internists, surgeons, and even a chiropractor. She had had two years of psychiatric treatment. She had undergone two operations.

Each doctor made a different diagnosis. She was told she had low blood sugar, an asthenic heart, an anemic condition. One doctor suspected cancer of the pancreas and operated on her; there was no cancer. Each time a doctor succeeded in relieving one symptom, another appeared. She had dizzy spells, palpitations, headaches, stomach pains.

I asked her what troubled her now. "I feel terribly tired,"

19

she said. "My legs are heavy. I can barely get through the day. I can't stand noise. I can't stand crowds. I have indigestion no matter what I eat. I have no energy . . ."

Of the many symptoms of which patients complain, this seems to be the one that doctors hear most often: "I have no energy." Many, like the anxious ones we have already seen, are conscious of tensions, nervousness, inner fears. But whether or not they are aware of their anxiety, most of them know that they are always tired.

These tired people often speak with envy of someone they know who seems never to be tired, who moves and talks with inexhaustible vigor. They wonder at such an abundance of energy. They are jealous of anyone who can eat and digest, who can fall asleep and arise refreshed.

"With me," they say ruefully, "I wake up more tired than when I went to bed!"

Resignedly they console themselves with the thought that fate has favored the envied one with more energy, as it grants some an elegant figure, a handsome face, or an outstanding talent. They are dashed to learn that the vigorous man does not necessarily produce more energy, but only uses it more effectively, that his energy is not dissipated but channeled.

With these weary men and women, energy seems to ooze away. It disappears like a river which vanishes underground, leaving barely a trickle on the surface. It is a law of physics that no energy is lost. Where does it go then?

A man in conflict is like a country in a state of civil war. He is battling desperately against rebellious forces within himself.

A man who commits suicide is one who has surrendered to this inner enemy, and by his own hand completes his destruction.

A mental patient has surrendered not his body but his mind to the enemy. A schizophrenic has given up reality in order to survive; this is his expression of the will to live. Dr. Karl Menninger has reported startling evidence of this from his Topeka, Kansas, clinic. He finds that psychotics as a rule enjoy the most robust health, and that they do not begin to suffer physical illness until they are on the way to regaining their mental health. As they return to reality and engage once more in the struggle of living, they become once more vulnerable to illness of the body.

A man whose illness is of the body has not given up. He may surrender organ after organ to disease, as a retreating army surrenders town after town. He may give up, step by step, his capacity for active living. He is fighting, but it is a losing battle. He turns to the physician for help, only to find too often that the physician is as helpless as himself.

Until the sick man and his physician confront the cause of the struggle as well as its damage, his sickness will not be healed.

For each man has within himself the power to destroy as well as to preserve himself.

The Destructive Drive

To understand the woman whom we have left sitting on the edge of her chair in my office, as well as the millions of sufferers like her, let us investigate this potential enemy within each one of us.

Einstein once declared, "the grand aim of all science is to cover the greatest number of empirical facts by logical deductions from the smallest number of hypotheses or axioms."

Applying this definition to medicine, we find just such a grand aim accomplished. One man, almost at the end of a long life of study, arrived at a single formula which seems to explain the great and infinitely varied array of man's symptoms of illness.

The man was Sigmund Freud; the formula, his theory of the instincts. The thesis stated in his last papers is still a subject of argument. Yet it has the potency of an all-embracing, masterkey conception. It seems to give the only single logical explanation for man's otherwise incomprehensible involvements and dilemmas.

Long before Freud, it was known that man's strongest drives are instinctual; that is, they are born within him and constitute an essential part of his nature. It is important to remember that the instincts are not conscious or reasoned, although they are guided or controlled to a degree by the conscious mind.

Scientists engaged in the study of man have named a large number of instincts. They have debated whether this or that one is actually an instinct, a product of man's environment or experience, or an instinct modified by experience.

Freud came to the conclusion that although there are an indeterminate number of instincts, we may trace all of them to a few fundamental ones.

And so he wrote: "After long doubts and vacillations we have decided to assume the existence of only *two basic instincts*, Eros and the destructive instinct."

Eros, named for the god of love, is the creative instinct. We think of love as principally bringing together man and woman for the purpose of procreation. But the instinct for the preservation of man and his species is only one aspect of the fundamental instinct of creation. Love in its all-embracing sense, as the Bible speaks of love, is the creative instinct.

This instinct is the father of all man's creative works. His devotion to his crafts and his arts, his intellectual and scientific achievements, his ceaseless struggle to advance himself and to improve his world—all these untiring efforts are further expressions of this one compelling force, the creative instinct. It is the will to live and to nurture life in all its varied flowering.

The destructive instinct is to most of us a new and difficult concept. Freud called it the death instinct, and sometimes Thanatos, after the Greek god of death. It is that smoldering belligerent force within us which aims directly and wishfully to destroy us so that we may be decomposed into an inorganic state, so that man may be returned to the dust whence he came. It is nature's instrument to end life. The ending of life, as the physiologist Rubner observes, must be a necessity since it appears everywhere in the kingdom of the living.

If we would understand the dynamics of the destructive

force, we must regard it as an active principle, checked only
by the creative force. We can observe how in nature these two
balance each other. We can also observe how, in nature as
in man, the destructive force gains momentum as the creative
powers in an individual are exhausted. This is the natural
progress of all living things toward dissolution or death.

The awareness of these two forces in the world is probably
as old as man's first thought. The Greek philosopher and physician Empedocles, more than two thousand years ago, taught
that two dynamic principles determine the phenomena of the
visible world. He called them Friendship and Strife.

Freud himself stated the parallel: "The analogy of our two
basic instincts extends from the region of animate things to
the pair of opposing forces—Attraction and Repulsion—which
rule the inorganic world.

Whether we call them attraction and repulsion, fusion and
fission, friendship and strife, love and hate, peace and war,
good and evil, the concept is the same: two forces are pitted
against each other, in the vasts of the universe, in the miniature
cosmos of the atom, and in the inner world of every man.

Freud did not formulate his theory of the instincts until he
had delved deeply into one man's inner world. First he had
made his tremendous revelation that all of us live another
life beyond our conscious life, beyond our reason and our conscious control. He had traced how the unconscious impulses,
the fears and desires hidden in that dark continent of man's
mind, actually influence and guide the conscious acts. He had
shown how reason often follows meekly after, hurrying up with
explanations and justifications—rationalizations, we have come
to call them—of acts and opinions determined upon in the unconscious sphere.

Thus it was in his later years, when genius had been mel-
lowed by wisdom and experience, that Freud came to the cul-
mination of his researches with his theory that two dynamic
principles, one creative and the other destructive, are the basic
forces from which all other instincts emanate.

Many who have followed Freud object to calling these forces

instincts, although they do not question the existence of unconscious creative and destructive powers. In this interpretation, such forces are not born in us, as instincts are, but develop
as responses to environment and experiences.

Whether we call them instincts or responses, we are aware
of these two opposing drives.

How they function in each individual, in harmony or dis-
harmony for health or sickness, for long life or early death,
for the fullness of living or the poverty of it, depends upon the
individual himself.

There are those who believe that we determine not only
our end but also the means by which we die. As Menninger
stated it: "In the end each man kills himself in his own selected
way, fast or slow, soon or late."

The Enigma of Health and Illness

How does this theory help us to understand health and illness? How does it explain the weary sufferers who drag their
pain of body and anguish of mind in vain from doctor to doctor?
Or the woman, tense, on the edge of her chair, with whom we
began this chapter?

What Freud pointed out to us, and what we are only beginning to understand, is that man turns his creative and destructive instincts not only upon the world around him *but also
upon himself.*

Let us examine this idea further. We understand how the
creative impulse is exerted upon the world around us. We see
it everywhere. From a Michelangelo painting his frescoes to a
housewife baking a good pie for her family, in whatever work
we do, if we do it with a loving purpose, we are following the
drive of the creative instinct.

The destructive drive is not always an opposing force. It
also moves hand in hand with the creative instinct. Hercules
in his cradle killed the serpent which would otherwise have
killed him. We cut down a living tree to build a house. When
we eat we destroy; that is, we convert matter from its original

form to another form, for the sake of our own survival. The act of sexual love, the universal symbol of creativity, usually has in it some element of the destructive impulse, as for example the conquest of the loved one.

We have still to answer the crucial question: How do we turn the drive to destroy against ourselves? And the further question, why does an individual seek to destroy himself?

Look in any newspaper for the account of a suicide. The deceased, it says tersely, had suffered a reversal in business, a rejection in love, a frustration in his career.

We readily understand a man or woman who seeks, at the end of a rope or through an open window, with a drug or by turning on the gas, *escape from a situation which cannot be changed or endured.*

Cannot the same be true in illness, the slow suicide?

In suicide the act of self-destruction is dramatic and final. In illness perhaps the creative force, though not strong enough to maintain health, is yet strong enough to hold back the final fatal resolution of a dilemma. It is yet strong enough to turn us again and again toward life, toward our friends for understanding, toward the doctor for help.

If we could find and remove what is crippling the creative drive, if we could restore it to its normal power, then we should be able to halt the slow suicidal trend and turn the patient back toward health.

The Inner Struggle

Let us return now to the anxious patient in my office. We need not go deeper into the physical particulars of her suffering. If we are right, and her illness is an evidence of an inner battle between her will to live and a drive to self-destruction, then we should find her in a situation which she can neither accept nor resolve. We should discover reasons why she has turned against herself, in an unconscious effort to escape from an unendurable dilemma.

She had suffered no serious illness except appendicitis, and no nervous disturbance, until her marriage at the age of twenty-two. She had continued her job after marriage.

With her marriage a sequence of troubles began. Every evening before she left her work she fell into a fit of weeping. It was only after this release that she was able to travel home. She had been married barely six months when she developed an ovarian cyst which required an operation.

Could there be a connection? She was so depressed each evening at the moment of going home that she broke down and wept. In six months she had a growth which demanded surgery.

Surgeons maintain that "medicine does not know the cause of growth." But medical literature challenges this. Kehrer, a noted German gynecologist, wrote in the mid-twenties:

"Every patient with a fibroid tumor has a history of chronic psycho-sexual disturbance. Women leading satisfactory sexual lives remain free from fibromata. . . . Furthermore, from the size of a myoma and the degree of certain other accompanying manifestations of chronic sexual hyperemia [congestion of blood] even the duration of the psycho-sexual disturbance can be judged with striking accuracy."

This was the statement of a physician who had elsewhere declared himself "free from such teachings of Freud and his school as rest on exaggerated emphasis of the sexual life." By an entirely different path, that of gynecological examination and observation, he had arrived at virtually the same conclusion.

In our patient's story, not only the growth which required surgery but the entire medical picture suggested that she had an emotional difficulty which was brought out by her marriage. Her illness had begun with marriage; until then she had been well. Obviously we needed to know more about her in relation to her home life and her husband.

Her husband was a fine man, she said, a man of good character. He was a lawyer, conscientious and punctual in the pursuit of his profession. He left home for his office at the same time each morning and returned home with the same regularity at night. Four nights a week he went out, to a club meeting or an evening at cards. Once a week they went together to a neighborhood motion picture. He was a shy man, she added.

Twice during her marriage she had become pregnant, once on the advice of a doctor, the second time by her own decision in an effort to regain her health. Those were the only periods during the fourteen years of her marriage when she had felt well. Why? Because of biological changes? Even so, are not those very biological changes the consequence of creative activity in the body, expressions of creative forces? Indeed, her well-being lasted only until the end of each pregnancy, when she had given life to a healthy child.

We talked of her sexual relationship with her husband. She was not quite sure what sexual satisfaction meant. She might have experienced it occasionally at the beginning of her pregnancies. She was certain she had not, in the years since.

One of my medical teachers used to say that the shortest definition of frigidity was "wrong partner." This may or may not be correct but it is certainly superficial. Frigidity or impotence reveals something more fundamental about the individual. Both are expressions of the destructive drive turned against the self.

Freud explained how the two basic instincts function harmoniously in the sexual act. A surplus of sexual aggressiveness will change the lover, he says, into a sexual murderer. An inhibition of the aggressive factor—through conscience or fear—will lead to shyness or impotence. When the aggressive factor is prevented from expressing itself outwardly, it turns against the self, in an unconscious effort to curb the guilty impulse. Thus sexual shyness, frigidity, and impotence are seen to be expressions of the destructive instinct, in the sense that they seek to destroy or to deny a part of the self.

As our patient's personality emerged it became clear that she was denying herself not only sexual expression but also expression in other creative directions. Although she had had a job before her marriage and for a while afterward, she had never had an interest in business as a career. She had no interest in artistic or intellectual pursuits. She did not join her

husband in his social life because she had never cared for
cards and she found groups of people exhausting. Like a child
she expected to receive but not to give. She felt no obligation
to return interest or affection to her husband or to others, nor
to exert herself in any way upon life.

As she talked about her marriage, she herself realized how
barren and unsatisfactory it was. She was a Catholic and had
not thought of divorce.

Apart from religious or moral scruples, a physician would be
oversimplifying a situation if he advised a patient to dissolve
a marriage in order to cure her ills. Divorce is not always a
solution. We take ourselves and our difficulties with us. People
divorce and marry again, and all too often they confront the
same situation in the new marriage that they fled from in the
old.

We had begun medical treatment for the patient's symptoms.
As her visits continued over the weeks and our talks proceeded,
her negative response toward her marriage became ever clearer.
She was a dutiful wife and mother, but the active, loving,
creative impulse was lacking. Though outwardly submissive
to her marriage, she was in unconscious rebellion against it,
unconscious because her religious scruples would not permit
open protest. This was her conflict: she rebelled against her
marriage while at the same time accepting the commandment
that marriage is indissoluble except by death.

She thus had only one alternative left. She must accept her
marriage. In order to survive there was no other solution except to make a positive adjustment.

She had never faced this decision. She had never realized
that she had a decision to make, until she saw her situation
clear in the light of our discussions. She thought she had accepted her marriage, since she had no thought of ending it.
But in her heart she had rejected it. In all the creative aspects
of marriage, from sexual union to social companionship, she
had remained withdrawn and negative.

This troubled soul reminded me of an experience I once had
during a hurricane in the Indian Ocean, when our ship was

slowly sucked into the low barometric center of the storm. Though this woman's progress was less obvious and less dramatic, she was just as surely being drawn toward the whirlpool of final destruction. By refusing to face the issue, she had set loose within herself a force which was destroying her happiness, her health, and might end by destroying her life. By choosing to live in indecision, by negating the creative impulse which she might have exerted in her marriage, she had unconsciously chosen to go down the path of slow suicide.

It mattered little how her situation had originally come about. She recalled that she had married with a feeling of relief that a man wanted to marry her, but with no awareness that she was entering a new relationship in which she had an active part to play. She and her husband had had to live with her parents for the first year. Whether her original decision to marry had been ill considered or immature, whether she had married out of infatuation or on the rebound or for whatever irrelevant reason, whether the crucial first year spent in the inhibiting atmosphere of her parents' home had set or developed the pattern, the result was an unhappy marriage.

The fact that her husband spent so much of his leisure time away from her could be understood as his unconscious answer to her inability to love him. The effect on her was still further discouragement, still further withdrawal. She could not share a normal social life with him. Crowds upset her; parties exhausted her. She was too sick—or too preoccupied with herself—for any enjoyment. Her illness, which began as a retreat from a life which she could not accept, now was its own reason for her further retreat from life. This is the vicious circle of illness.

Behind the Veil of Time

It is always painful to awaken from self-deception to reality. If the reality turns out to be a trap with no hope of escape, it is frightening and can lead to deep despair.

A decision we cannot make, an obstacle we cannot surmount

is pushed down below the level of consciousness where we no longer feel its pain. Time lays veil after veil over hurtful events, so that when we later come to a crisis or a point of decision the source of our difficulty is obscured from understanding and beyond the reach of conscious reason.

If a man does not even know what troubles him, how can he know that this trouble is making him sick? Confused, he exhausts himself in futile search for a way out. The harder he tries, the weaker he becomes, the wearier and the more haunted. A new depth of depression acknowledges each new attempt to break out and each consequent realization of defeat.

Each defeat has its effect both consciously and unconsciously. As his physical energy is depleted, his problem grows to monstrous proportions. Sleepless nights or nights spent tossing in fitful sleep end in still greater fatigue, deeper depression, darker hopelessness.

Though the struggle may seem to end in resignation—as with our patient who seemed to resign herself to her marriage —in the unconscious mind it continues, exerting its subtle pressures on the body. Eventually the tortured man or woman joins the throng of fellow-sufferers who crowd the waiting rooms of the famous specialists, to be treated for their asthma, their heart trouble, their colitis, gastritis, bursitis, neuritis, arthritis, and the many other varieties of *itis*.

One who is physically depleted by this inner struggle moves like a spiritless, beaten army.

But we can restore his physical strength. And we may succeed in revealing to him the clash of forces within him in which he can take a positive part.

So it was with our patient. Clinical medicine had ways to alleviate her physical and nervous symptoms. But now she knew that the approach to her illness had to be double-pronged, that treatment was aimed not only at the symptoms but at the cause itself. The physical part of her new regimen was directed at repairing the disturbance of her bodily functions. But the main strategy was to build up her strength to deal with her inner enemy, the conflict within her marriage. (For the full story of how modern medicine can rebuild strength in both body and mind to meet the real enemy, the emotional cause of illness, we must wait for a later chapter.)

The day when this patient discovered that her attitude toward her marriage was the source of her trouble was the day on which she began her upward climb. Such a revelation is, of course, not fully absorbed at once. She needed time to examine and evaluate her behavior. She had to be reassured again and again. She had to understand that she had buried her discontent because she could see no escape from it. She had to confront the only two alternatives open to her: either adjustment to the responsibilities of marriage—or slow suicide.

She made her choice. Obviously a pattern followed for fourteen years, especially one which has traced the path of least resistance, could not be reversed overnight. Between visits she was filled with self-doubt; her courage often wavered. But the truth of what she had learned about herself was compelling. She did not want to be half alive. She wanted to live and be well.

Once she could recognize her many ills as the many-headed forms of self-destruction, she knew the direction she must take to escape the specter of suffering which had haunted her for fourteen years.

Little by little, creative energies began to flow. In her duties toward her husband and her children, which before she had performed as a burden almost beyond her strength, she now saw a vista of new opportunities. She began to take pleasure in the simple tasks of making a home.

I had called her husband in, to enlist his help. We discussed what mutual interests he and his wife could develop, what ways they could find to build a better companionship. He came to see me again later.

"For the first time, we are beginning to have something like an enjoyable family life," he confessed, and added significantly, "I am losing my fear of coming home."

_____ SUMMING UP _____

Tiredness without exertion is a sign that energies are be-
ing used up in an inner struggle between self-destruction
and the will to live.

❈   ❈   ❈

Illness is an unconscious temporary surrender of the will
to live.

❈   ❈   ❈

Repeated illness is a form of slow suicide.

3

Some Live on Love

I could not have found a mightier ally.

I WAS called to see a patient occupying a small suite in a fashionable hotel. The patient, I was informed, was suffering from an advanced tuberculosis of the lungs. She was under the care of a reputable specialist. But a new symptom, a recurring pain in the abdomen, had led her friends to consult me as an internist.

A nurse ushered me into the bedroom. My patient was a young woman in her thirties, plainly emaciated. Her face seemed withered by pain, the lips livid, the light freckled skin pallid. She had thick red hair and lively, observant eyes.

She answered my questions thoughtfully but without apparent reserve. Her speech revealed intelligence and education. I gathered that within the year she had gone through a divorce, her second. Her first marriage, entered on the rebound from an earlier attachment, had lasted only a few months.

She had never been ill except for the usual children's diseases. Her parents and one sister were well. There was no tuberculosis in her family.

Her present illness had begun less than a year ago while she was living in California. The symptoms of coughing and tiredness were first diagnosed as a bronchial catarrh resulting from nicotine poisoning. When she continued to complain of her unusual fatigue, the physician attributed it to an inflammation of the genital organs and hinted that a gynecological operation might be unavoidable.

Alarmed by her rapid loss of weight, her friends insisted that she be X-rayed. The films revealed an extensive tubercular process in the right upper lung, with two cavities, signs of complete tissue destruction. A consultant was brought in who at once admitted her to a hospital for pneumothorax treatment, the injection of air into the chest to collapse and rest the diseased lungs.

At first she improved; her temperature subsided, her coughing lessened, her appetite increased. After a few months, however, the treatments became increasingly painful and also lost their efficacy. Her temperature rose once more and coughing and sputum grew worse. New X-rays showed that the infection had not been arrested, that indeed a third cavity had developed. She was advised to have an extensive operation in which several ribs would be removed to force a collapse of the infected lungs.

Now she faced a grave operation with a long convalescence to follow. In New York she had friends, or rather she had the friends of her recently divorced husband with whom she still maintained emotional ties. Out of a need to be near him and the group of people to whom she felt closest, she decided to fly East for the operation.

The New York specialist confirmed the California doctors' opinion, and after a few weeks passed without change in the patient's condition he insisted that the operation must be no longer delayed. A date was fixed.

The night after that decision was reached, the patient suffered an attack of abdominal pain which the doctor was able to control only with a narcotic drug. From then on she was more or less in constant pain. At that point I was summoned.

I found no pathological condition other than the active process in the lungs; the abdominal pain was apparently of a psychogenic or "nervous" nature. It was routine to assume that in the absence of any other evidence, the new stomach symptom must be due to anxiety about the prospective operation. At that time—before World War II—the thought that there might be connections between the emotions and an infectious disease such as tuberculosis seemed very farfetched.

Patients in a state of stress generally reject a diagnosis that their pain is the result of psychoneurosis. "Your pain is just nerves," sounds like a scolding, as though the doctor were accusing you of being a poor soldier. The patient resents not being taken seriously, and at the same time he feels himself accused of having caused a sort of false alarm.

Therefore I explained to the patient that purely physical pain is comparatively rare, and that it is fear which builds up pain into agonizing suffering.

The young woman accepted my explanation with surprising readiness, and then she burst out in a tirade against her own doctor. She declared that she had no confidence in him, that he lacked personal interest in her, that he was a cold scientist. She pleaded with me to take over her case. I told her I could not, because the rapidity and destructive character of her disease required a very experienced specialist. There were also the usual ethical reasons. I promised, however, to meet with her doctor.

I met him the following day. He showed me the chest films, including the latest series. They spoke an unmistakable language. A third cavity was visible and there were signs of a fourth one beginning. The doctor took a grave view of the situation, predicting that unless the lungs were immobilized (that is, collapsed) by surgery, the patient would probably not live six months longer. Even the operation offered her comparatively little chance.

The specialist's pessimism was not unjustified. For clinicians generally agree that if a cavity shows no evidence of closing by itself after six months it is unlikely to do so at all. Its resistance to treatment and to the natural healing processes of the body is proof of the malignancy of the disease—or of the patient's lack of recuperative powers.

Thus on my next visit I advised the patient that the operation seemed to hold the safest and probably the only promise of recovery. She received this advice quietly.

But she pleaded eloquently for time. She said she was feeling very much better. She had just begun to catch her breath. She needed yet a little time to get "mentally" ready for such a far-reaching decision—this despite the fact that she had come to New York for the express purpose of an operation, and had already allowed some weeks to go by. Finally she persuaded me that a delay of a week or two more would not matter.

The next morning her former husband called on me, bringing with him two friends. At the sick woman's request he had arranged matters with the specialist, most amicably, he assured me. Would I now take full charge of the case? Again I declined.

But the ex-husband had another question. He and his friends had observed the patient's sudden and unforeseen change for the better. One of his friends was a Columbia professor, the other a research man. Men of trained and criticial minds, they were puzzled. How did I account for the reversal against all clinical predictions? I answered truthfully that I had no clinical explanation.

We agreed that another specialist should be consulted. The patient was outwardly cooperative but it was soon evident that she was fighting a stubborn battle for delay. When the consultant was at last able to examine her, we had X-ray and other physical proof that the tide had in fact begun to turn.

Against all odds and all predictions, the hitherto precipitous course of destruction had come to a standstill. The final objective proof came when the sputum repeatedly failed to show tubercular bacilli. The operation which had been so urgent was now indefinitely postponed.

With the first warm days of spring a new problem arose. The young woman became uneasy at the prospect of a summer in

New York's humid heat. I proposed Saranac Lake. She feared a change in treatment might jeopardize her progress.

Good fortune came to our rescue. For some time I had nursed a plan for a little country clinic accentuating a more individual approach to the patient. I had found hospitals, as a rule, reserving to surgery an undue priority over the medical division. Also the impersonal atmosphere of a large institution dedicated to efficiency is depressing to many patients.

Pursuing my idea on a modest experimental basis, I succeeded in leasing a country estate large enough and suitable for my purpose. Since my tubercular patient had become non-infectious, I could take her there with about a dozen other patients for the summer season. Her former husband, who continued to feel responsible toward her, moved into a cottage nearby with his new wife and another member of the same circle of friends, so that she would not find herself entirely alone among strangers.

Some six difficult weeks went by. It was not easy to fit this rebellious and moody patient into the routine of an institution. She was constantly striving to win for herself the position of a favored child.

Then one evening, driving back from New York, I saw her walking lightly along the country road. She recognized my car and waved. Exuberant joy radiated from her face, a face amazingly transformed. Her hollow cheeks had filled out and a fine tan had smoothed away the lines of bitter resignation. She confessed that she was crazily happy.

It seemed that our patient had fallen in love again. The man was a celebrated artist who had come to the little country clinic for a convalescence. Whether it was his physical attractiveness, his fame, or his responsiveness to her—in any event, to the lonely woman living the life of an involuntary recluse he represented the fulfillment of all her longings.

I could not have found a mightier ally in our battle against illness. Three months later, when the time came to close the little clinic, our patient seemed cured, restored, filled with hope and confidence in the future.

But after a few months in New York she protested that she
was bored with her restful life. She missed the companionship
of the other patients in the clinic and their open admiration of
her as a witty and attractive woman. Most of all she missed
her new love, who had moved to California. Perhaps to make up
for lost time, or perhaps to conceal from herself the growing
suspicion that he was becoming indifferent, she plunged into
more active living. She took a part-time job. She began to go
out socially, and to stay out late at night. Her visits to my
office became increasingly irregular.

Until this time, X-rays and other tests showed consistent
healing of the lungs. Then one night of a blizzard, after an unsatisfactory evening at a concert, our young woman was unable
to find a taxi and walked home through the snow in silk san-
dals.

The next day she had the grippe. It was her first temperature
in six months. A bladder complication prompted me to take
her to the hospital. I feared a relapse of the tubercular infection, but the urologist found the infection nontubercular and
her bronchitis showed no evidence of her old disease.

Recovery, however, was slow, and again I urged her to try
Saranac. But the man who had become the keystone of her
life was in California. I warned her against Los Angeles, which
did not have the high altitude generally advised for her illness. She compromised for a point between, a sanitarium in
Colorado.

But soon she wrote to me, complaining about the sanitarium.
After several weeks she wrote again, saying that she had
coughed up blood. She sent me her new X-rays. They showed
a beginning process on the right side and a new cavity on the
left.

She continued to write, one day in despair, the next with
renewed hope. She left the sanitarium, but was undecided
what to do next. She took a cottage and engaged a nurse.

She went rapidly downhill. She contracted laryngitis, an
ominous symptom.

At last she had a visit from the man she loved. "I held out

until you came," she told him exuberantly, unaware of how shockingly emaciated she had become. He stayed with her a little while, and then he left the room.

Almost immediately the nurse called him back. When he re-entered the sickroom the patient was dead.

The Emotional Dynamics
of Illness

A closed case invites critical analysis. Usually this means a comparison of one's own findings with those of the patholo-gist, a study of the autopsy to find wherein it sustains or dis-proves one's diagnosis.

But let us make our analysis from another point of view. Let us review this case to discover, if we can, how this tragic young woman miraculously conquered her malady. Let us also try to see why, after she had regained her health and had nearly as good a chance, medically speaking, to live out her years as any one of us, she succumbed once more. Let us try to penetrate the double mystery of miracle and martyrdom.

A medical chart records any illness a patient has had in his life. Everything from whooping cough to German measles is duly registered there. But events of striking force, such as the birth or death of a love, the beginning or the end of a life's work, all of what we might now call manifestations of the creative or the destructive drive are considered too unscientific, too irrele-vant to be noted.

Yet these are the events which turn and twist a life. Indeed, the wider our experience, the more certain we become that these are the verdicts of life and death.

Let us recall my first visit to the tuberculous patient in her hotel suite. She had answered the routine questions about the beginning of her illness: the approximate time, the initial symp-toms, the first erroneous diagnosis. Then, apparently under the impact of revived emotions, she revealed something really important: she knew the very day when "it" began.

She said "it" in a half whisper, as if she were talking to herself or suffering embarrassment at voicing a deep feeling. Perhaps it seemed useless to try to convince a physician of a connection of which she was herself only half aware, only half convinced. The "day" was not the day of her divorce but the day on which she felt the full significance of her divorce, the day when her former husband married his secretary.

A few minutes later she made another of these almost involuntary revelations. She was speaking of the first X-rays and the extent of the lesions in her lungs which they revealed. She ridiculed the doctor who had treated her for nicotine poisoning. She said, with a flash of anger, that she knew all along how sick she was.

"I did not demand X-rays earlier, because I did not care," she said. And she added, with quivering lips, "Because really, I did not want to live."

Did she want to die? Or did she want to be sick, to frighten her former husband, to make him feel sorry for her, to punish him for abandoning her, like a child who fancies himself dead and his parents sorrowing?

Words are sometimes used to hide rather than to reveal. On later occasions the patient talked freely about her husband's shortcomings, about her good fortune in being free and financially secure. She protested too much, I thought, as though she were trying to convince herself of the advantage of her new life, when what she really saw before her was loneliness, emptiness of purpose, gray nothingness.

I did not then, as I do now, see an acute illness as a sort of protective act of nature, a defense against an attack which, unless the victim is forced to conserve energy, may lead to total collapse. Or as a needed period of withdrawal during which a patient may come to a decision on some deep-reaching problem or make peace with a difficult situation. Nor did I realize at that time that illness might be a cover for failure, an escape from an unendurable position, a physical expression of emotional struggle within, possibly a gesture toward suicide.

Emotions and the Tubercle Bacillus

In brief, the thought of emotional factors possessing any casual relationship to illness had no practical significance for me. Despite Thomas Mann's *Magic Mountain* or Dumas' *Camille,* despite lectures by various psychoanalysts, I would have rejected flatly any suggestion that a disease like tuberculosis could have been brought on by emotional conflict.

The intimations of poets and writers I dismissed as "interesting" but fictional and therefore incompatible with the demands of scientific reality. Psychoanalytical theories also seemed too farfetched for serious consideration. My approach differed in no respect from that of a majority of physicians: that tuberculosis is, after all, an infectious disease, that it is caused by a specific bacillus, and that it is transmitted by contact.

We have known this since 1882 when Koch presented his epochal discovery of the tubercle bacillus at a short and dramatic meeting of the Berlin Medical Society. In the last seventy years a mass of research has been accumulated on this disease, but little change has been made in the conclusions drawn by Koch from his original investigations.

Obviously, then, when my patient suddenly confounded the clinical evidence and made her about-face toward recovery, I was just as baffled as her friends. True, I had experienced miracles in medicine, and had learned to rate them somewhat higher than merely the exception to the rule. I had not, however, experienced the healing power of words. I did not suspect that the words one speaks as a release from an intolerable burden, in those rare moments when one feels one is understood, are not like the words of ordinary speech. I did not know that words of explanation and reassurance, born out of compassion, may be as healing as potent drugs.

To be sure, I had had intimations of something like this. And the idea again came to mind when I discussed the case with the specialist. But a fleeting—and unscientific—glimpse of

truth could not stand against the force of X-rays, plus the knowledge that a patient in advanced tuberculosis releases from
one and one-half million to four million bacilli every twenty-
four hours, plus the probability that she could have brought
the infection home on her shoes, or petted a dog, or inhaled
the bacilli on the street, in a department store, or riding in a
railway car.

And added to all this was the well-known fact that almost
every child or adult living in a city experiences a tubercular
infection, recognized or unrecognized, at one time or another.
And finally statistics show that some twelve per cent of the
world's population die of this universal scourge.

Why Does One Survive and Another Die?

But how did science explain this phenomenon, that one individual survives the infection with no apparent bad after-
effect, and another becomes ill and dies?

Predisposing factors have been named, a long list of them,
with environment near the top of the list. Poorly ventilated
dwellings and work shops, slums, asylums, damp and dark tene-
ments have been described as breeding places of the bacillus.
Constitutional factors have been named. Hippocrates long ago
portrayed the predisposed victim of the disease as "the smooth,
the whitish, that resembling the lentil; the reddish, the blue-
eyed, the leucophlegmatic, and that with the scapulae having
the appearance of wings."

But my patient did not have scapulae, or shoulder blades,
like wings; she was well built. And her environment had never
been dark and damp. She had grown up in sunshine, with all
the material good things in life.

Later, when I had gained more insight into the emotional
dynamics of disease, it was as if a curtain had been raised. Re-
reading the medical literature, I found much to question, much
that was contradictory, much that seemed one-sided, even superficial.

For example, a classical medical textbook says of the predisposition to tuberculosis of one sex rather than the other: "Women are perhaps somewhat more frequently attacked than men, possibly from the fact that in a more sedentary, indoor life they are more liable to infection." Could one not just as readily deduce that women should be less liable to infection because they are less exposed to it?

All authorities agree on the theory of lowered resistance. The parable of the Sower is quoted by Sir William Osler: "In a large proportion of us, the seed falls by the wayside. In others, the seed falling upon a rock or on stony ground withers away as soon as it springs up. In the last group, in which the seed falls on good ground and springs up and bears fruit a hundred-fold, are the cases in which the disease progresses and the unfortunate victim dies of tuberculosis."

The Vulnerability of Youth

But in spite of the generally accepted theory of lowered resistance, modern statistics agree that tuberculosis is more frequent during the adolescent years, and that the years between twenty and forty show the highest mortality.

Are not these our best years? Are not men and women in their prime between twenty and forty? If lowered resistance means that of the body alone, why should the disease be more often fatal during the years when the body is at its peak? May there not be factors other than purely physical ones, which act upon the body during these years?

We speak of the adolescent years as the most difficult in our lives. Parents dread them, expecting the sunny child to change overnight into a moody, difficult, unstable youth or young girl. We know these years as years of confusion and emotional restlessness, years when all the disturbances of childhood may raise their heads again. They are the years in which we must at last accept the realities of life in an adult society; no further postponement is possible.

Consider the years that immediately follow adolescence. Are not those the period of grim and relentless struggle to suc-

ceed, to make one's place in the adult world, to achieve economic security and emotional independence? Are not those
the years which often bring defeat to the less ruthless, to "the
smooth, the whitish"? Cannot defeat shatter the inner man?
Cannot defeat lower the body's resistance? It seems significant
that these are also the years of the highest suicide rate—in
men, between the ages of twenty-five and twenty-eight, and
in women between twenty and twenty-two.

Still another factor, that of environment, is supposed to play
an important role. If this is true, then the children of tubercular
parents would be greatly endangered. But the medical literature reports that infants from a tubercular milieu show no
higher mortality during their first years of life than other children. Older children living in a home where tuberculosis exists
also show the same rate of infection and mortality as children
of healthy homes, no higher. Perhaps the suggestion that these
parents take special care may adequately explain the contradiction. Or perhaps there are other reasons.

In apes and monkeys in a wild state, tuberculosis is unknown. In confinement it is the most formidable destroyer
with which these creatures must contend.

Among men, North American Indians show a proneness to
this disease more than double that of white Americans, and
Negroes in the United States are second to the Indians. The
unhygienic living conditions to which these two groups of Americans have been generally subjected are given us as the reason.
But these minority groups are also subjected to other depressing conditions, of a social and psychological rather than a
physical variety.

When the Irish emigrated in large numbers to the United
States they were better fed and had better prospects for em-
ployment and comfortable living than at home in Ireland. Yet
the death rate from tuberculosis among the Irish in New York
was 100 per cent higher than in Dublin at the same time.

The physical conditions were surely better for the Irish in
New York. But man does not live by bread alone. For many of

them the break with home ties and the demands of a new way of life were insurmountable difficulties.

Scientifically—that is, studying the physical evidence critically—we have no absolute explanation of what causes the predisposition to tuberculosis. All we have are hypotheses. We seek the answers in laboratories, concentrating on tissue, studying the serum reactions of guinea pigs, trying the same techniques on human beings. But reports of research projects often betray their disappointment at man's refusal to act like a guinea pig.

No Life Without Love

We will go back now to our suffering young woman. During the first phase of her illness she asked in detail about the technique of the operation which was so urgently recommended. She was only curious, she said, and I thought no more about it at the time. But another case threw new light on this facet.

A young woman, a fashion model, came to me with an obvious malignancy of the breast. An immediate operation was necessary, but instead of the surgeon I suggested, she chose a plastic surgeon. The night after the operation she collapsed. With blood transfusions and medication she rallied, but soon afterward she collapsed again. She had chosen the plastic surgeon in the hope that he would merely remove the tumor. Instead he had removed the entire breast.

The patient had suddenly awakened to the realization that she had been "mutilated." To her this meant that she had ceased to be a competitive female. It would be futile to attempt to evaluate her reaction objectively. The depth of this shock can be understood only from the subjective point of view of a woman.

Within a year this patient died of metastasis in the brain. Now statistics show that a patient has a good chance if breast surgery is properly performed and done in time. Perhaps in this particular case the operation was not performed with the necessary skill; possibly all axillary lymph glands were not completely removed. As a matter of fact the plastic surgeon did operate a second time after a few days.

But today we can imagine another, more significant possibility: feeling that she was no longer a desirable woman, the patient did not wish to live.

Our latter-day Camille had, I believe, the same fear. Her initial improvement from tuberculosis may have been a heroic effort to escape what she too would have considered a mutilation. She fought a delaying action against the second specialist, needing time to make enough progress so that he would not doom her to the operation. Her summer love affair gave her new confirmation that she was again a desirable woman. By finding a man who wanted her, she had achieved a victory over the husband who had rejected her. The future glowed again. New hope drowned out the clicking of time.

Sir William Osler declared: "What happens to a patient with tuberculosis depends more on what he has in his head than what he has in his chest."

Thus we can understand that when the tragic woman approached the end of her renascent happiness, there came the relapse. She had to face reality once more.

She was a quiet sufferer. Hers was not a positive, not a fighting spirit. She was at the same time rebellious and submissive. She day-dreamed vengeance, but she retreated into martyrdom. She was without direction, without inner security, without the belief in her own worthiness of love which would spur her to fight for love. Instead she surrendered not only love but life itself.

_____ SUMMING UP_____

The birth or death of a love may determine the victory of the will to live or the wish to die.

❖   ❖   ❖

Emotional stress, like physical stress, lowers resistance to disease.

*   *   *

Youth is the time of greatest physical vigor, but it is also a time of great emotional stress, when the individual first confronts the realities of life on his own.

*   *   *

Love is as healing as potent drugs.

4

Man Dies When He Wants to Die

Conscious or unconscious, we make our own choice.

LIFE holds many doubts but only one certainty, the certainty of death. This is the one certainty which all human beings share. Although animals too must die, as far as we know they cannot foresee their own death, and therefore they do not fear it. Man, however, can envision his own end. His fear of death is one of the prices he pays for the intellect which entitles him to call himself *Homo sapiens*.

The fear of death seems to be universal, at least in our culture. Most of us make our first acquaintance with death in some form quite early in life. A pet dies. An animal lies dead in the road. Or, more disturbingly, there is the dark hush which falls over the house because of a death in the family.

These experiences take deep root in childhood. They are a lightning glimpse into an awesome secret, an instant of revelation instantly cloaked again in darkness. The silent mystery with which death is fearfully shrouded for us in childhood may haunt us all our life.

When we fear death, what are we afraid of?

Do we fear the pain of dying? Physicians know that most people suffer far more pain, both physical and mental, in living than in dying. Death is characteristically serene, and the face of a dead man is peaceful.

"Calm and gentle is the death of every good person," wrote Schopenhauer. "Come, sweet death," sang Bach. And the great physician Sir William Osler testified:

"Most human beings not only die like heroes but, in my wide clinical experience, die really without pain or fear. There is as much oblivion about the last hours as about the first, and therefore men fill their minds with specters that have no reality."

Perhaps what we really fear is that life may end *before we are ready,* that we may sink into nothingness before we have made our mark. Standing in the midstream of life, full of the things we have only begun and the things we have yet to begin, do we not fear that we will be cut off before we have finished with living and doing?

If this is what we fear, then there is a single answer to banish fear: it does not happen that way.

We die only when we are ready to die. We die when we want to die. We die because unconsciously we want to die, although consciously we may believe that we have everything to live for.

If we truly wish to live, if we have the incentive to live, *if we have something to live for*—then no matter how sick we may be, if we have not exhausted the last of our physical resources, we do not die. We live *because* we want to live.

But the incentive must be one in which we inwardly, utterly believe. It is not the "everything to live for" in the eyes of the world that keeps us alive, but the something which meets our own uncompromising measure of what is worth living for.

A very old lady, one who had accomplished a pioneer work in education during her lifetime, once told about a dangerous illness she had suffered in her middle years. She lay hovering between life and death, in the twilight of half-surrender, when she overheard two of her co-workers talking just outside the open door of her hospital room.

"If we could only reach her! If we could only make her understand," one of them said passionately, "how much we need her!"

Such a message may resurrect the will to live. It is not one single factor which brings an individual close to death, nor one single factor which rescues him. But when the balance of many factors hangs undecided, one significant word may swing the weight of a complex decision. The words this woman overheard concerned her life work, for which she had made many sacrifices. In a moment of discouragement and wavering faith, the intensity of her colleague's plea reassured her and gave her courage to take up the struggle again.

Something to Live For

Doctors are aware of many "miracles" of healing, of patients snatched back to life against apparently hopeless physical odds. But they have some difficulty in finding a medical explanation for these "miracles." I had such a case in my earliest days as a physician.

One night I was called to attend a man who lay dying in an apartment across the street from my brand-new office. His regular physician, who happened to be my chief at the hospital was out of town. The patient was in his sixties, a pharmacist who enjoyed a very fine standing among the top doctors of the city.

His brother met me at the door with a frantic plea. "Doctor you must keep him alive until morning"—he pursued me breathlessly—"until we can get a marriage performed. He must not die until he has legitimatized his son!"

Then I learned that this ultra-respectable man had been living with his housekeeper for more than twenty years. But he had never had the courage to publish his transgression of the proprieties by a marriage. True, he had provided well for his son, who was even then studying at the university, preparing to enter his father's pharmacy. But without legal status, the young man could not succeed to his father's name in the business. The patient had postponed the necessary formalities until there was little hope that they could be performed at all.

I struggled through the night against a myocarditis in its last stages, until the threatening rattle of fluid in the lungs subsided. When a minister finally arrived, the dying man had gained consciousness enough to take part in the ceremony.

Then came the "miracle." My former chief met me some time later and asked, "What did you do? That fellow was a dead man! And just now he waited on me himself in his pharmacy!"

The druggist lived two years longer and saw his son graduated from the university. The old man was not in very good health, but well enough to spend a few hours almost every day watching over the business and introducing his son to the clientele, especially the distinguished medical customers. Then, peaceful and content, he died.

I was much abashed by my chief's excessive praise. Actually I was unable to claim any technique beyond those outlined in the textbooks, plus the zeal of a young doctor who cannot bear the thought of losing a patient. Now, after many such wrestling matches with death, some won and some lost, I think I can understand why that sick old man was first willing to die, and then determined to live. He had doubtless been torn for years by his inability to overcome a rigid social code. Deprived of the satisfaction of acknowledging his son, he must have suffered from a deep sense of failure.

Once the decisive step was forced on him by his brother, he found he had a new and happy task to fulfill. He had to live to participate in his son's graduation, and to give the boy a good start in the business. Obviously medicine helped to keep life in his failing body. But medicine alone could not have brought him back to life without the powerful resurrection of his will to live, by that formal act which blessed his union and gave him a son to carry on his name and his work, that promise of immortality for which most men long.

The Biological Will to Live

Each of us has a goal, conscious or unconscious. The goal may change, or become confused. Other purposes may arise which conflict with it. At such periods we may be in danger, as will be seen in later chapters.

Deep within every living thing there exists the will to live, that inborn dynamic principle whose purpose is to preserve the individual as well as the race. It is the keystone of every organic existence. So strong and passionate is this force, that man and animal alike will battle desperately when life is endangered, however starved, wretched, and deprived that life may be.

An individual who has little zest for living, whose life is plagued by anxieties, who may even wonder if it is worth struggling any longer, may be the very one who is first to jump when the house is afire, first to take to the lifeboat when the ship is sinking. The shock of sudden, real danger can shake a person out of his emotional confusions, so that he is moved only by the reflex of his primitive will to live.

Yet this biological will to live seems not enough to support us through the complexities of life in a civilized world. We need a moral and emotional force to make the struggle endurable. The will to live in civilized man is a combined biological and psychological drive. As long as we have something to live for, the will to live carries us through the moments of crisis which are inevitable in every life.

A Mission in Life

The poet Goethe expressed the belief that every extraordinary man has a mission which he is called upon to fulfill. Once he has fulfilled it, Providence no longer requires him on earth. Demons trip him up again and again until he succumbs. The composer Mozart and the painter Raphael, both of whom died

30/7/1950

Ayot Saint Lawrence, Welwyn, Herts.
Station : Welwyn Garden City, 5 miles.
Telegrams and Phone : Codicote 218.

4, Whitehall Court (116) London, S.W.1.
Telegrams : Socialist, Parl-London.
Telephone : Whitehall 3160.

From
Bernard Shaw

The will to live is wholly inex-plicable. Rationally I ought to blow out my brains; but I dont and wont. No use asking me why : I dont know.

Haydon cut his throat when his eyesight and hand failed. He lived only for painting.

Edmund Gurney did himself in because his neuralgias were unbeara-ble.

These were cases of voluntary euthanasia, quite justifiable. Cancer cases now die of morphia poisoning " to control the pain". This also is euthanasia.

But most people hold on to the last moment and die "a natural death" as I mean to do, though at 94 I ought to clear out. my bolt being shot and overshot.   G. B. S.

at thirty-six; Shakespeare and Byron, even Napoleon who pursued his destiny through a lifetime of heroic exertion without fatigue, were among the extraordinary men whose death, in Goethe's theory, came when they had accomplished the purpose designed for them.

Goethe himself was a living example of his own hypothesis that man dies when his work is finished. He began *Faust*, his masterpiece, when he was a youth of twenty-four. He wrote the last line of Part Two fifty-eight years later, in 1831. In 1832 he died, without ever seeing it in print.

George Bernard Shaw wrote on a pad on his night table, "The will to live is inexplicable. Rationally I ought to blow my brains out; but I don't and I won't. . . . Most people hold on to the last moment and die a 'natural death' as I mean to do, although at ninety-four I ought to clear out, my bolt being shot and overshot." That was the day, according to a friend, when he suffered his last accident and died of complications some weeks later.

Obviously this extraordinary man was in a struggle between his will to live and his conviction that for him there was no longer any purpose in living. Consciously he rejected the idea of ending his life, but the events that followed suggest that unconsciously this is precisely what he desired.

Philosophers and poets often express intuitively what science later confirms. We can restate Goethe's comment in modern psychological terms.

For his "extraordinary man" we may consider the ordinary man and woman, you, myself, the neighbor to whom you just now said good evening. For Goethe's "mission" we can understand the self-assigned goal of each human life. His "demons" we can translate to mean that unconscious drive to destruction which balances the will to live in each of us, Freud's destructive instinct.

Let us put it this way. From birth and through the years of struggle toward maturity, each human being aspires toward some achievement, clear or clouded, conscious or unconscious. Toward this he strives, through the entanglements of life, its success and defeats, until he reaches his mark—or until he becomes convinced that he can never reach it. Then he dies.

Exceptions leap to mind. The fulfillment of a great task does not necessarily mean the end of life. With each new eminence which a man may reach, new perspectives may beckon him to new endeavors. One man may exhaust himself with a single great effort. But another gains conviction in his purpose, and continues onward.

There are apparent exceptions at the other end of the scale, for example the pauper who lives to a ripe old age in an institution, aspiring to nothing and accomplishing nothing. Such a man, however, has resigned from the struggle to achieve, and asks nothing of life but a vegetable existence. Presumably we could all live longer if we were content with less. Many a farmer lives long and in good health, creatively busied with the succession of the seasons, measuring his aspiration to the harvesting of each year's crop. Those who drive themselves to a premature grave might well be found to be people whose goals were from the first unrealistic and unrealizable.

To Each His Own Goal

For it is within ourselves that we set these goals. We weigh ourselves in scales of our own devising. Each of us is his own judge. The world has laid its highest tributes at the feet of some men whose ambition was never satisfied, men, who still strove to achieve some greater position, some mightier power, no matter what they had already won. And by the same token, many a man or woman has lived in modest content with little that the world would hold desirable, but for them it was enough.

Most of us fall somewhere between the man with insatiable ambition and the man with little or none. But with all of us, the deciding estimate of our accomplishment is not society, nor any group of persons or set of standards outside ourselves.

Too often it is not even our critical or reasoning mind which passes judgment on us. Unless we strive toward that maturity of mind which makes these judgments conscious and reasonable, they remain unconscious, and they remain the immature judgments of childhood. To keep our goal clear and to judge it by rational standards is the task of our conscious, reasoning mind.

Conscious or unconscious, we make our own choice. No human being is spared the struggles of life, but each human being has his unique way of reacting to them. The pain of adjustment, the awareness of the world's misery and inequity, cry out in a Beethoven symphony. Throughout the ages there have been those who grieved over the bitterness of life but felt themselves helpless to improve it. Yet in each age some individuals have rebelled against what they would not endure, and have exerted themselves to change it. When the dynamic energies of the rebel have been translated into action or teaching for the benefit of others, the world has found another of its great leaders and reformers.

Whether the individual accepts life with its inexorable conditions, or rejects it, will determine his course. The individual who accepts life, whether or not he protests, strives to adapt himself to situations which he cannot avoid. He begins in infancy a long series of adjustments, and the more readily he adjusts himself the greater his capacity for living.

We must be careful not to confuse such a positive acceptance of the joys and responsibilities of living with the familiar pattern of conformity or resignation. To conform to others' standards is to surrender one's identity, and to resign oneself to the will of others is to surrender one's own will. Each of these is a death of at least part of the self. To do this knowingly is one thing. But to surrender unknowingly, and to rebel at the surrender without knowing that we rebel, is to live in perpetual inner conflict.

Each battle in this lifelong struggle of adjustment takes an individual nearer to his goal or further from it. Sooner or later in every man's life, and perhaps not once but many times through the years, there comes a moment when he despairs of ever reaching his goal. Occasionally, like Goethe's extraordinary man, he becomes aware of having reached it. He has achieved his utmost. He cannot surpass himself. There is nothing left for him to do.

These are the moments in which we may become battle weary. We may yearn to withdraw from a struggle which can have—or so we believe—no satisfactory outcome. At such times the body begins to lose its ability to make adjustments, or its resistance to disease. When the longing for peace outweighs the joy of struggle for achievement, when the determination to seek peace becomes irreversible and conclusive, then we die.

This is what is meant by the statement that man dies when he wants to die, that he dies *because* he wants to die. Death can no longer be looked upon as a visitation, coming without warning, before we are ready.

A Medical View

Traditionally we have considered death from disease to be death from "natural causes," as contrasted with death by violence or accident. Now there is medical authority for believing that death from disease is not natural, and that the only natural death is from old age.

Pathology is regarded as the most exact and conservative branch of medical science, and it is from a pathologist that this interpretation comes. Dr. R. Roessle holds the same chair of pathology at the University of Berlin from which the great Virchow published his theory of cellular pathology, locating disease in the cell changes, a theory which has become a guiding principle of modern scientific medicine. His study of growth and aging seems to bring medical science to the support of the poets and philosophers.

Dr. Roessle defines natural death as physiological death, the result of the aging of tissues. The long-lived, he points out, are those whose tissues wear out at a harmonious rate, so that no one organ or function of the body succumbs prematurely. The long-lived are also possessed of a high degree of adaptability.

This interpretation of natural death deepens our understanding of the diseases of old age, and suggests new ways of pro-

longing life and guarding health in our later years. Traditionally, the family and even the physician strive to find an exact
organic diagnosis of an aged person's illness, and are likely to
treat the failing heart, for example, to the exclusion of other
considerations.

But as Roessle points out, even when a person of advanced
age dies of an infection, such as pneumonia, allowance must be
made for his lowered resistance because of age, and the infection should not be regarded as the cause of death no matter
what the doctor's certificate may say.

To prolong life, therefore, we ought to regard the whole
person, his interest in living and his adjustment to life, instead
of devoting ourselves exclusively to his physical symptoms. Indeed, in the new science of geriatrics, many of the traditional
complaints of old people have been found to disappear when
social activities, interests, and a generally happier adjustment
could be provided.

Carrying the Roessle findings in longevity a step further, we
may say that the individual whose tissues wear out at a harmonious rate is one whose destructive drive does not take a
toll of one or another organ of his body. The adaptable individual may be one whose acceptance of life makes him willing and
able to adjust himself to the changing, and often none too favorable, conditions of life. One who fails to adapt himself is
following a destructive trend.

This brings us back to the death wish, and the time and the
manner in which we choose to die.

The Triumphant Death Wish

How does the power pass from the creative to the destructive side? Why does the will to live weaken and bow before the
wish to die? What are the reasons for those sudden events in
illness which confound physicians, those lightning changes between night and morning, in which a patient on the road to
recovery at evening is seen by the light of the next day to be
marked for death?

One story of the many which we might tell may demonstrate this turning from life to death, this shift of power obscure in its origin and discernible only in its effect.

The man whom I was called to see, on a sweltering summer night, was no stranger to me although I had never met him. His name glittered with international renown. As a creative producer and director in the theater he had been an unrivaled genius for decades.

Before I entered his room that night, his son described to me the incident which had precipitated his illness. The day before, vacationing on an island some distance from New York, he had gone into a telephone booth to make an important call, setting a date to begin rehearsals for his new production. While he was telephoning, his Scotch terrier was attacked by a larger dog. The terrier sprang at its master to escape the attacker and, fixing its teeth in his arm, hung there howling while the larger dog locked its jaws on the terrier. Trying to separate the two animals in the narrow, dark, steaming telephone booth, the patient had become fearfully overwrought. When the excitement was over he found it difficult to speak.

He returned to New York the same evening. His difficulty in speaking had increased and his right arm felt heavy, as though paralyzed. A doctor, sent by a friend, came immediately but the patient showed the physician the door. His son feared I might receive the same treatment, and suggested I give his father some excuse, such as that a city law required me to cauterize his arm against rabies.

I found the patient sitting in an armchair, reading a paper, a gray-haired man with penetrating eyes and a sharp-featured, arresting face. He looked at me keenly, holding his head in a characteristically proud way with his pointed nose high. Answering the question in his look, I merely said I was a doctor who had come to examine him. There was a pause during which he continued to fix me with his critical gaze. Then he mumbled inarticulately and his left hand waved me to a chair.

The right corner of his mouth was visibly drawn down, indicating paralysis of the facial nerve. When he answered my questions he tried to cover his partial loss of articulation by accenting the final syllable of every word. The right arm showed a mild motor disturbance. His blood pressure was rather high. His heart was normal in size and its function was good.

I explained to him that the excitement of his experience with the dogs had apparently caused a spasm in certain arteries of the brain, which rest and treatment would cure. His face disclosed the fear that he had suffered a stroke, and to erase any doubt I explained the meaning of "spasm." He seemed convinced and somewhat encouraged.

My report to his son was optimistic, depending on developments in the next few days. We decided against moving the patient to a hospital. He passed a quiet night, and after a few days he began to show signs of improvement.

But time began to press. My patient was on the threshold of a Broadway production, one of the elaborate, costly dramatic spectacles for which he was unequaled in Europe or America. He had important decisions to make. The rehearsal date which he had been about to set with his telephone call the preceding Sunday was already past. Urged to set a date when he would be well enough to begin his work, I strove to win time for him. I asked for a consultation with one of New York's most distinguished neurologists. The consultant corroborated the diagnosis of cerebral spasm.

A week later, noting his general improvement except for his speech, which was better one day and worse the next, the neurologist and I held a second consultation. As a result a specialist was called in to give the patient speech lessons. Far from successful, the lessons seemed to depress him, and presently I advised against their continuance. The patient visibly relaxed. He enjoyed listening to music. He took to writing little messages on slips of paper. He was pleasant and cooperative. He missed his cigars and his coffee but was cheered by the progress he was making.

One morning, taking advantage of his nurse's absence in the kitchen, he dressed to go out. The day was a religious holiday, requiring fasting and attendance at services. Our patient refused food and was adamant in his decision to fast and pray. The nurse, unable to deter him, called me. I tried to give him an intravenous injection of glucose, although a day of fasting would not in itself be seriously weakening. He went to attend services.

That night one of those inexplicable changes took place. In the morning the nurse, hearing a shattering of glass, hurried into the patient's room. He had prepared to shave, but with his first glance into the mirror he had discovered the extended paralysis of the right side of his face. The mirror had crashed to the floor.

As though to drive himself deeper into the realization of his disability, he set himself the very next morning to answer the many messages of reverence and respect which had come from all over the world on his seventieth birthday, some two weeks before he fell ill. He found that he could not write. The discovery excited him so that his speech, which had been much improved, deteriorated once more. He was gradually losing sensation and mobility in his right leg and arm.

When, a few nights later, he complained of a pain in the right side of his chest, I called in a cardiologist. The doctor found heart and circulatory system in "excellent condition," and blood pressure well down to normal. He shared the opinion that the patient was suffering a spastic disturbance, and agreed that the prognosis would have been very favorable if there had not been a recurrence of the initial spastic attack.

Out of consideration for the family's growing anxiety, a neurologist was summoned from Boston. Before this doctor began his examination I asked him specifically not to test the patient's ability to write. Nevertheless, as the specialist proceeded with a very thorough examination in an atmosphere of growing tension, I saw him place a writing pad before the patient. No doubt the neurologist wished to determine whether the damage had occurred in the sensory writing center in the brain, in the nearby motoric center of the right arm, or in both.

The patient took the pen. He hesitated, and one could see evidence of a rising resentment against the doctor's relentless pursuit of his symptoms. He began to write. He used force, bearing down on the pen. His face flushed. Again he hesitated, evaluating the distorted letters of the single line he had scrawled. Once more he tried, but in the middle of a frustrated upstroke and with a damning mumble he flung down the pen. Thus ended this examination.

The patient now sank into a deep depression. During the days which followed the nurse frequently surprised him in the act of testing his writing when he believed he was unobserved. The first neurologist now took a serious view of the situation. The paralysis in the facial nerve remained unchanged, and though the patient's speech had worsened into a completely inarticulate mumble, his bodily functions remained for a while in good order.

But it was obvious that the sick man was going through a series of strokes. There were two more consultations, but all medication, all suggestions, all efforts failed to halt the downward course of the disease. A difficulty in swallowing appeared and it became obvious that the entire anterior central gyrus, the area in the brain which harbors all these centers, was involved. We had before us the classic picture of cerebral hemorrhage.

The patient sank into a coma from which he did not awaken. Pneumonia developed, and on a Sunday, just five weeks after the onset of the illness, he died.

"Death That Is the Cooling Night . . ."

As spectator to this man's struggle between his will to live and a wish to die which grew steadily to overwhelming power, the reader needs to understand not only his state of mind at the time but also his physical condition. Although, as we have learned, both are interwoven, we must know whether he had ever shown himself particularly susceptible to this or any other illness.

Actually up to the date of the initial attack the patient had been in perfect physical health. There were no symptoms of trouble, no storm signals of any kind. A clinician might point out that overindulgence in nicotine and strong coffee could have affected the condition of the arteries. Yet a cardiologist of great repute found, three weeks after the beginning of the illness, "the heart sounds are excellent . . . the heart itself not dilated . . . the electrocardiogram shows a normal tracing in every respect . . . blood pressure is normal . . . liver not enlarged." Physically, this man was in as good condition as a man can be at his age.

But now let us turn to the emotional picture. When he came to the United States for the first time in the early twenties, laurels strewed his path. He was acclaimed as an unsurpassed master in his field by both the press and the public.

He returned ten years later, a refugee fleeing the Nazi terror. The laurels had faded; the reverence had become perfunctory. The guest of honor was now a competitor, and his welcome accordingly diminished in ardor. One must weigh the effect of this on a man accustomed to living like an uncrowned king in his native land.

After a few years of moderate success he determined on a production which was to be his masterwork. I was told by his friends how much effort, enthusiasm, and devotion he put into his work. The opening night critics dealt him a crushing defeat.

One producer told me that this production was too far ahead of the times to be a success. The reason for its failure, however, is immaterial. The effect on the patient is what counts, and that was devastating.

The Symbolic Three Score and Ten

Shortly afterward he had his seventieth birthday. If success had continued to shine on him he might not have observed that this birthday marked the end of his three score years and ten.

It is possible to imagine the emotion with which, following the failure of his crucial production, he greeted the significant day. Suddenly, and for the first time in a life filled with creative activity, he must have known himself to be an old man. People no longer understood him or, what was worse, he had gone beyond understanding them. There was no prospect of rising to a higher peak than that from which he had fallen. Every new attempt would be at best an effort to recapture a lost eminence.

He went to the seashore, brooding. He had every reason to believe that his show was over.

But he had financial obligations. His possessions and his very considerable fortune had been either confiscated by the Nazis or frozen because of the war. He was urged to revive a production which had been an outstanding success abroad. His name had great drawing power, and many people stood ready to back him in this venture. He let himself be persuaded.

Yet this was only a technical resurrection of showy craftsmanship which he was undertaking to produce. From his point of view it was bare of creative art; it was to be done only for the sake of money. He was a proud man. He was tired; he had no wish to resume the battle. He had abdicated.

When he went to make the telephone call, to set the date for those rehearsals which he surely wished might never take place, the conflict within him had doubtless reached its climax. The dog fight was really unimportant except that, being an expression of hostility, it kindled his own hostile impulses which otherwise he had been able to control. Any ordinary occurrence, a loud voice in the street perhaps, might have precipitated the spasm. It might have come upon him during the night, or during rehearsals or at any stage in the preparation of the production. The emotional setting for illness was ripe.

The prospect of giving his talents to a work without creative possibilities was the death knell of his creative instinct. Significantly, the destructive drive thrust its dynamic power against those centers in the brain where are located the skills of gesture, of motion, of speech, those very skills which had been the medium of this man's genius. Modern psychoanalytic psychology has gathered a wealth of evidence to convince us that the choice of the organ or organs to be attacked by illness is not accidental, but is related to the whole personality.

Now we can see why elementary speech lessons upset him;

he had been the acclaimed master of speech, skillful with every nuance. Now we understand why the test of his writing threw him into a black depression. His whole life had been devoted to the arts of communication of ideas. Now he could communicate neither by speech, by gesture, nor by the written word.

His constitution was strong, his will to live a powerful force. But he refused to continue life as an invalid, either in the physical or the artistic sphere. The outcome was inevitable.

Emotion Defeats Reason

The power of reason is formidable. It gives logical grounds for hope; it whips up new activity by revealing new possibilities. These were the days during which the patient showed outward improvement.

When reason and emotion are locked in battle, however, emotion eventually wins. There was the relapse, for which we physicians had no medical explanation. Coming the day after the patient's fast, the relapse might have been the result of physical exertion. Although through most of his life he had not observed the solemn holiday, this time he had chosen to fast against all the efforts of his physician and his nurse to dissuade him, as though he were preparing himself to meet his Maker. That very choice was a self-destructive act, in unconscious obedience to his triumphing destructive drive.

Later I learned that the holiday was also the anniversary of his father's death. I have observed that, just as a word of reassurance at a critical moment can inspire the creative instinct and raise a man once more to strive in his own behalf, so an alluring mental image can encourage the destructive drive and cause the patient to succumb. Especially when a system has already suffered strain, the thought of one's dead father or mother, of a wife or other beloved person who has gone before, beckons one to follow.

The death wish promises peace and surcease from struggle. But it does not rely upon lure alone, nor upon its power over the unconscious centers of the body. It pleads its case convinc-

ingly to reason too. No man lives forever. Why stretch a bur-
densome existence for just a few years more? The reward is not
worth the effort.

And so a man shuts himself away from the outside world, not
to hear the voices of those who love him, not to see the tempting glitter of fame which has already betrayed him, not to fal-
ter in his resolution to seek eternal rest.

The strange behavior of the sick, often so perplexing to their
families and friends and even to their physicians, thus becomes
understandable. When a man on his sick bed apparently fights
with all his strength to recover, while his lips reiterate the as-
surance that he wants to live, the same man commits acts
which are aimed directly at his own destruction.

We who stand at the sick man's bedside are handicapped in
our effort to understand him by the very fact that we ourselves
are well. We attempt to evaluate a sick man's subjective experience, his feelings and his desires, with a healthy man's calm
and reasonable objectivity and a healthy man's involvement in
the work and relationships of living. But it is not what we
would feel or desire, but the hidden inner resolution of the sick
man which will determine the outcome.

When death comes, it comes as a wished-for end. It comes as
a natural event for which body and mind are prepared. It is a
deliverance, as in the words of the visionary poet Heine, which
Brahms set to music:

> *Death that is the cooling night,*
> *Life that is the sultry day.*
> *It is growing dark already—I feel drowsy—*
> *The day has made me tired.*

How Not to Shorten Life

Can we guard ourselves against this shift of power away
from the life-preserving force? Can we sustain the will to live?

The physiologist Rubner declared a generation ago that the
best way to prolong life is not to shorten it. Today we are be-

ginning to recognize that the first danger to length of life may not be the invading germ, nor any physiological process beyond our control. We are beginning to understand that the first line of defense is in our emotional health.

If we are emotionally sound, we will be physically sound. Body and mind are one. When we truly want to be well, to live long and in health, we have the power to do it.

If grown children, who have long left their parents' home to live their own lives, come to a parent's bedside and say, however sincerely, "Live for our sake. We need you," the parent may be touched, but not really convinced. A mother whose children are immersed in their own lives knows when she is no longer needed as a mother. If she has not carried forward into her later years an interest apart from her children, something really meaningful to her, then she will not want to live.

The same may be true of a man who has retired from his business or profession, if he has lived solely for his work. When his work is finished he may have nothing left to live for.

We need not come to this pass. If we live to our full capacity, not merely as parents, not merely as workers, but as mature, well-rounded human beings, then we will have something yet to live for even when work and parenthood are ended.

There are measures we can take, if we so desire. We can learn to guard our emotional health as we guard our physical health. We can make every effort to develop our fullest capacity as human beings. We can strengthen every link that joins us to work, to other human beings, to the world around us. These are our safeguards against illness and against premature death. They are the deeper roots of our will to live.

If we want to live, we can nourish the will to live at these roots. It is within the power of every normal human being to do this, sometimes alone, and sometimes with the aid of medicine.

_____ SUMMING UP _____

No one needs to fear death because we die only when we are ready to die.

❖   ❖   ❖

We may have reason *to live, without the* wish *to live, and in a struggle between reason and emotion, emotions seem always to win.*

❖   ❖   ❖

In order to live long we must guard our emotional health as we guard our physical health.

❖   ❖   ❖

To keep life we must strengthen all our links with life and living.

❖   ❖   ❖

If we are really working at living we need not be afraid of dying.

❖   ❖   ❖

The best way to prolong life is not to shorten it.

II

The Pathways
of Illness

*Life is a continual adjustment
of internal relations to
external relations.*
HERBERT SPENCER

5

Why Doctors Disagree

Operation successful; patient died.

WHY do doctors disagree?

If medicine is a pure science, why is there not a single scientific answer to an illness? How is it possible for a patient to go from one doctor to another and receive a different diagnosis and a different treatment from each for the same set of symptoms?

People talk about good and bad doctors. But we cannot dismiss the problem by saying that an individual doctor doesn't know his business.

The confusions and contradictions in the practice of medicine today have tempted many a layman to dismiss the whole profession. When a man goes to a doctor, he delivers himself into another man's hands for what may be his future good or ill, perhaps his life or death. He may be forgiven if, confronted first by one and then another opinion, he calls down a plague on all doctors and tries to get along without any medical help, or even if he turns to quacks and fads.

The patient remembers that until a few years ago the medical profession issued grave warnings about "focal infections." Tonsils and adenoids were ripped out, teeth were pulled, and appendectomies were performed, all as preventive measures, to protect health, not only to cure disease. A man still in possession of his appendix was afraid to undertake a long journey, and one who still had his tonsils was in a class with savages in primitive lands who resist vaccination.

A newspaper story of the late 1920's told of a young man and his wife who had decided to renounce civilization and were going to live on a romantic Pacific island. Before they went, however, both these young people had all their teeth pulled and dentures made, to be sure they would be safe from "focal infection" in their primitive paradise.

Today it is once more fashionable to wear your tonsils, and the surgeon who used to recommend an appendectomy as a health measure, like a circumcision or a good set of false teeth, has now become somewhat more conservative.

Fundamentally, however, little has changed. Instead of tonsils, the scalpels of today are harvesting gall bladders, fibroid tumors, sections of stomachs and colons, cystic ovaries and wombs. Appendectomies are old-fashioned but hysterectomies are in style.

Yet it is unjust to question the surgeon's good faith. It is unjust, and furthermore it solves nothing, to make the individual doctor the villain of the piece, be he surgeon or internist, gynecologist or any one of the dozen specialists we have today.

The doctor is no villain, any more than the patient with "imaginary" symptoms is a naughty child to be scolded and sent home with the injunction that he must be a good boy and stop bothering busy physicians. Doctor and patient are both victims, and while the patient suffers, the doctor's dilemma may be just as difficult to bear. The doctor stands bewildered, perhaps dismayed, and often on the defensive, at a crucial turning point in the history of medicine.

Technological Medicine

The technological revolution, which gave us engines to do the work of muscles and delicate machinery to replace the skill of hands, penetrated every lane of human activity, and medicine was no exception. While the nineteenth century was crowding farmers and cottage craftsmen into city slums and teaching them to run machines, and incidentally killing them en masse with infectious diseases, it was also transforming the art of medicine into a precise, disciplined science.

The century up to the First World War was one of stormy progress. When man turned the lens of a telescope upward against the heavens he knew himself to be no more than a speck of dust in the universe. But if he turned a similar bit of ground glass downward, in the tube of a microscope, he was a giant, and he made giant strides toward knowledge of the physical factors in illness.

Now the scientist actually saw disease: he saw the changes in the diseased cell. And now the *cause* of disease was assumed to be this cellular change. "Illness," said Virchow, "is life under changed conditions." This is probably the shortest definition of illness in medical literature, and a masterpiece of scientific neutrality as between illness and health.

In infectious diseases the man with the miscroscope was fortunate. He could see the invading disease germ. But in certain diseases, such as cancer and arteriosclerosis, he saw tissue changes, but no germ. And the "functional diseases," the gastric disturbances, the asthmas, the heart seizures, were still more baffling. The miscroscope failed to reveal either germ or cellular change; the malfunctioning organ persisted in remaining physically normal and healthy.

Dedicated scientists hoped that they would one day discover the physiological cause of the tissue changes in the one group of diseases, and that with still more refined technique and still more sensitive instruments they would see tissue changes to account for the abnormal behavior of the organ in the second. But for the answers to these two physiological mysteries, the organic and the functional disease, the man with the microscope is still seeking in vain.

The infectious diseases, however, offered a ready battleground for the new scientific warfare on man's afflictions. The invading army of teeming microorganisms could actually be seen; the filterable virus, invisible under the optic microscope, came only later to baffle the researchers until the electronic microscope was invented.

On every hand ancient superstitions began to dissolve before the searching light of science. Serums were developed before the plagues which had terrorized man for centuries. For the first time in history it became possible for millions to live crowded together, free from the fear of epidemic. Without modern sanitation New York City could not exist.

Walter Reed with his heroic human guinea pigs proved that a mosquito carried yellow fever, and sanitary engineers attacked the breeding places of mosquitoes and showed how that curse of the tropics could be eliminated. Wassermann came forth with his serum test for syphilis. Ehrlich introduced its first effective cure. Schick produced not only an immunization for diphtheria but also a test for susceptibility. And Salk developed an effective vaccine against poliomyelitis.

Pharmacology labored to perfect scientific methods of testing old and producing new remedies, and a sort of alchemistic renaissance revived the medieval belief that against every ill there grows an herb. New drugs mushroomed out of test tubes, some of ephemeral value only, but others of enduring and even miraculous properties. Without these patient and precise men taking step after cautious step in the laboratory, checking and rechecking, and without the impressive pharmaceutical industry which has grown out of their efforts, we might not have today first the sulfa drugs, then the antibiotics, the antihistamines, the synthetically produced hormones, and finally the tranquilizers.

But as the mass of detailed observation and experiment, of theory and procedure, of scientific data, grew even larger, the individual physician became dwarfed before it. No one man could absorb so much knowledge and put it to use. Specialties sprang up in research, and inevitably specialties sprang up in medical practice. With so much known and so much yet to learn, it was all a man could do to keep abreast of the new knowledge of a single organ or system of the body.

The End of the Family Doctor

Thus, as a logical next step, the family physician disappeared before the onrushing need for specialization. The man who had known all about his patient's life, his work, his family; who had perhaps delivered him into the world, had seen him through childhood measles and adolescent disturbance; who had received his confidences and who, more than any other living person except possibly the priest or minister, knew his patient's mind as well as his body—this man became extinct. He was sacrificed to the aseptic tidal wave of scientific data and scientific precision. The art of healing became a standardized scientific technique.

In the old-fashioned doctor it had been a virtue to make do with little, and to depend on his sharpened observations, his experience with people sick and well, and his knowledge of his patient in particular. The new scientific man, the specialist, approached a case with an arsenal of equipment. He saw not a sick man but a sickness. He concentrated on the diseased organ like a mechanic working on a worn or broken part of a machine. He treated an organ but not a suffering human being.

Indeed he had little opportunity to observe the human being. As more and more chemical and mechanical aids—blood tests, biological tests, basal metabolism tests, electrocardiograms, fluoroscope and X-ray examinations—entered into a diagnosis, as more and more specialists were called upon for their special knowledge, the relationship of doctor and patient became increasingly remote. More than this, the doctor was sternly warned against allowing merely human factors, his own or the patient's, to corrupt the purity of his scientific data.

Patient on an Assembly Line

And so we have the picture of the patient ushered in and out of a doctor's office as though on an assembly line. He gives his history to an assistant or a crisp nurse with a printed form, perhaps, which provides blanks for only physical information: age, height, weight, previous illnesses, operations, symptoms.

He is prepared for examination, again by a nurse or assistant. The doctor himself, held to a schedule of appointments as tight as a railroad time table, comes in only when the patient lies stretched on a table under a sheet, a completely dehumanized, deindividualized object for examination.

The patient is asked to breathe, to grunt, to sit up, to lie down, but never, on pain of breaking the doctor's scientific concentration, to talk. And when the time comes for discussion of the case, for diagnosis and a survey of the treatment to come, it is the doctor, not the patient, who talks.

The doctor, surrounded by his charts, graphs, chemical analyses, specialists' reports, undertakes to tell the still mute, still dehumanized sufferer what is wrong with him and how he is to be cured—or that there is nothing wrong with him and he must go home to live with his pains and his fears as best he can.

If the patient enters the hospital he is likely to be still further stripped of his human individuality. One patient protested for all, "I'm *flesh* Number 1040! When my doctor finally gets here, he is followed by his retinue—the bigger the doctor, the longer the tail!"

The examination is public, with hardly a word to the patient. Then comes the bright, "And how are we today? Feeling better? That's fine. Take it easy." And the doctor is gone.

Busy as he is, important as he may be in the profession, the doctor would make time for the few minutes of private conversation for which the patient longs, if he believed it would help the case. But all his training is against permitting the variable, unreliable, *unscientific* human element to confuse or sway his handling of the illness.

Dr. Carl Binger describes the traditional "grand rounds" of the hospital in his book *The Doctor's Job:*

> We would assemble in our white coats around some hospital bed with a chart hanging at the foot of it so that the patient could not read it. There usually was learned discourse about livers and lungs and respiratory quotients, serum proteins and urea indices. Much of it did not need to be said at the patient's bedside, but it was and is the tradition to talk about patients on rounds in their presence. Of course, the patients did not understand. What does a red-faced cop off his beat, lying in bed in a short, white cotton nightshirt tied in the back, know or care about hemoglobin? The less he knows the more he will misinterpret. . . .
>
> Is it *scientific* medicine to consider his liver or his bone marrow and not him? Actually one has to consider both and one is not less of a scientist but more of one for doing so, because the first task of a scientist is to observe and describe phenomena as they occur in nature. And a cop's emotions, even when off his beat, lying in bed, are none the less natural phenomena.

The Surgical Approach

Above all, in the race for more and more refined specialization to deal with the growing accumulation of physical data, surgery triumphed.

To enlightened people surgery was the most progressive, the most rational and direct method of dealing with illness. The question of what had brought on the illness was not within the domain of the surgeon. The surgeon's business was to do a clean-cut job of removing the offending organ. And that he did.

All around him, technicians came forth to support him with better tools for his exquisite skill. Blood chemistry, anesthesia, drugs to prevent and to combat infection, drugs to encourage and to discourage blood clotting, painstaking procedures for preparing the patient before the operation, for keeping him alive through it, for hastening his recovery after it, were developed—and are still being developed—by battalions of diligent scientists.

An entire branch of medical science grew up around the surgeon, to perform like a symphony orchestra in a concerto of which he was the virtuoso. Hospitals focused their most concentrated attention on the drama in the operating room. Even the human body cooperated, demonstrating that a man or woman could get along minus a kidney or a gall bladder, with half a stomach, one lung, or part of the sex organs.

In Europe one woman was reported to have had twenty-three major abdominal operations. *Furor operatius passivus*—passive operative madness—was the ironic name the reporting physician gave to the craze for surgery. When I was a student, a story went the rounds of the hospitals about a man, suffering from epilepsy, who had this plea tattooed on his belly: "Don't take out my appendix. Was taken out twice."

No one questions the incomparable skill of hand, eye, and brain of the surgeons, and their courage in the performance of their stellar role in the climax of the drama, when they are called upon to do a precise violence upon a living body under pressure of time by the clock.

But one can question a development in medicine when the physician becomes so engrossed in technique that he sees nothing but the area of operation. One can question a science, presumably dedicated to healing and the preservation of life, which until about a generation ago could complacently accept the terse verdict at the end of a report: "Operation successful; patient died." This was, to many, the logical absurdity at the end of an uncompromisingly "scientific" mechanization of medicine.

Illness in the Mind

Toward the end of the great century of mechanistic progress in medicine, resistance to this rigid formula began to grow.

Doubts were expressed whether the sharp line between body and mind, between "scientific medicine" and neurology's young brother, psychiatry, could be maintained.

Psychiatry was the scorned orphan of medicine because its area, the diseases of the mind, stubbornly refused to give physical evidence of their presence. Psychiatrists endeavored to find the cause of mental disease in brain tissue, but all their brilliant anatomical research came to nothing except, for example, in general paralysis resulting from syphilis, and in senile dementia, the deterioration of the brain in old age. In these, at least, some physiological damage was discovered. Otherwise the most serious psychotics were found to have brains anatomically no different from that of any normal man.

But if brain anatomy proved to be a blind alley, progress was being made in the psychological research laboratories. Pavlov demonstrated scientifically by his conditioned reflex experiments that physical functions originate in a psychic impulse. Neurologists sought the nerve pathways by which the subjective idea in the mind is translated into physical action.

In France, Charcot brought order out of the chaos of nervous disturbances. His pupil, the young Freud, followed him through the chambers of the Salpetriere, observing the many unhappy human beings whose illness was not understood, because it was of the mind.

From the neurology of his day Freud set forth in new directions to explore the dark world of the unconscious. For all that he was hooted at in the streets of Vienna, the early teachings of psychoanalysis had a dynamic impact which could not be ignored for long.

In 1914 a brilliant cure of toxic goiter (hyperthyroidism) by psychotherapy was reported in Germany. This was a case in which surgical treatment had been completely unsuccessful.

Signs of a change in medical thinking began to emerge, especially in gynecology. Freud's revelations of the depth and power of the sexual impulses gave pause to thoughtful medical men.

"There is too much minor gynecology and too little etiological [causal] thinking," wrote a leading professor of gynecology at the University of Berlin in 1925.

". . . Their illness is a psychic conflict sailing under a gynecological flag, which has escaped the attention of the quacks," declared the director of the Woman's Hospital of the University of Tubingen.

Elsewhere, and in other branches of medicine, the same questioning voices were heard. In such prevalent ills as heart diseases and gastrointestinal disorders, a literature began to grow on the possibility of psychic causes of physical illness.

Both in this country and abroad, some doctors were even then in rebellion against the often unnecessary resort to surgery. The gynecologist Dr. Ernst Graefenberg wrote in a medical journal in 1929:

> Correct recognition of psychogenic pains [pains of psychic origin] is of great importance because such pains often result in major operations. Many an appendix has been sacrificed to a harmless . . . pain [in the lower portion of the small intestine]. If the pain happened to be in the left lower quadrant, the left adnexa [ovary] were doomed . . . Back pains were at once associated with displacement of the uterus . . .

Today we recognize that the victims of a surgeon's rash diagnosis are legion. Patients in a state of emotional as well as physical distress are poor judges of a situation. They and their families are ready to take the pain of the body for the cause of the illness.

Unnecessary Operations

A sick man will follow, though fearfully, anyone who promises a way out of his misery. And many a sufferer from emotional conflict, as Menninger and others have pointed out, will willingly, even eagerly, place himself on the altar of the operating table and sacrifice a part of his body to the terrible feelings of guilt which unconsciously dominate him.

Every doctor can draw out of his files cases of operations, the necessity for which might be questioned. Here is one out of my own, a young woman who because of abdominal pain had undergone an appendectomy which resulted in adhesions. Three years later, after a miscarriage, she had hemorrhages and a painful pulling in the lower abdomen. Again an operation was performed, during which a small cyst on the left ovary was discovered. The ovary and part of the uterus were removed.

The patient recovered from the operation, only to find her pain still with her. The next year the other ovary, also revealing a cyst, was removed. And so at the age of twenty-six she had been deprived of ovaries and uterus—and she still had her pain.

Uterine hemorrhages resulting from psychic trauma have been reported many times in medical literature. In this case the young woman had gone through the emotional shock of an unsuccessful marriage and a divorce.

The Problem Child of Medicine

Despite the growing knowledge of the interrelationship between mind and body, the doctrinaires of medicine remained unyielding, and many of them do to this day. Some admitted a certain "mental overcast" in illness. But on the whole the practicing physician was careful not to become infected by the "mental" trend.

This is not surprising in the face of their medical training. One of my professors was a consistently objective, sober scientist, except in one lecture.

"Gentlemen," he said with unaccustomed emotion on this occasion, "if I have failed in having taught you anything else, I hope I have succeeded at least in implanting in you a critical mind. For that, gentlemen, is the only guarantee against mysticism, against all this metaphysical nonsense which whirls about us these days. I want you to believe in facts and facts only. I want you to believe in what you can see, what you can feel,

and what you can demonstrate. In the making of a satisfactory
diagnosis, I shall tolerate no escape into the nebulous realm of
the mental!"

Words like this, spoken conjuringly over a pair of oval-shaped
glasses, penetrate deep into a future doctor's consciousness.
They give definition to a doctor's integrity. They set limits
which he cannot overstep without betraying his medical honor.

To influence the mind or attitude of a patient is called "suggestion," unworthy of a good doctor. Dr. Flanders Dunbar il-
lustrates this confusion in the practicing physician's mind:

> A colleague of mine once said, "Of course I can give Mrs. X
> a sedative, but if I do so, I shall tell her that it will not do her
> any good because I don't know what is really the matter with
> her, and she has had all the tests I know. It will only make her
> feel better for a time" . . . Another physician cured Mrs. X
> with the use of mild sedatives and sound advice, but was con-
> sidered dishonest or at least unscientific . . . The scientific
> way is to tell the patient to "buck up," that there is "nothing
> the matter except his imagination," that he seems to have "one
> of those troubles we do not yet understand."

Americans, in many fields the foremost apostles of technique,
at first resisted the theory of emotional factors in illness, although Freud received an enthusiastic welcome here in 1909.
In Europe, on the other hand, clinicians attempted to find ways
of admitting the emotional side of illness into their practical
work while at the same time rejecting its deeper significance.

In an effort to keep psychiatry out of the doctor's examining
room, doctors returned full circle to the old-fashioned physician, the bedside manner, the *art* of healing which had flour-
ished before the science of medicine had swept the doctor's
personality, along with a good many of his humane practices,
onto the junk heap.

The days when the doctor, after examining the patient, was
invited into the parlor to have a glass of wine and talk things
over with the family, were gone forever. But it was beginning
to be felt that perhaps some of that old-fashioned doctor's ways

with sick people were not altogether useless. Let the doctor be a little kinder, a little more sympathetic—or, when necessary, a little more of a Dutch uncle, making it clear, of course, that it was all for the patient's own good. Then the physician would not need to get involved with this vague, unscientific, unseeable and untouchable, mental stuff.

Other schools came up with other answers. But they were all a desperate effort to whittle down the new science, to take bits and pieces of it into their own practical handling of illness so that they would not be obliged to accept the whole. School medicine presented an almost united front against the mounting influence of the teachings of Freud.

Today it is no longer enough to restore a little of the art of healing into the practice of medicine. Today we have the mounting evidence of the neurologist, the endocrinologist, the very scientists themselves, to support the psychiatrist's plea that the mind be no longer excluded from the science of dealing with illness.

Dr. Franz Alexander, in his book, *Psychosomatic Medicine, Its Principles and Application,* states the case eloquently:

> The fact that the mind rules the body is, in spite of its neglect by biology and medicine, the most fundamental fact which we know about the process of life. This fact we observe continuously during all our life, from the moment when we awaken every morning. Our whole life consists in carrying out voluntary movements aimed at the realization of ideas and wishes, the satisfaction of subjective feelings such as thirst and hunger.
>
> The body, that complicated machine, carries out the most complex and refined motor activities under the influence of such psychological phenomena as ideas and wishes. The most specifically human of all bodily functions, speech, is but the expression of ideas through a refined musical instrument, the vocal apparatus.
>
> All our emotions we express through physiological processes: sorrow, by weeping; amusement, by laughter; and shame, by blushing. All emotions are accompanied by physiological changes: fear, by palpitation of the heart; anger, by increased heart activity; elevation of blood pressure, and changes in car-

bohydrate metabolism; despair, by a deep inspiration and expiration called sighing.

All these physiological phenomena are the results of complex muscular interactions under the influence of nervous impulses, carried to the expressive muscles of the face and to the diaphragm in laughter, to the lacrimal glands in weeping, to the heart in fear, and to the adrenal glands and to the vascular system in rage. The nervous impulses arise in certain emotional situations which in turn originate from our interaction with other people. The originating psychological situations can be understood only in terms of psychology—as total responses of the organism to its environment.

In the laboratories meanwhile, biological scientists are seeking the evidences of mental illness in the body's altered chemistry. The walls between psychiatry and the other branches of medicine are collapsing under the combined attack from both the biological and the psychological sciences, under the new term, psychobiology.

Thus the doctor, reminded every day that the mind and body are one, can no longer resist the next logical step in thinking: if mind and body are one in normal functioning, namely in health, cannot mind and body be one in illness?

That it can be so, and by what pathways it is so, we shall try to understand in the following chapters. Only thus can we grasp the true picture of what makes illness, and only thus can we find our way back along those pathways to the cause of illness. We must find our way, not as doctor alone nor as patient alone but as doctor and patient together, working toward an end deeply desired by both, the safeguarding of health.

—————————— SUMMING UP ——————————

The knowledge that the body cannot be cured without the mind goes back to about 500 B.C. "There is no illness of the body apart from the mind," said the Greek philosopher Socrates.

❋   ❋   ❋

Medical knowledge of the body and its ills progressed by giant strides through the age of science and technology. Medical knowledge of the mind and its ills is making equal strides today.

✿   ✿   ✿

The oneness of mind and body holds the secret of illness and health.

6

Warning Signals

Abnormality is only the normal to an excessive degree.

THE DESTRUCTIVE drive, as we have learned, is an everready force lurking in the unconscious mind. When the climate is right—when, for example, we are caught in the toils of emotional conflict—then the destructive force can become an active threat to our health.

But if it is unconscious and inaccessible to reason, then how can the average man and woman recognize it? Is there any way to detect this danger to our health in time to save the body from harm? In a word, can we prevent illness?

Once we accept the fact that man wages war not only against others but also against himself, once we begin to look for the signs of this inner war, then we can find them. For the signs are there. We can say with conviction that illness does not come as a bolt out of the blue, a thief in the night, a visitation without warning. Even a heart attack sends its messages before, if we can only read them.

We moderns find these warnings difficult to read because we tend to think in mechanistic terms. We are accustomed to dials and indicators. For example, a man came to me recently, shaken by a friend's sudden death from a heart attack. What upset him most was that his friend had had an electrocardiogram taken only a few days before, and the findings had been negative.

"Now we can't rely on anything!" my visitor protested.

Many of the warning signals are subjective and do not register on dials, and therefore we ignore them as a passing depression, or as hypochondria. Let the pointer of our bathroom scale swing upward, or the mercury in the doctor's blood-pressure machine climb, and we pay attention. When the fever thermometer reading reaches the red mark, we are frightened. But when our inner feelings warn us that all is not well, we reject the warning as superstitious nonsense. We are almost too well educated in the scientific method. If a symptom does not meet the rigid standards of science we dismiss it entirely.

But what we thus dismiss may be an inner perception of danger. Why, for example, did this man's friend go to have an electrocardiogram taken? Had he perhaps caught the whisper of anxiety from his unconscious mind? Most of our actions are instigated or influenced by some inner motive. When we are baffled, it is because we are not trained to listen to these muted voices from our unconscious. But we can learn to listen.

The Riddle of Fatigue

Fatigue is one of the most frequent of these warnings from the unconscious. Fatigue without cause, without apparent physical reason, fatigue which often exists in the absence of any exertion whatever, is an experience which almost all of us have shared. Which of us has not known a moment of weariness, inertia, indifference—and which of us has not jumped up full of energy, our weariness forgotten, at the summons of a telephone call, provided it is the call we were waiting for?

We are on familiar terms with fatigue. The patient in a doctor's office speaks for millions with the words, "I don't know why, but I'm tired all the time." A man, giving his case history,

says, "I was working too hard. I was overtired." Of one who
succumbs we say, "He died of overwork. He wore himself out."

Yet we know both from daily experience and from laboratory
experiment that a man or woman of average physical development can carry on heroic exertions over long periods of time
with little or no rest, and yet suffer no greater fatigue than a
night's sleep will repair. We have only to think of rescue workers in flood or earthquake, carrying on around the clock, often
with the added emotional strain of fear for themselves or anxiety for their families.

During the blitz over London, Winston Churchill writes in
Their Finest Hour, it was feared that plague or epidemic must
result in a population living under such strain, with little sleep,
crowded together in shelters every night, struggling to keep
home and work going under unimaginable difficulties. Meanwhile the shattered sewers were pouring possible epidemic into
the Thames River.

"The fact remains," he reports, "that during this rough winter the health of the Londoners was actually above the average. . . . The power of enduring suffering in the ordinary people of every country, when their spirit is aroused, seems to have
no bounds."

But we do not need a war to unlock the dynamic resources
within people. Everywhere, every day, people go about their
tasks without weariness if they have a goal and are supported
by enthusiasm and belief in what they are doing.

The chronic sufferers from fatigue do not have the excuse of
unusual exertions. They are wearied by a day of normal activity. They are weary before they begin the day's work. They
are weary whether they work much, or little, or not at all.

Medicine has tried to define the symptoms of fatigue but has
immediately run into trouble. The objective symptoms, when
any exist, are not exclusively symptoms of fatigue. Low blood
pressure, low blood sugar, secondary anemia, loss of weight can
be symptoms of numerous other disturbances. More often there
are no measurable symptoms at all. The weary man or woman
describes a subjective state, a feeling which pervades his mind

and body but which rarely registers on a doctor's instruments. Yet the fatigue is none the less real because it is subjective. It is real, and it is a warning.

There is also a whole group of people who refuse to admit fatigue. It is painful to their pride to admit such weakness. They want to be the captain on the bridge who never sleeps. They are the people who push themselves without mercy, often until illness strikes them down in earnest. Theirs is an unrealistic heroism, childish and wasteful. There is no shame in admitting weakness. We must admit and face it before we can take rational steps to deal with it and its causes.

Fear Without Cause

Anxiety is another signal that we should heed. Freud defined it as "internalized fear." Fear is a healthy mechanism. It is an alarm bell, a warning of impending danger.

When an animal confronts danger, he pauses for an instant —Fight? Or flight? In that instant, in which he must make the decision on which his life may depend, he suffers fear. Not only does he subjectively feel afraid. The subjective feeling is at once accompanied by physical changes. The heart beats faster; the blood pressure rises. Impulses stream along the nerves. Messages race to the glands. The adrenal glands pour their hormones into the blood stream, energizing the body. The entire physical system is galvanized into preparedness. Whether the decision is to battle the enemy or run from him, in that instant of alarm the body is mobilized for action in its own defense.

Man, a more complex animal, does not need to confront present danger to feel fear. He may fear a hurricane many miles away as he reads the storm warnings. He may fear an employer, a teacher, the loss of his job, or an impending examination, or a war that threatens across the world. So long as the fear is justified by external circumstances, so long as there is a real threat, his fear is healthy as the animal's fear is healthy, because it prompts him to preparedness.

When the danger is over, fear disappears and the body relaxes. Heart, blood pressure, glands and nerves return to normal.

But when the danger does not exist in reality, when it dwells only in the fantasy of the sufferer, when it does not subside with the passing of its apparent cause—then the fear is no longer healthy. Then we have morbid fear, that internalized, destructive fear which we call anxiety. We have a diffuse state of uneasiness, a general feeling of worry, of pressure, of tension.

All these subjective feelings are real, though the danger which arouses them is not. They can lead to such physical symptoms as higher blood pressure, faster pulse, without apparent organic cause. The body is in a permanent state of preparedness to meet danger. Because it is not related to reality, this is a neurotic state.

The causes of anxiety vary with the individual, his innate self, the environment into which he was born and grew to maturity, the fortunate or unfortunate circumstances of his life. Usually these causes are buried deep within the unconscious. To unearth them, psychiatrists often must probe for many months. The psychiatrists speak to us of infantile dependency, hostility, aggression; of feelings of inadequacy and inferiority; of guilt.

The Burden of Guilt

Why guilt? What has the average, decent, law-abiding citizen to reproach himself with? Most of us can say, with justification, "I have done my best to be a good son, a good husband, a good father, a good member of society—why should I feel guilty?"

The answer is, conscience. Conscience is the voice within us which tells us what is right and what is wrong. Psychoanalysts call it the superego, the part of the self which sits in judgment on both the conscious intelligent self—the ego—and the deeper, instinctual self, the self composed of instinctive needs and desires, termed the Id.

It is not necessary to discuss here all the varied and some-times desperate struggles of the inner man with his superego, his conscience. It is important to understand, however, that the pattern of that conscience is laid down in childhood. Its judg-ments and evaluations of right and wrong are often a child's judgments and evaluations. And the sins for which our con-science castigates us in maturity are often sins only according to the limited, inexperienced, sometimes grievously mistaken interpretations which as children we may have made of the adult world and of adult standards.

Here is an example: Suppose a child has been naughty, and a father has spoken harshly to the child; the child has rebelled against the rebuke. Shortly afterward the father may fall sick, or even die. For the rest of his life, the child may carry buried within him the conviction that it was he, by his naughtiness and rebellion, who caused the illness or who outright killed his father. Coupled with the unfortunate sequence of events, the child in his deepest self may have wished his father dead; this is not unusual, and at some stages of growth it is normal.

This is only one simple reconstruction out of many possible early experiences which may instill an underlying guilt feeling. Guilt may grow out of a child's interpretation of sin or crime. It may result from any of the violent impulses and unsocial acts of childhood. It may be born of a misunderstanding of any in-nocent childhood experience which was accompanied by emo-tional shock.

Whatever the forces which conspire to bring it into being, the guilty feeling is there. It is a burden which the superego lays upon the individual throughout his life, unless it can be exorcised by understanding and emotional maturity. To be mature, in this sense, is to be able to revise those childish mis-interpretations with the understanding of an adult.

Guilt implies punishment, and the superego is relentless. The individual expects punishment, fears punishment, and at the same time longs for punishment to expiate his "crime" and free himself from his guilt. We have cases of neurotic criminals who commit crimes in order to be caught and punished; the punishment which society visits upon them assuages in some measure the guilt they feel for some inner crime. The relief, even eagerness, with which these men accept their sentence is a source of wonder to those around them. In prison they are model inmates.

Freud observed that "the sense of guilt offers an explanation of the cure or improvement of severe neuroses which we sometimes observe after real accidents; all that matters is that the patient should be relieved—in what way is of no consequence . . ."

Abnormality is only the normal to an excessive degree; almost everyone carries into his adult life some remnant of guilt from his childhood struggle to adjust to the rules of society. In extreme cases we have suicides, those who come to a point where they can no longer endure their guilt and their fear of punishment, and who at a stroke free themselves by giving life itself in expiation. Less dramatic are the martyrs who punish themselves throughout life by making undue sacrifices for others.

Most of us carry our burden of guilt more easily. We give ourselves the friendly advice which is given and taken many times in adult life: "Forget it." Yet we do not really forget anything; we only bury it. Some day, when we are under pressure, our feeling of guilt may raise its head again as anxiety or depression.

We have pointed to the pattern of guilt only because it is a very common cause of anxiety, but there are many others. Suppose an infant's craving for love has been met by a cold, unresponsive parent. Throughout his life that individual may be anxiously seeking love, with the bitter conviction that he can never succeed, that he is forever unworthy of love because even his mother could not love him.

Feelings of inadequacy drive him to set impossible, perfectionist standards for himself: he must be ever richer, more successful, more worthy of love. Feelings of hostility creep between him and those from whom he craves love; they cannot love him, says his inner voice, and therefore he dare not love them.

And so on into the infinite variations of which the theme is capable. The infant, struggling to live and grow, strives from the moment of his birth to adjust himself to a real world which is at best no paradise. He must learn to curb his desires, to make friends with his environment, to meet the standards of his parents so that they may love him and continue to care for him in his helpless, dependent state. His tiny personality takes on the shape determined by his innate strengths and weaknesses in this struggle to survive. It is no wonder that he takes with him into manhood some burden of conflict and misunderstanding, and that this should emerge at some time during his life, generally in a period of crisis, as an undefined state of disturbance.

To Eat or Not to Eat

The list of ailments which are now recognized as arising from emotional distress grows every day. "Headaches as Much Psychological as Physical," "Life Stresses Tied to Osteo-Arthritis," "Love Conquers All—Even an Ulcer," "Tooth Health Tied to Emotional Tone" are a few of the headlines gleaned from the newspapers from time to time. All are reports of studies made by medical and other scientists of high repute. In our search for the warnings of inner stresses which may lead to illness, let us look at the advance signs of some of the more common ailments.

Obesity is now widely considered a consequence of emotional disturbance. The craving for food, for sweets, is interpreted as a sign of insecurity, a craving for love or a gratification in place of love.

There is no reason to wait until we have actually arrived at what the doctors call obesity, to take notice. We can draw the inference that we are inwardly troubled while the scale still tells us that we are only "putting on a little weight." Real obesity is difficult to cope with, and physicians regard it as a serious threat to health in itself. We can cope with the tendency before it goes that far, if we are willing to seek the inner cause.

People who are gaining weight generally protest that they eat very little. Their inability to keep track of all the guilty nibbling they do is part of the same picture, an inability to face the real problem which plagues them. Doctors often find a gland disturbance, and offer this as the cause of the overweight condition. The patient gratefully accepts this physical explanation, since it relieves him of the necessity of facing the real problem. But the glandular disturbance is in fact only another symptom, an earlier step in the chain reaction set off by emotional stress.

Too careful eating, like overeating, is also a sign to heed. In any restaurant some of the customers are studying the menu not for what they like, but for what will not disagree with them. Health foods, health farms, food fads of all kinds flourish as a consequence of the widespread nervousness about eating.

It is well to understand that we are careful about food not because we have a delicate stomach, but because an inner disturbance is actually causing the delicate stomach and the nervousness about food, either one at a time or both together. In many people, food fussiness may be a harmless safety valve for emotional tensions. But the prevalence of digestive ailments, up to and including gastric ulcer, leads us to believe that the safety valve is not really safe, and that illness may be the end result of food fussiness.

Trouble with Love

Sexual difficulties of many kinds are evidence of the destructive drive at work. These disturbances are widespread; Kinsey reports that sexual maladjustments are a factor in perhaps three-fourths of the upper-level marriages which end in separation or divorce.

Occasional or chronic loss of sexual power in a man is sometimes caused by diseases of the nervous system, but these cases are rare. Except for these cases, sexual impotence is given a variety of familiar explanations. A man is told that he is run-down, that he is preoccupied with pressing problems, that financial difficulties or family worries are the cause.

These superficial explanations may be true as far as they go. Specific pressures may have brought his inner difficulty to the surface and caused impotence. But the real trouble goes deeper and has existed long before.

A youthful fear of venereal disease instilled by a fearful parent; a childish belief in the immorality of sex, engraved on the immature mind; an attachment to a mother which was never properly outgrown; general fears of inadequacy; even a fear of impotence itself. These and other factors may unconsciously check or suppress entirely the normal capacity for a pleasurable sexual relationship. Whatever its cause, impotence is a form which the destructive drive may take.

Frigidity in women, a similarly self-destructive sign, is astonishingly widespread. The accepted estimate has been that fifty per cent of women are frigid; Kinsey found it to be seventy-five per cent. Frigidity, which one authority calls the "hateful response," can scarcely be other than psychological in origin, and it has been so reported in countless studies.

Why is a woman frigid? She may be suffering from the same fears which bring about impotence in men, plus the added fear of pregnancy. She may be thus unconsciously expressing her acceptance of the role of a martyr who must submit to masculine aggression. She may be showing her hostility toward men in general, or toward her marriage partner in particular. Or without knowing it she may be unable to accept the mature role of wife or mother. Or she may unconsciously reject her womanliness altogether and wish she could be a man.

Certainly the large number of women who are sexually dissatisfied demands attention, considering the possible illnesses which may result. Perhaps this is the real explanation for the current frequency of hysterectomies. Most so-called "women's troubles" can be traced to an emotional origin, of which frigidity may be an advance sign.

Some Like Splints, Some Like Scalpels

The accident habit has received wide attention as a menace to life and property. The National Safety Council's report for 1956 lists 95,000 persons killed, nearly nine and one-half million injured, and a loss of $10.8 billions worth of property in the one year.

The German psychologist Marbe was the first to observe, more than a quarter-century ago, that having accidents was a habit, that a person who has had one accident is more likely to have another than a person who has never had an accident. Dunbar found in a study of accident cases that eighty per cent of fracture patients had had two or more accidents.

This psychiatrist suggests that there is a broken-bone personality; healthy, happy-go-lucky, cavalier toward sex and family, with a planless, live-for-the-moment philosophy. The accident type has a cousinly resemblance to the juvenile delinquent. Both are in rebellion against society, we are told, but while the criminal breaks the law, the other breaks his leg.

A patient of mine, an actor, is never seriously ill, but every now and then he has an accident resulting in one or several fractures. One season, in a play which he had performed hundreds of times, he broke a bone in his foot. The next year he fell and broke his leg. The third year he fell out of a third-story window onto a paved street. By the law of averages he should have been killed. He suffered multiple fractures, but he will probably be in shape again for his next accident.

Almost any woman remembers days on which she has suffered a series of minor mishaps in her kitchen, when things spilled and dishes slipped out of her hands. Sometimes the accidents turned on herself, and she cut her finger or burned her hand.

Another sign of emotional disturbance is the addiction to surgery. The man or woman who has not just one but many operations to talk about sometimes seems to enjoy not only the memory of past operations but actually to welcome the prospect of more such experiences in the future.

Recently I received a telephone call from a patient who had seen me a few months before. On that occasion she listened for nearly an hour while I explained about a gall bladder condition that she was then developing. After that I took great pains to point out to her exactly what changes she should make in her way of life. She asked me then whether she needed an operation. My answer was an emphatic negative.

But now on the telephone she said, with a note of triumph, "You never told me about the gall bladder. I need an operation."

"I don't think you do," I repeated.

"Oh, I must have the operation!" she exclaimed, alarmed and indignant that I might try to forestall it.

Similarly on another occasion when I was examining the dowager of a distinguished old family, I expressed astonishment at the number of surgical scars which crisscrossed her abdomen like the map of Europe. She took my comment for a compliment, and enumerated her operations with pleasure, labeling each scar with the name of one or another eminent surgeon and the enormous fee that went with each. She had forfeited to the scalpel every organ that it is possible to live without.

Menninger interprets this repeated submission to the surgeon's knife as an expression of unconscious guilt. The sufferer, anticipating punishment for his unknown crime, repeatedly offers a part of his body in expiation, hoping that life itself will be spared to him. After the operation, Menninger points out, there is a marked period of relief and well-being, as though the criminal were enjoying a reprieve. Whatever the unconscious reasons may be, it is certain that the almost aggressive demand for surgery is a symptom of the self-destructive force on the rampage.

Sometimes we do emerge from the hospital with a serious

problem solved or a needed adjustment made. How much better, if we can, to attack the problem and make the adjustment
without sacrificing an organ in the struggle!

Older Than Your Years

Premature signs of aging present us with another group of
warnings that the destructive drive is at work. We age, not by
years, but by events and our emotional reactions to them. One
man loses his money and becomes gray overnight. Another man
suffers reverses, struggles for a period, and then finds a new direction and forges ahead once more. He may show the scars
of his bout with adversity, a few new lines in his face, but he
has refused to submit. Instead he has exerted himself to put
forth new creative efforts.

Among our millions of widows in the United States we have
ample opportunity to observe the effect of the same experience
on different women. Chronological age seems to have little to
do with the difference in reactions. One woman who loses her
husband regards her life as ended, and gives outward evidence
—in her gradual withering, her graying hair, her shrinking posture, the querulous tone creeping into her voice—that she is
preparing for death. Another woman, actually older, begins to
blossom. She may enter into the competition for a new husband,
or she may embark on a career in business, or she may do no
more than busy herself with interests for which perhaps she has
not had the leisure and freedom until now. In any or all of
these creative ways she is expressing her vigorous will to live
and enjoying its fruits.

When graying hair, coarsening skin, the shambling walk and
stoop of age come before their time, we may be sure we are
confronted with a man or woman wearying too soon of the
struggle and willing to submit to the lure of self-destruction.
Sometimes the retreat into old age is clearly a defense against
what can no longer be borne. A very sick man, stooped, shuf-
fling, with trembling hands, came to me for treatment, and I

incidentally asked him when he became deaf. He gave me the approximate year.

Was he married then? Yes, he was. Did his wife complain a great deal, perhaps loudly?

"Oh, it was intolerable!" he exclaimed.

A European doctor reported an experiment he tried some years ago on a deaf patient who liked to sing. Once while she was singing a song the physician accompanied her softly on the piano. At the change from one verse to the next, he suddenly began to play in a different key. The woman, giving no sign that she noticed the change, continued to sing, but in the new key.

The doctor in this case expressed his doubt whether the patient was really deaf. But such doubts are irrelevant, merely because she seemed to hear only what she was interested in hearing. Many of us have known deaf persons who can hear nothing which is said to them directly unless it is shouted, but who catch even a whisper if it is something about themselves. It is too easy to smile at such deafness as a sly device, an escape from responsibility or a mischievous way of causing inconvenience and trouble to the family.

While all this may be true, the deafness itself cannot be dismissed. It is real. It is a warning that the sufferer is in the toils of self-destruction and has already sacrificed part of himself, his sense of hearing, to the ravaging force.

The physiologist Rubner observed that peasant women who work as cheap labor in the fields in some parts of the world are given to early withering of the face, but they suffer no loss of physical strength and endurance. Here is an example of specialization in aging. We can reason that these women have relinquished their competitive role as women. They have resigned themselves to the life of the working bee, which needs no beauty of face but only physical competence.

A witty friend of mine once said, "Nobody is responsible for his face up to the age of thirty. From then on he shapes it." Emerson remarked: "A man finds room in a few square inches

of the face for the traits of all his ancestors, the expression of
all his history, and his wants." Rubner, whose approach was
not philosophical but scientific, wrote that aging of the features
depends on facial expression.

Facial expression is, of course, an expression of the inner self.
It is the barometer of the emotional climate in which we live;
it is the record of our most private life. Effort, grief, worry may
leave their indelible marks even on a comparatively young face.
There can be no question that behind a face which looks older
than its years an emotional struggle is being fought, and perhaps lost. The marks of defeat and surrender to age are a warning.

At Odds with Work

There is a whole group of minor ailments which might be
called occupational, like the waiter's flat feet. A medical textbook (Von Mering-Krehl: *Internal Medicine*) mentions a sickness dating from pre-typewriter days, called mogigraphy, the
inability to write. Students, clerks in business firms, and others
who spent long days pushing a pen across paper were its victims.

With the characteristic medical approach, the text suggests
physical reasons for the disability: probably the penholder was
too thin, or the pen itself was too sharp or too blunt. Not for a
moment was it suggested that the victim might be protesting
against his dreary lifelong task.

After much research, in the course of which he only rarely
found a periostitis (inflammation of the bone) or a neuritis
(inflammation of the nerve) a leading neurologist of the time
came to the conclusion that "these individuals are neurasthenic"
and probably worry and grief were involved and some such
"psychic influences" as embarrassment and excitement. His
verdict, by the way, was: incurable.

The same textbook talks of "occupational spasms" which affect pianists, violinists, flutists, tinsmiths, and watchmakers. But
in the case of milkers, in whose hands there was only rarely

found a neuritis or other anatomical cause, the condition was called an occupational neurosis, and the milker a "man of neuropathic condition."

The neurologist Moritz adds, parenthetically and with a question mark: "(Anxiety may be primary?)".

The annals of great creative workers are full of tragic evidences of the self-destructive drive. Renoir, plagued by gout at the prime of his life, withdrew from Paris to Provence where he spent his last years painting with his brushes strapped to his crippled hand. He doggedly persisted against the unconscious destructive drive, defeating himself and yet painting, displaying himself to the world in the heroic role of a martyr to his work.

Sometimes the destruction has a creative end result. Lovis Corinth, the German impressionist, at fifty suffered a stroke from which he rallied, and afterward achieved his finest work. Beethoven's deafness ended his career as a virtuoso, but he went on to write his great symphonies.

Still the destructive signs are there and must be heeded. We cannot count on great symphonies emerging from deafness and great paintings from a paralytic stroke. The conductor who has neuritis in his arm, the singer with his sore throat before a critical performance, the teacher with laryngitis—all give evidence of the self-doubt, or dissatisfaction with his work, which every normal person occasionally suffers. When the disability becomes frequent, or chronic, it may be more than an occasional self-doubt. It may be a sign of conflict taking a destructive direction.

Inner Fear Turned Outward

One more group of warning signs remains to be included. Sometimes an anxiety of which we are not conscious may become externalized in the form of an unreasonable, baseless fear. One wakes in the night, certain there has been a noise and convinced an intruder is in the house. A patient told me of such an experience, one night when she was alone in her Connecticut farmhouse. She awoke, got out of bed, grasped an ax, and walked through the house, following the sound of footsteps, only to discover that the sounds were those of her frightened heart. She was able to laugh at the picture of herself, a very tall, thin, sophisticated city woman stalking through the empty house with an ax in her manicured hands. The cause of fear was all within herself.

Inner fear, or anxiety, may be turned outward and fixed on some external object or condition; we call this a phobia. We speak of acrophobia, the fear of heights; agoraphobia, the fear of open spaces, and claustrophobia, the fear of closed spaces; astrophobia, fear of thunder and lightning; dromophobia, fear of crossing streets, cynophobia, fear of dogs and rabies, and even triskaidekaphobia, fear of the number thirteen. This list could go on and on; the unconscious mind seems endlessly imaginative, and human beings in trouble find any number of outward causes, relevant and irrelevant, on which to fix their fears, including phobophobia, the fear of fear itself.

A real phobia is a sign of deep disturbance, and most of us settle for less. But we do externalize our inner anxiety; we do fix it on trivial causes. We worry about a business appointment the next day, or a dinner menu, or next month's bills (or perhaps last month's bills). We worry about anything, and then we worry about losing sleep worrying. The worry habit is definitely a sign of inner anxiety, and it is destructive.

Dangerous Crossings

In our campaign to find the danger signals before illness strikes, we can be helped by a knowledge that there are also dangerous periods in life, and dangerous seasons of the year.

Troubled people have a narrower margin of resistance than those who are at peace with themselves, and the more troubled, the narrower the margin. An individual may go along for years without apparent difficulty while environment and circumstances are favorable; he may give no outward sign that he is carrying on a war within himself. But at a time of crisis or pressure the personality must call upon its reserves, both physical and emotional. If these reserves have been depleted by continuous inner conflict over the years, the individual discovers that when he most needs his strength it is not there.

This is why we have breakdowns over a death in the family, a failure in marriage, a setback in work. This explains the varied illness growing out of war, either during the pressure of war itself or in the readjustment to civilian life afterward. One who is already teetering on the edge needs only the push of circumstance to topple him over.

Therefore it is well to consider those periods in every human life which are likely to provide the push. We have said that no man, woman, or child can avoid the pain of growing up. Adjustment is struggle. The need for adjustment is continuous. One must adjust oneself to environment, to family, to society, to the responsibilities of adulthood, to the realization of one's own limitations.

At certain ages this struggle becomes intensified. These are the dangerous periods. Medically speaking, these are actually the times of life when we find more people falling ill.

Adolescence is known to be a difficult time. The young person in adolescence is confronted not only with the changes in his own body and personality, the new demands made upon him by his need for independence, by his awakening sexual appetites. He must also face for the first time his responsibilities as a member of the adult world. He will soon be called upon to choose a career, to choose a marriage partner. The thousand demands of maturity are now just ahead of him.

As he emerges into his twenties he may have found the work of his choice or he may not. Some decisions may have been made for him. In any case his need for adjustment is now pressing. Rare is the fortunate young man or young woman for whom the path of the twenties is smooth. We may even question whether a smooth path is fortunate, for a struggle to mature at this age may avert more serious difficulty later.

Adolescence and the early twenties are the years of our freshest strength, our most abundant physical vigor. They are also years of great emotional pain and stress, years of anxiety and indecision and fear. They are the years in which a number of acute illnesses—among them tuberculosis, rheumatic fever, and pneumonia—are particularly likely to strike.

Let us say that our young man and young woman have made their adjustment in the twenties and embarked on the career and family life of their choice or as close to their desires as they could achieve. Now comes the danger period of the thirties.

Whether we accept the Bible's three score and ten as fact or symbol, the concept of a lifetime of seventy years has all the power of tradition. Most of us consciously or unconsciously approach the thirty-fifth birthday as a milestone; some begin to meditate even earlier. At this accepted halfway mark we take stock of what we have done with half our lives. If the accounting falls short of our ideal or desire, we become frightened. Time presses. Half of life is gone, the stronger, better half. From now on, our anxious self reminds us, we are on the downhill side. In the distress of hurry we ask, can we do what remains to be done? Can we overtake the success, the love, the happiness which is still just out of reach? The mid-thirties are a time when many functional disturbances begin to emerge.

Time moves on. The young man and young woman who have weathered their thirties are now in their middle or late forties. Climacteric and menopause are either upon them or in the near future, a physical reminder that one aspect of life—in the woman, the physically creative aspect of child-bearing—is ended.

For a man, and for a woman whose career or profession is important, this is also the time when success should have been achieved. Most people feel that if they have not reached the peak by the time they are fifty, they are not going to get there.

This is the time of the greatest number of breakdowns and the most serious. Especially in women, the belief that life is over, that they are now old and useless, no longer competitors in the sexual race, no longer physically productive, is often overpowering. Mental depressions are frequent at this age. In men the crisis is more subtle, but the number of men who suffer their first heart attack at this time is impressive.

Stormy Weather

The idea that two seasons of the year, spring and fall, are dangerous periods may sound fanciful, more in the realm of poetry than medicine. But every doctor knows that he has more sick people to take care of in the fall. As for spring, it has for centuries been the time for blood-letting and dosing, the traditional brimstone and molasses season.

Hellpach, a professor of medicine in the University of Frankfort who later became minister-president of Baden, wrote extensively on what he called "cosmic influences on the psyche." He was one of the first, some twenty-five years ago, to seek a connection between the change of seasons and the sudden increase in pregnancies, sexual crimes, suicides, and admissions to mental hospitals which occurs between the thirty-fifth and the sixtieth parallels from April to June, and below the Equator from October to December. Among both school children and working adults, he observed, physical activity increases and intellectual activity declines.

He described the species of intoxication which seems to infect the human race in the spring, the increase of instinctual activity and the submergence of rational considerations and inhibitions. But he confessed that the physical explanation was not clear. He suggested that the physiological effect of the increasing warmth of the weather was "intellectually paralyzing, the increase of light motorically stimulating." Science takes the long way 'round to define what any schoolboy knows is simple spring fever.

In normal persons, basal metabolism reaches its peak of the year in the spring, and thyrotoxicosis—the disease of over-active thyroid—is most frequent in spring, least in fall. We also know that hot or cold temperature can change the basal metabolism by fifty to one hundred per cent.

If the resurgent blossoming time of the earth is, as Hellpach says, instinctually stimulating, its opposite season is depressing. Troubled souls are inclined to be despondent in the autumn.

The end of growing things in the fall carries their spirits down to depression and often has a noticeable effect on their physical condition.

Years ago I had a neighbor, a hard-working farmer who in the spring and summer was a most responsible and respectable citizen. But on the day his field work was finished, his tools and machinery cleaned and put away, his sheds and barns made secure against the winter, this man began to drink.

"Why does this happen to you year after year?" I asked him once.

"Just wait till spring," he said. "I'll go on the wagon in the spring."

The explanation of his conduct is, of course, obvious. In the spring and summer, when he is creatively occupied, his inner conflict is stilled. But when the fall comes and creative work is ended, when he has nothing but the dull winter months of routine chores to look forward to, then his dissatisfactions rise to plague him and he escapes them via the alcohol route.

Certainly, as creatures of nature, we are affected by natural phenomena. Dogs bay at the moon, respectable house cats refuse to come home on moonlight nights, and somnambulists walk in their sleep under a full moon. Cattle become restless before a storm, and wild herds actually stampede. It was observed during World War II that fliers became drowsy and listless at high altitudes, and this phenomenon was explained by the decreased functioning of the adrenal glands.

Arrhenius, the Swedish chemist who was director of the Nobel Institute and who won the Nobel Prize for his theory of electric ionization, gave medicine the scientific connection between electrical charges and the autonomic nervous system. Efforts have been made to find a relationship between changes in static electricity in the atmosphere and in the nervous system which controls the visceral organs and the ductless glands.

Whether or not the exact train of psychic reactions to physical phenomena will some day be explained, we know pragmatically that as the earth turns in its course it brings changes in our natural environment to which we are vulnerable. At such times those who are at odds with themselves may see the signs of inner struggle. The symptoms are there for them to see—that is, if they wish to live in health.

SUMMING UP

There are critical seasons in the year, critical ages, and times of crisis in everyone's life.

* * *

People who are at odds with themselves have a narrower margin of safety and are ready victims of illness at critical times.

* * *

Under stress the unconscious gives warning signs to be heeded by those who wish to live in health.

7

The Chain Reaction
of Illness

*It is not enough to repair the link in the
body's system of defense.*

THE NATURAL world presents to our senses an infinite variety of detail. We know also that there are worlds beyond our own, both too great and too small to see with the unaided eye. Yet despite this labyrinthine complexity, there arises one day an Einstein whose penetrating intellect brings harmony out of massive chaos and reveals to us a universal majestic order.

So with man, nature's most complex and contradictory child. The apparently unrelated patterns of illness, of which we have sketched some of the advance symptoms, also fall into a revelatory orderliness. Chaos does not exist in nature, but only in man's imperfect understanding.

Physiologists, endocrinologists, and psychiatrists, working in their separate fields, have been converging toward a single theory. The human being, they tell us, reacts to stress—that is, difficulties in life—in one of two basic ways. Either he deals with it aggressively as an animal deals with an enemy, by fight or flight. Or else he evades the difficulty, turning like a child for help and protection to a parent or the equivalent of a parent.

Whichever way he chooses, he may be blocked by an obstacle, either external or within himself. If he sets out aggressively to deal with his difficulties he may be stopped by circumstance, or he may be stopped by his own fear—of failure, of punishment, or some unhappy consequence of his action. If he seeks parental protection, he may be rejected by the person from whom he seeks it, or he may be halted by his own pride or guilt since he is aware that he is no longer a child.

But in each case a series of reactions has been set in motion in the body. These, blocked, now turn aside from their original goal, which was to act in some way on the difficulty.

The aggressive impulse, fight or flight, sets up a chain of reactions which when blocked may lead to one group of diseases. The regressive impulse, the retreat into infantile dependency, may lead to another set of diseases.

Thus we see emerging two great groups of illnesses resulting from the two basic emotional responses to stress.

The aggressive personality is susceptible to heart disease, high blood pressure, arteriosclerosis and other circulatory disorders, migraine, rheumatoid arthritis, hyperthyroidism. Diabetes, many skin diseases, and certain allergies also possibly belong here.

The regressive personality reacts with fatigue states, functional disturbances of the digestive tract such as indigestion, diarrhea or constipation, colitis and a whole train of gastrointestinal complaints including peptic ulcer, plus certain allergies and respiratory diseases.

So far we have in bare outline an explanation of why energetic, dominating Aunt Martha has migraine while Uncle Henry, meek and timid soul, suffers from a chronic dyspepsia. We mention Aunt Martha and Uncle Henry as symbols for the many couples whom all of us know.

Take Mr. and Mrs. S for example: Mrs. S, a strong personality, is a public speaker and a leader in community-organization work. Mr. S is the conservative, cautious vice-president of a corporation. Mrs. S suffers from migraine. Mr. S has chronic gastro-intestinal disturbances and bronchial catarrh.

Mr. and Mrs. T are in business together. She is outgoing, at ease with people, active, enthusiastic. He is somber, heavy, easily irritated, withdrawn, and in private depends on his wife for every trivial decision. She has rheumatic pains in her neck. He has persistent stomach trouble.

And Mr. and Mrs. N. She had a hyperthyroid condition and he had a stomach ulcer—until they separated and both illnesses disappeared.

At the Command of the Emotions

To grasp the full promise of this approach to illness not only for cure but also for prevention, we must trace the course of the chain reaction of the emotions through the physical mechanisms of the nervous system and the internal glands.

We have within us three nerve systems, the central, the peripheral, and the autonomic. The one of which we are aware, and by which we walk, talk, laugh and cry, eat when we are hungry, cover ourselves when we are cold, is the central or voluntary system; that is, it is controlled by our conscious will. The peripheral system deals with the sense organs.

The autonomic nervous system is the one with which we are now concerned. This system is involved entirely with internal activity. It controls the so-called smooth muscles, those of the visceral organs, the veins and arteries; its branches reach into every tissue and every cell of the body. Our heart beat, our breathing, the expansion and contraction of blood vessels, the mechanism of digesting food, storing it, and releasing it for the body's use—all this is the business of the autonomic nervous system.

This system cannot be commanded by our conscious will. *But it reacts automatically to our emotions.*

The autonomic nervous system has two divisions, both essential, which must function in harmony for us to remain in health: the sympathetic system and the parasympathetic system. They work in opposition to each other. One dilates and the other contracts; one stimulates and the other inhibits.

The parasympathetic system (also called the vagus system) runs a steady conservative course, preparing food, storing sugar, protecting the body against cold by contracting the blood vessels, making you cough in a smoky room. The parasympathetic system is the peacetime governor.

The sympathetic system deals with emergency conditions. Let us say you hear a burglar entering your home. Alarm sends its message through the sympathetic system, and the organs are at once activated to war production. Blood is driven out of the abdominal cavity to the lungs, the muscles, the brain, bringing them their needed increase of energy for action. The blood pressure rises. Carbohydrates are moved out of storage in the liver and muscles and converted into fuel. The adrenal glands, the fighting glands, pour their stimulating hormones into the blood stream. The body is made ready for a fight—or for flight.

Since these systems work in opposition to each other, whichever is in control—depending on the situation or on the emotional state of the individual—determines the condition of the body. Under the dominance of the parasympathetic system the body tends to withdraw into a vegetative state: after eating we rest; after working we sleep. The body conserves and prepares itself for the demands of living. The sympathetic system is for action. When it is in control the peaceful, upbuilding functions of the body are arrested. All is mobilization, production, the spending of reserves and resources.

Now we begin to see once more the outlines of two personalities within the one human being, two possible basic reactions to life. In a well-integrated, well-adjusted individual these two systems function in harmony, each assuming control as the situation demands. But when the individual is in conflict emotionally, this harmonious cooperation is disturbed.

Two Reactions to Emergency

Let us again create an emergency, a situation demanding decision and action. A burglar is entering the house.

Aunt Martha, the energetic, the aggressive, whose sympathetic nervous system is the dominant one, leaps out of bed, seizes whatever weapon comes to hand and descends to meet the intruder. Uncle Henry, a parasympathetic type, covers his head with the bedclothes and lets Aunt Martha handle the emergency.

So far so good. If there is a burglar, Aunt Martha's highly energized heart, muscles, and brain have their outlet in action, and Uncle Henry enjoys the protection he craves.

But suppose there is no burglar. Suppose the situation is not such an absurdly simple fiction as we have concocted, but one of those complex, emotion-tangled snarls which form the real pattern of human living.

Suppose that, instead of a burglar, Aunt Martha must face, day in and day out, the truth of her marriage to a timid, indecisive man. Suppose that Uncle Henry must confront through the years his inability to make an outstanding success in business, to achieve the stature of a man in his own and his wife's eyes.

Aunt Martha, driven by the need to deal aggressively with life situations, is in a state of continuous preparedness for action—and cannot act. It is contrary to her ethical standards to act on her dissatisfaction with her husband; she can neither abandon him nor accept him as he is, and her efforts to change him into a more aggressive personality are frustrated by his inability to change, as it were, from the inside out. She is caged, filled with thwarted drives, with the rage and hostility which are the products of continuous frustration and which she buries in her unconscious because it is wrong to have such feelings toward one's marriage and one's husband. When her inner tensions become too great, she has one of her violent migraine headaches.

There are people who go about in a state of perpetual preparedness for a battle which—because of fear, of conscience, of family obligations, of social standards—they can never fight. That is, they cannot fight the real battle, and so instead they burst into rages over a trivial cause.

The repeated rise in blood pressure may lead to hypertension and possible embolism or stroke; the disturbance in carbohydrate metabolism may tend to diabetes; the chronic muscular tension may cause rheumatoid arthritis; the constant state of vigilance may bring on toxic thyroidism.

Uncle Henry meanwhile lives in unconscious longing to withdraw entirely from the struggle into a state of childish dependency. He cannot meet the demands made on him by the world, by his wife, or by his own ambition. Nor can he in reality creep back into his mother's arms. He wins some comfort and protection from his wife's stronger personality, but at a price. Shame castigates him, guilt tortures him, and his sense of inadequacy follows him as his shadow. Indigestion is his fate.

Why indigestion? Why do dependent personalities react with digestive disorders?

The infant's earliest sensations of comfort and protection are related to food. His first physical discomfort is hunger, his first satisfaction is eating, and both the hunger and the relief of it are identified with his mother. So is his feeling of being safe and cared for. Hence the infantile pattern of seeking relief from emotional discomfort through food.

In nature, an animal first fights and then eats, dining on his victim. But a dependent personality, figuring there's a tough job ahead, says, "We'd better have a bite first." Frustration and guilt in seeking relief through a dependent pattern take their toll on the same organs. The digestive system is the target.

Before we are misled into dividing the human race arbitrarily into two categories, however, let us keep in mind that man with his complexities does not lend himself to simple classification. Each of us has his differences from every other. To press any of us into a preconceived, rigid scheme, however logical, is an affront to our uniqueness.

Any man or woman may be aggressive and regressive. Or, unable to go either way, one may simply sit still and remain passive. The body may be mobilizing to fight while the child within whimpers for protection. We can use our knowledge of the two types of emotional response and the two groups of illness as a guide, but we must be prepared to find the line between them crossed and recrossed, and symptoms of both reactions existing in a single individual, side by side, even at the same time.

The Significance of ACTH

This interpretation of illness—that a given disease falls into one of two groups, arising from one or the other basic emotional response—is presented by the psychiatrist Franz Alexander in *Psychosomatic Medicine, Its Principles and Applications*. It is drawn not alone from psychiatric findings but from a vast array of clinical and laboratory research by biological scientists, especially Doctors W. B. Cannon, George Draper, and E. Moschcowitz.

The truth of this approach is being daily confirmed, most compellingly by the endocrinologists, whose field of study is the ductless glands. It was of the endocrinologists that Freud long ago warned his students, remarking that this biological next-door neighbor was close on the heels of psychoanalysis and might one day overtake it.

A great event in this field occurred in 1949 when scientists gathered in Chicago for the first conference on ACTH. Out of this meeting came the story of what appeared to be a miracle; arthritics who had been helpless for years rose up out of their wheel chairs and walked; some of them danced. There were films to reassure the skeptical that the wonder was a fact. Newspaper headlines trumpeted the hope that sufferers from rheumatoid arthritis could be cured. The discoverers were awarded the Nobel Prize.

Since that October day the brilliance of this news seems to have dimmed. Relapses of arthritic patients after treatment have been reported in a percentage of cases. Doctors have suggested that the miracle hormones might be of benefit only to a limited group of people and only if administered periodically, like insulin to diabetics. ACTH is a treatment of symptoms, *not a cure*.

At first glance these reports seem discouraging. We remember the excitement generated by Steinach and Voronoff's work with the sex glands, and the latter's famous "monkey-gland" operation which first sent a wave of hope across the world that the secret of youth had been found, and then became a popular joke. Is the miracle of ACTH dwindling too under the critical eyes of the experimenters and clinicians?

Not so. The significance of ACTH and cortisone is not so much whether they cure. Their significance is that they reveal to us a most important link in the chain reaction of illness.

What Are Hormones?

The system of the internal or ductless glands, functioning with the sympathetic and parasympathetic nervous systems, is constantly engaged in meeting the changing conditions to which the individual is exposed. It does this by means of glandular secretions, which are called hormones.

The sex hormones were for a long time the hormones predominantly used in medicine, and for this reason people tend to identify hormones with the product of the sex glands only. They say, "My doctor gave me hormones," but this is like saying, "My doctor gave me capsules." There are probably hundreds of different hormones produced in the body.

Hormone is a general term, meaning the secretion of any one of the ductless glands, and there are a number of these glands. We call them "ductless" to distinguish them from the glands which have ducts or canals. Sweat glands, tear glands, salivary glands all have ducts and empty externally, on the outside of the body. Other glands, like those in the digestive system, empty within the body into an organ. The ductless glands empty directly into the blood stream.

The theory that inner fluids regulate the functions of the

body goes back to Hippocrates, who named four cardinal fluids responsible for health or illness: blood, phlegm, yellow bile and black bile. The four humors, as they were called from the Latin word for moisture, survive in our language as descriptive of four types of personality. A cheerful, confident person we call *sanguine,* from the Latin for blood. A stolid one is *phlegmatic.* A man easily angered is *choleric,* a word derived from the Greek root chol for bile, and a gloomy man suffers from melancholy, which is *chol* plus *mela* meaning black, or "black bile."

The theory of the humors dominated medicine through the Middle Ages and into modern times, until it was abandoned in favor of Virchow's cellular pathology. The French physiologist Claude Bernard, studying the digestive juices, discovered the functions of the liver and pancreas, and stated his belief that health depended on the *milieu interieur,* the inner condition, by which he meant the balance of these fluids.

This idea was carried forward by the American physiologist Cannon, who coined the term "homeostasis" to describe the tendency of the body to maintain balance. Thus the theory of the humors returns in a new, scientific form.

Among our ductless glands are the sex glands, the thyroid, the pancreas, the thymus, the pineal, the adrenals, and the pituitary. Each of these produces its specific hormone or group of hormones. We know the functions of *some* but not of *all* of them.

The adrenal glands, which lie just above the kidneys, produce a powerful hormone under conditions demanding physical action. We have long known that that area of the body was a source of physical energy and courage. One of Shakespeare's characters calls out for "strength in my kidneys." The familiar adrenalin is the trade name for this adrenal hormone, and is used as a stimulant.

The pituitary is the master gland, the switchboard through which impulses are directed toward the other glands. For all its importance, it is a small gland, seated at the base of the brain in a protective bony cradle called the Turkish saddle. It has three lobes. In the interior lobe are tiny centers of specific hormones which go out to stimulate the other glands. The sex glands, the thyroid, the adrenals do not go into action unless the pituitary sends to each its specific activating hormone.

The word *tropic*, from the Greek word pertaining to turning, is used to describe these anterior pituitary hormones which turn toward or are directed at specific glands. What Hench and Kendall isolated in the anterior lobe of the pituitary was the hormone directed at the cortex or outer layer of the adrenal gland. They called it the adrenal-cortico-tropic-hormone or, briefly, ACTH. Cortisone is one of a group of twenty-eight or more hormones in the adrenal cortex which are activated by ACTH.

The physiological chain of reactions appears to follow this course: a stimulus is carried through the hypothalamus (a part of the interbrain between the cerebrum and medulla) to the anterior pituitary, which then sends out its tropic hormones to the glands.

Stress Gives the Alarm

Stress is the term now used in medicine to cover all the conditions—external or internal, physical or emotional—to which the body is exposed. Hans Selye, professor at the University of Montreal, in his book *Stress,* lists three diseases as outstanding examples of the effects on the body of our modern stressful life: thyrotoxicosis, a disease resulting from excess activity of the thyroid gland; duodenal ulcer; and hypertension, or high blood pressure, of the variety which comes from causes other than diseased kidneys. He groups these three under the name, "stress diseases."

The stress diseases are often described as "wear-and-tear diseases," and medicine adds several more to the list: obesity, underweight, diseases of the heart and blood vessels, and some others.

These diseases occur under the strains characteristic of civilized life. They are comparatively rare in primitive society. In fact man is not alone in suffering these penalties of his civilization. His companion, the dog, having accepted whole-heartedly his dependence upon his human master, also gets ulcers. The cat, though domestic, remains essentially independent—and cats do not get ulcers!

Stress, whether an emotional disturbance or a physical one such as injury, exposure to cold, fever, in short any noxious condition, sets up an alarm reaction in the body, a chain of functions designed to meet the condition. Selye calls this series of reactions the "general adaptation syndrome," a syndrome being a group of related symptoms. A continuance of this syndrome eventually brings about one of the stress diseases.

Selye demonstrated by experiment that any stressful experience, physical or emotional, as well as an overdose of certain hormones, can bring about the same diseases. Rats exposed to jingling noises, flashing lights, and other stressful experiences rapidly developed symptoms of the various stress diseases: rheumatic, allergic, and hypertensive disorders, especially severe arteriosclerosis and persistent high blood pressure.

When the rats were given ACTH and cortisone, the symptoms subsided. The diseases were checked, and actually reversed.

Dr. Selye concluded that the body has a unified defense mechanism which operates by way of the ductless glands and their hormones. This theory is based on Cannon's teaching of *homeostasis*, the term that this great American physiologist used to mean the body's mechanisms for restoring and maintaining internal balance. Health depends on the balance of these hormones. When stress continues too long, a breakdown may occur in this integrated defense system, at the point of production of one or some of these hormones. Thus when we supply these hormones medically, we attempt to restore the broken link so that the defense system can again function.

"They are the first natural agents," the *Journal of the American Medical Association* points out, "by means of which it is possible to demonstrate the potential reversibility" of a number of diseases which up to now have been considered incurable.

ACTH and the Two Basic Reactions

Further experiments with ACTH and cortisone seem to lend support to the theory of the two groups of illnesses proceeding from the two basic emotional reactions, the aggressive and the regressive.

ACTH, cortisone, and a variety of cortico-steroids which are more potent and have fewer side effects, are now an established treatment for rheumatoid arthritis, osteo-arthritis, rheumatic fever, inflammatory and allergic eye and skin diseases, and others of the group known as collagen disorders (collagen is a substance in the tissues of bone, cartilage, skin, and hair). All these diseases, as we have learned, belong to the group stemming from the *aggressive response* to stress.

On the other hand, three cases of peptic ulcers were treated with ACTH. The ulcers, far from improving, became much worse. Peptic ulcer is one of the leading diseases in the list of those belonging to the *regressive response*.

Another report revealed that cortisone increased the susceptibility to infantile paralysis. This seems to indicate that a breakdown of the glandular system opens the way to *infectious* diseases, as well as to diseases of "wear-and-tear."

This recalls one of my own cases of several years ago. A young man, whom I had treated some time previously for stomach disorders, came to me and asked to be examined for polio. He showed no symptoms, and I was obliged to tell him that we knew of no way at that time to test susceptibility to the disease, of which he was extremely fearful. The following year he went to another physician and again demanded to be examined for polio. Again he was reassured that he did not have the disease.

The third year, he contracted paralytic polio.

Much more research along these lines is needed, and is being done, to set us firmly on the track of this new, and perhaps revolutionary, approach to illness by way of endocrinology and biochemistry which dovetail so closely with the theory of the emotional background of illness.

A patient of mine had suffered intensely from headaches for many years and was totally blind in one eye, when the other eye began to fail. The optic nerve of the second eye was found to be inflamed and badly damaged. This man had an old case of syphilis which had been treated unsuccessfully with the classic medications, plus massive doses of penicillin. Five injections of cortisone restored vision in the failing eye, and there was no recurrence.

Why Not a Cure?

Yet these powerful hormones are not a cure. Hench has explained: "Both agents (ACTH and cortisone) affect not the cause of a disease but the reaction of the tissue to the irritant or cause."

ACTH and cortisone come close to a cure. They restore a broken link in the body's effort to maintain or regain balance, at the point where continued stress has caused a breakdown.

But obviously, hormones cannot cure, if the underlying emotional pattern remains unchanged. Hormones, impressive as their brief record has already become, may still do no more than repair what the inner conflict will again break down. We cannot expect a cure if the individual continues a course of self-destruction.

It is not enough to repair the link in the body's system of defense. We must get at the source of stress which is forcing the body to make this continuous excessive effort.

We have a fair chance of avoiding physical stress, except in abnormal situations, because we are aware of it. Of emotional stress we may not even be conscious, or we may evade or seek to escape the necessity of becoming conscious of it. But there is no substitute for the rational effort to deal with emotional stress. Hormones are a weapon against disease, but the preservation of health remains, and must still remain, within ourselves, because it depends upon the individual's own specific way of reacting to the stress of living.

We now know that the body can restore itself if we will only allow it to do so. The body is not so fragile as we sometimes fear. It is capable of forceful resistance. It can be pushed far, very far, and still find resources to recover. If the body has exhausted these resources, we can supply medically the help which will restore it. This restoration is, however, only temporary. It is a lift on the way back to health. The true recovery is still in our hands.

In Philip Barry's play, *The Second Threshold*, young Doctor Wells muses, "Wonderful stuff, these new drugs. But in many cases, if I had to choose between them and the will to live, I'd take the old original . . . All the same, it's nice we have both."

There is a conscious, rational role which each of us can play in the defense of our health against the stress of living. The body is constructed to endure this stress. The human organism is the product of thousands of years of selection and adaptation, and it is built for hard usage. From the stress of living *by itself* we have nothing to fear.

It is when we permit stress to continue indefinitely, or repetitiously, without taking rational steps to relieve it, that we suffer damage. It is when we permit ourselves to follow a neurotic pattern, that we ourselves defeat the body's resiliency. When we fight the same battle over and over *in fantasy*, when we fear disaster *in fantasy*, when we run for protection *in fantasy*, then we wear out the body's mechanisms for maintaining balance.

This we must remember: whether we fight the battle in reality or only in dream, whether we labor physically or in the mind, the demands on our body in all these instances are real.

Once we make a decision and set a course, once we take action in the world of reality, then we relieve the body of that emotional stress which is as real as physical stress. Positive decision, realistic action in the direction of adjustment, are steps on the road back to health.

The infantile dependency pattern is not an effort at adjustment; it is a passive state, an evasion of the need to do anything. The aggressive pattern, on the other hand, is an effort at adjustment. But it must be carried through. We must deal with the real difficulty by means of real action, either fight or flight.

Fight means changing the situation, or changing oneself; that is, positive adjustment. But flight from the situation is also normal and therefore healthy. Flight is not necessarily cowardice; it may be self-preservation.

The choice is ours. A chronic state of indecision is an expression of the destructive drive. By positive adjustment, by supporting mind and body in their efforts to adjust—which is not the same as compromise or resignation—we can achieve the satisfactions of healthy living.

_____ SUMMING UP_____

Life confronts everyone with stressful situations and stress causes wear-and-tear in the body.

*   *   *

Whether the stress is external or emotional, the wear-and-tear is real.

*   *   *

We may not be able to change the situation, but we can change our emotional response to it.

*   *   *

The body will restore itself if we will only allow it to do so, for it is built for hard usage.

8

We Select Our Illness

We must learn to understand and respect the elementary forces within us if we wish to understand what makes illness.

WE HAVE examined the two basic emotional reactions to stress. We have seen that two groups of diseases emerge according to these two emotional patterns. But within each group of diseases, what brings on one disease rather than another?

Out of the research of physicians exploring the relationship between mind and body, a formidable truth appears: within the framework of our individual constitution, we ourselves choose the time of illness, the kind of illness, the course of illness, and its gravity.

Of course we do not make these choices consciously. We do not *reason* ourselves into illness. The decisions are made in the unconscious court of judgment which sits, waking and sleeping, within us. They are arrived at by way of involved and turbulent argument without words, the language of the emotions. Also we must remember that these decisions are not irrevocable. We can and do change our minds. We can and do reverse our course, and turn back from illness to health.

But the important new knowledge we have gained is this: that while the choice for illness or health is made emotionally, it is carried out through the physical mechanisms of the body.

Against doubts, questioning, and ignorance, against the natural resistance of the reasoning mind, which is reluctant to believe what cannot be seen or touched, it is necessary to repeat, time and again, that we poker-faced civilized people are moved by impulses and inspirations, by feelings and emotional drives which our clear reason can never understand so long as we employ only physiological methods to examine them.

Physiology describes subjective experiences such as hunger, fear, rage, pain, in physiological terms. Psychology studies the motivation of these emotions. With our present methods, psychological study depends on verbal communication. We can penetrate another person's subjective experiences only if he can be led to talk about them. Only by inviting him to communicate, by giving him freedom to talk, can we gain insight into the dynamics of emotion, idea, fantasy. Those are the inner drives which, when intefered with, lead to physiological and eventually to physical changes; in other words, to functional and at last to organic illness.

We must learn to understand and respect the elementary forces within us if we wish to understand what makes illness. Love, hate, fear, guilt, pride, vengeance are the values by which we are moved. Also, as Cicero said, "There is something so penetrating in the shaft of envy that even men of wisdom and worth find its wound a painful one." Our emotions fill us with dynamic power to deal with the problems of living, or they block our intelligence, paralyze our will, and hypnotize our consciousness.

Illness Hits its Target

The need for a way out, for escape, sacrifice, or self-punishment, drives us to single out an organ to destroy by illness. According to our emotional standard of values, we make the choice for a determined suicide or a half-hearted one, or for merely a gesture. The emotions have their own compelling logic. A man with sickness in his body follows a chosen route which the high command of the destructive drive has determined.

Medicine speaks of tissue memory. A part of an organ which has been injured in the past is said to retain a memory, and that is the part which will give the first sign of trouble when the individual is under stress. Medically this is explained by the principle of the point of lowest resistance.

Now we may seriously consider whether it may not be a case of returning to the attack on the same part or organ as, under stress, we attacked before. The same emotional pattern which fixed on that organ in the past fixes on it again. An obvious example is that a man who gets a stomach ulcer is likely to have a history of gastric disturbance. But there are less obvious ones. If you hurt an arm once long ago, it is in that arm that you are likely to have neuralgic pain in a time of stress.

The first time that a part of the body was involved in difficulty may go back to childhood, and we are not likely to remember too clearly what the emotional situation was then so long ago. But all indications are that the part of our body which suffers attack from injury or illness has a specific emotional significance within the framework of our whole personality.

Retreat into Blindness

Mrs. De S., for example, is a city woman of highly cultured background who married and went to live in an Indian village in the high Andes of South America. Her husband brought her back to the United States after a few years, very ill. She had a blood pressure of more than two hundred, pain in the neck and temples, a choking sensation in her throat. In particular she was almost blind; she had developed cataracts on her eyes.

When she came into my office she was near collapse. An old

friend, she stayed to dinner. In the next hour or two she became young, animated, charming, telling witty anecdotes of
her life in South America. The transformation was astonishing.
In the course of the evening's talk she let fall, not once but several times, the remark, "I couldn't bear to look at that wall of
mountains."

The cataracts were removed, the patient's health became
better, and then the time came to return to the Andes. Now
her blood pressure suddenly shot up again to two hundred
forty. But because her relationship with her husband was a
close one she would not remain in the States without him. She
barely made it alive to their mountain home, and in less than a
year she was back in New York, this time with a detached
retina.

She spent months in the hospital and underwent an operation, which was unsuccessful. Meanwhile her husband began
negotiations for the sale of a large tract of his mountain land.

Gradually she improved. The eye began to heal itself.
When they flew back she was hopeful that with the sale of the
land they would at last be able to live again in New York
where she could once more enjoy the life she longed for, the
music, theater, and friends she had missed.

With the promise that she will one day be able to scale that
mountain wall and enjoy the world beyond it once more, my
patient no longer needs to shut out the very sight of her prison
walls. Now she has the support of hope in curbing her destructive drive and rekindling her will to live. Nor does she have to
wait for the actual day of escape in order to begin to live. She
can afford to live more fully now, and enjoy the beauty of the
majestic peaks.

We Choose the Time of Illness

I have said that we select the time of our illness. A high-
spirited Irishwoman of forty-three came to me with a variety of
complaints. She had been well and strong, she told me em-
phatically, until she was twenty-two. She was happily married,

loved her husband and her two children, loved living in the United States.

But since the age of twenty-two she had been plagued by a series of physical miseries: infected tonsils, inflamed gall bladder, pains, nausea, a virus infection, an eye infection, an infection in her arm. Her tonsils had been removed, and both her children had been born by Caesarean operation. She had been a healthy, robust girl—why should she be so troubled by illness, she demanded.

I asked her in turn, what had happened when she was twenty-two. She said at that time she had left her home in Ireland, left her village, her youth behind. Memories, longing for places and people of her girlhood, and perhaps some unconscious protest against adjustment to her new life, not only in a strange land but with the responsibilities of adulthood—all these were present in the background of her many illnesses. Actually her real disease was homesickness.

The time we choose for illness may have symbolic significance. A man and his wife were celebrating the golden anniversary of what had been an apparently perfect marriage. Standing at his wife's side, accepting the congratulations of his friends, the man was all at once aware of something amiss with his body. Later he discovered that he was suffering an internal hemorrhage. He had never been ill in his life. The urologist diagnosed an inoperable growth involving the prostate gland and the bladder, probably malignant.

Under questioning, this vigorous and highly respectable man confessed that his wife was frigid, and that he had had a mistress during his younger days. His wife had known it and reproached him with the fact through the years. As he grew older and more dependent on his wife, she used her increasing power over him to torment him with his offense.

Menninger tells us that feelings of guilt are especially strong in connection with violations of the sexual conventions, and it is not surprising that organic lesions should occur in the genitourinary organs.

Symbols too have a potency over us. So in this particular

case the golden wedding, a significant milestone, brought to a critical stage a condition which must have been developing over a period of years.

Treatment with opposite sex hormones had here, as in many similar cases, a deterrent effect on the tumor, and the old man lived in comfort for nearly seven years.

But the death of one whom our superego tells us we have injured brings a new access of guilt. So when the patient's wife died his disease became suddenly reactivated. A biopsy—that is, a laboratory examination of a section of diseased tissue from the patient—showed that he did indeed have a malignancy, which had been held in check until the new crisis occurred. Then medicine could no longer countermand the verdict of the superego, and the destructive drive carried out the sentence.

The following story suggests how infectious disease also may be purposefully, though unconsciously, sought.

Two men friends were celebrating a reunion after one of them had been absent overseas. At the end of the evening they dropped into a bar, and presently noticed an attractive young woman alone. The more aggressive of the two men, on the insistence of his timid friend, invited the young woman to their table and afterward to his home. Both enjoyed her favors.

The timid man came later to be treated for a venereal infection. He complained bitterly that his friend, who had taken no more precaution than himself, had got off scot-free.

Says Menninger: "I am convinced from my observations that even venereal disease is sometimes acquired partly because the victim invited the infection not only by his behavior (e.g. carelessness) but also by some unknown subtle modification of tissue resistance."

Significantly it was the timid man, the one with the stronger inhibitions and hence stronger guilt feelings, who suffered punishment. The germ which attacks the cells of the body is no more accidental than the tree in the path of the speeding driver who is unconsciously toying with suicide.

The Man Who Needs His Ulcer

How determined is the wish for self-destruction?

We have said that it might be half-hearted, or in earnest, or merely a gesture. A record of 2,030 deaths in Manhattan, covering a period of seven years, shows that forty-five per cent of all "natural" deaths were due to heart disease, twenty-three per cent respiratory, eighteen per cent caused by nervous disorders, and only six and one-half per cent digestive.

Digestive disorders are rarely fatal. A man may live in sorry discomfort with his stomach ulcers, but he is not likely to die of them, without the assistance of other troubles.

This bears out the theory of the digestive disorders as resulting from the infantile dependency pattern. These people do not want to die. They want to live and to be loved. They long to be cared for. When love is denied them, or when out of pride and guilt they cannot accept love, then they suffer pain and eventually damage to the tissues of the digestive system.

It is only when guilt and anxiety are overwhelming, or when hostility is acutely sharpened by the denial of love, the more dangerous processes enter in and the tendency toward self-damage becomes a drive toward self-destruction. Otherwise theirs is likely to be a repetitious nagging self-torture rather than a struggle to the death.

An elderly man, a grandfather, came to me with peptic ulcers from which he had been suffering for thirty years, the major part of his adult life. If he could only be rid of them! It was all he asked of life he said.

"Suppose tomorrow you woke up cured—what would you do?" I asked him.

"Why, I would enjoy life," he answered.

"How would you enjoy it? What would you do?" I persisted.

"Why—" he floundered, "I would enjoy it—like other people."

He could not be more specific. He had no plan, no purpose,

no driving desire to be well in order to accomplish something that was important to him. For thirty years he had built his life around this illness. His colleagues in business catered to him, praised him for his devotion to his work despite his handicap. His family at home cushioned him with attentions because of his "condition." The bowl of hot soup was always waiting for him when he got home from the office.

To take away his ulcer would at one sweep deprive him of the special position he enjoyed, and all the attentions which served him in place of mature relationships of mutual affection and responsibility. Take away his ulcer and you take away the bowl of hot soup, his substitute for love. No, he could not say how he would enjoy life without his ulcer, because he could not even imagine life without his ulcer. He needed his ulcer.

So often this is true of chronic sufferers from digestive disorders. Ulcers are frequently cured by medical means, but too often they do not stay cured.

With these patients the need for love, or for the attentions which are their recourse in the absence of love, is stronger than any need to be well and to function at full capacity in the world of adult responsibility. With all possible sympathy for these sufferers, and with all possible understanding and tolerance for them as victims of adult domination in their childhood, we must still recognize the average chronic ulcer patient as one who suffers from emotional immaturity first and from ulcers second.

To say this is not to judge or blame him, but rather to understand and help him. It is beyond his power to help himself, since his growth into emotional adulthood is blocked by a power stronger than himself.

A youth of twenty once came to me with an acute ulcer of the stomach, for which he had been medically discharged from the navy. Going back through his history, I learned that he had had a series of accidents: a football injury to his knee at school, an injury to his foot at work, and finally an accident on shipboard during his navy service in which he suffered a concussion as well as injury to both knees. Then he revealed that he had already had his first ulcer at the age of fourteen.

This early start on the ulcer route is not average, but this boy's future as a chronic ulcer sufferer had better than average preparation. His father had chronic ulcers. When I visited him at home, I saw an environment which might have been contrived as a laboratory demonstration of what makes ulcers.

The mother, a dominating woman, was also restless, neglectful, apparently without the slightest impulse of warmth or a wish to care for her family. Though they were better than well-to-do, dinner was a hastily assembled mess from the delicatessen store because she had spent the afternoon at a card party—food out of cans and paper bags, food which required no forethought and no preparation, and an over-abundance of it, as though to make up for the time and care she had not spent on the meal. Too much food, to take the place of too little love.

The house in which this family lived was handsome and expensive, but it certainly was not a real home. There was, in fact, no permanence about this family's living arrangements. Every second year they moved. When the father bought a suburban house and furnished it, the mother tired of it in a year, expressing a longing to be back with her friends in the city. So they sold the house and moved back to town. A year or so later she wanted to get out of the city again. The father bought a house in another suburb. At the time when the boy became my patient the mother was already tiring of this second country place.

Eventually the father also became my patient. From him I learned that he was comparatively well all week. But almost invariably after each weekend he suffered a violent attack of ulcer symptoms.

What deep discontent drove this woman to behave this way to her husband and son? If we knew all there was to know about her we would understand that she had profound difficulties of her own.

Her husband's need to cling to the protected situation of

childhood led him unconsciously to choose a woman of dominating personality, and she, needing to dominate, married this
kind of man. But neither could be satisfied because, in the
light of reality, each also had opposite needs that the other
was unable to fulfill. He needed to be recognized as an adult
man, and she wanted to be loved as a woman. Thus their marriage resulted in deep emotional deprivations for both.

On the surface the typical ulcer sufferer is likely to be aggressive rather than dependent. The last thing he wishes to reveal about himself, or to recognize in himself, is his need for
love. Consequently he overcompensates with forceful, self-con-
fident behavior. The father in this family was energetic, driving, a very good provider. He demanded recognition, and was
inclined to be boastful about his business success. Away from
his work he was a fish out of water. He talked about liking to
have interesting people around him, but actually he was inclined to withdraw into a corner of a room, avoiding the necessity of extending himself socially.

This sort of individual characteristically does not gamble at
cards or the races. He needs most to be the center of his wife's
attention and feels deprived by her rival interests.

Hunger for Love

Ulcers can also be an acute, sudden development in a specific emotional situation, provided the contributing factors of
personality are present. An individual with a tendency toward
dependence may go along for many years without trouble until
a crisis occurs which finds out his weakness, his short supply of
mature resources to deal with the difficulty.

A report from a Swedish clinic in 1950 gives the results of
a psychiatric examination of 108 ulcer patients; fifty-four were
found to be suffering acute mental conflict; twenty-nine showed
chronic mental conflict; twenty-two had psychopathological
symptoms without conflict, and only three revealed no psychological factors whatever.

That ulcers, of the whole long list of man's ills, have an emo-

tional origin has been accepted for some time with little argument. What we are newly coming to understand is the nature
of this emotional background. The general statement that ulcers come from worry is no longer enough.

Clever and skillful as we may be in our medical treatment
of ulcers, the emotional setting of the patient's life, his need
for love and care will balk all our efforts until we can awaken
in him an understanding of himself, and an active, purposeful
will to lift himself out of the dependent pattern which makes
him ill. He will not live for his ulcer if he can find something
better to live for.

Rebuke, reproach, rejection of his inarticulate plea for love
will not help him. On the contrary, it will only drive him deeper
into conflict with himself and perhaps despair. An attempt to
"make a man of him" by force, without understanding, can
change a mild illness into a serious one.

We must recognize, too, the pressures of our society which
drive less sturdy individuals backward into this immature emotional pattern of dependence. H. R. Hartman, writing on "Neu-
rogenic Factors in Peptic Ulcer," observes that Chinese coolies
and Latin-American Indians never have ulcers, and suggests
that the explanation may lie in their attitude toward living.
They are free from the straining, driving ambition which char-
acterizes Western white civilization. The coolie expects little
of life, and when the day brings him his bowl of rice he eats it
zestfully. He does not complicate his body hunger with other
hungers since these other hungers, as far as we know, do not
exist for him.

But we Westerners, under the pressure to achieve individual
success, to "make good," need continuous confirmation of our
value as individuals, continuous recognition of our worthiness
to be loved. To us a bowl of rice is not merely food for the body
but also a reminder of the parent who first provided us with
both food and love. It becomes a symbol of love and also a
weapon when love is absent. Feeling rejected, we reject in turn,
refusing our food to punish the parent and ourselves.

In Indonesia I observed coolies who worked as longshore-

men. They habitually spent half the day's pay for food, and
the other half to enjoy the night with a girl. Each day provided
the whole answer to that day's needs, no more and no less.
Another day would bring another day's pay; if it did not, one
went hungry. A simple life, without many things which make
life meaningful—but also without ulcers.

Allergy, the "Strange Disease"

Among the attempts at self-destruction that may be termed
half-hearted, we may also rank the allergies, those assorted
afflictions which are rarely fatal but which give both patient
and doctor so much trouble. (Asthma, however, cannot be
called half-hearted, since it may take a serious course.)

The idea that the allergies may have emotional origins is as
old as medicine. Even Hippocrates related attacks of asthma
to violent emotions.

But then about 1915, bronchial asthma, hay fever, and skin
eruptions like urticaria and eczema were grouped as sensitivi-
ties to foreign substances. They were called the "atopic group,"
from the word *atopy,* meaning "strange disease."

In the next several years, serum sicknesses, contact derma-
titis (that is, irritation of the skin from contact with certain
substances) and hypersensitivity to certain medications were
added to the group of "strange diseases," and since then they
have been treated with the allergist's vast array of medical
techniques. The word allergy itself means only altered energy
or strength to react.

Today we are beginning to take a new direction in the understanding of allergies. More accurately, we are finding new
signposts pointing back to Hippocrates' ancient direction. In
one report in the *Journal of the American Medical Association*
during 1950, thirty unselected cases of urticaria were studied
to determine if there was any relation between a "stressful life
situation" and the skin processes that caused eruption.

The attacks of skin eruption were found to be "highly cor-
related with an emotional disturbance of a particular kind."

Contradicting the assumption of half a century, the researchers found "no relation between exposure to the allergens and
the attacks of the disease." In other words, the foreign substance to which the patient was supposed to be allergic, the
hair of the pet dog or cat or the vase of roses, had no effect
unless there was an underlying emotional disturbance.

What "particular kind" of emotional disturbance was found
to be present? "The traumatic life situations responsible were
almost exclusively those in which the patient felt resentment
because he saw himself the victim of unjust treatment about
which he could do nothing."

To put it crudely, the patient can safely stroke his dog unless at the same time he is having a frustrating argument
with his wife which *provokes his underlying pattern of buried
hostility.*

Intuitively, people have related their emotions and the sensations of the skin. Expressions in our everyday language bear
this out. While the allergists labor painstakingly over their
scratch tests, we tell a friend, "I feel like jumping out of my
skin," and our skin may actually break out in an ugly rash.
We feel like tearing someone—or ourselves—to pieces, and we
may really be plagued by a maddening itch. Many an itch can
be traced to confused emotions in sex; one seems to be saying,
as Flanders Dunbar suggests, "Love me but don't touch me."

In an allergy case among my own patients the woman's Si-
amese cat was named as the villain. She protested angrily,
"How can you get sick from anything you love so much?" As
it turned out, she was right. We had clear proof that her asthma
was due to a frustrating emotional relationship. In the eight
years since that relationship was resolved, she has not had a
single recurrence of her asthma.

A Background For Asthma

Do we unconsciously select among the "strange diseases"
the particular one which suits our emotional situation? There
is evidence that we do. The skin disturbances seem to occur

where hostility and resentment are the dominating emotional factors. The asthmatic attacks are most frequently traceable to situations of emotional dependence. Psychiatrists explain the asthmatic wheeze as an aborted cry of the infant for help.

A young woman in her thirties, a chronic asthma sufferer, described her childhood. "I was an only child and always had the best of food and care. I used to envy other children because they were allowed to eat hot dogs, jelly apples, cheap candy, and I was not. Later I thought I would have been better off if I had been permitted to eat any kind of junk. My playmates were never sick, while I always had these so-called 'colds.'"

She remembered, once as a child, testing her father's love for her by a trick. At the hour when he was expected home in the evening she lay down in front of the door, pretending to be dead. Her father, first frightened, then furious, gave her the first and only spanking of her life. She remembered the long and deep unhappiness she suffered over the loss of her first pet dog. She remembered "'way back, always being afraid that something would happen to my parents, especially to my mother."

Clearly this was a child marked by insecurity in her parents' love, by the overprotectiveness of her mother and by her own dependence.

This young woman's asthma was variously attributed to different kinds of dust, and to the hair of her pet dog which she loved. I asked her to keep a careful record of the time and circumstances of her attacks.

One report she gave me thereafter is typical and striking. By this time she was married, though she and her husband lived with her mother, now widowed, and they had no children.

On this occasion she was out for the evening with her husband. She was dancing, enjoying herself thoroughly, when suddenly she was seized with a violent asthmatic attack. The time was half-past ten in the evening.

What, I asked her, had happened at about that time?

Nothing, she said: she was having a wonderful evening. To

explain the asthmatic attack she seized on the first plausible physical explanation. Probably she had overexerted herself with too much dancing and laughing.

What had she been thinking of?

She struggled to recall, and then it came back to her. In the midst of her enjoyment she had thought anxiously and somewhat guiltily of her mother. She had wondered if her mother was all right at home alone, wanted to telephone home to make sure, rejected the idea because it was late and her mother would be awakened by the call. A few minutes later, when she had presumably put her mother out of her mind and gone back to her friends, she suffered the attack. Though a grown woman, she still had not gained freedom from her emotional attachment to her mother.

He Who Does Not Wish to Breathe

In general the respiratory diseases are a determined expression of self-destruction, at least at the moment of illness. We have been quicker to discover cures for these diseases than to understand their causes. Pneumonia is no longer a first-rank killer, now that we have penicillin and other antibiotics. The miracle drugs may prevent an illness from progressing to the point of no return, and thus give the patient time to change his mind and decide in favor of life.

The normal organism reacts protectively to an unwholesome atmosphere. Coughing in a smoke-filled room is the autonomic nervous system's protest against the irritating smoke, its effort to protect the bronchial tubes and the lungs by expelling the smoky air. Stating it another way, we say that the cough is caused by the physical or chemical irritation of the soft tissue in the bronchial tubes.

But how shall we explain the coughing spell in an air-conditioned room, or outdoors on a clear, fine day without wind or flying dust or pollen? Isn't the cause in this case due to an unwholesome psychological atmosphere?

On a visit to one of the General Assembly sessions of the

United Nations I listened to a speech by a delegate defending his country in what was, on the known facts, an indefensible position.

This man had proved himself on previous occasions an able and eloquent speaker. Yet on this day he was hampered by a continuous, racking cough which he could not control no matter how many glasses of water he poured for himself. He could scarcely be heard, choking through his speech, and all over the hall the nervous tension increased until at last he finished his address and sat down.

On the assumption that the man merely had a cold, I watched him assiduously through the remainder of the session, but in vain. He used his handkerchief only to wipe his forehead. If, trained orator that he was, his voice was for some reason strained by use that day, surely he should have coughed at least a little when he sat down, or when he talked with his colleagues, which he did frequently in the course of the day. But he did not cough again that afternoon.

We identify life with breathing. Life begins with the first breath and ends with the last; in legal medicine an infant is considered to have been born alive if its lungs have contained a single breath. The question of infanticide has in many cases been determined on this test alone. We are safe to take the next logical step and assert that a person who does not wish to breathe does not wish to live.

A statesman, who had been a courageous leader of his nation during the war, was to open an international conference on which much depended. On the eve of the conference he was laid low with bronchial pneumonia.

An actress, who had struggled long and unsuccessfully for recognition on Broadway, accepted a modest Hollywood offer and overnight became a movie star. She returned to Broadway for her first starring role in the legitimate theater. Just before the opening, she came down with pneumonia.

The path of retreat which an individual chooses in a stressful situation depends on his characteristic emotional pattern. The man with a profound self-doubt may fall victim to tuberculosis. One with only a momentary panic may be stricken by pneumonia.

In pre-penicillin days laymen and doctors alike used to observe that it was often the vigorous, healthy man, the strongly physical type who had scarcely suffered a cold, who would fall prey to pneumonia and succumb with shocking swiftness.

We did not ask, in those days, whether the patient faced a more critical decision or a more challenging task than usual at the time he became ill. These individuals usually impressed those who knew them as being equal to any situation.

Yet no one could know how they themselves felt about it. A man might well say to himself with the logic of the unconscious, "If I were to die at this moment, I need not take the risk of this next venture—and the success I have achieved until now will be safe."

Today we are more observant of emotional forces. Perhaps in time we may learn exactly how the ever-present *pneumococcus* suddenly receives the signal to attack.

————————— SUMMING UP —————————

The choice of a particular organ as a target for illness is related in unconscious ways to emotional experiences.

*   *   *

An emotional need and a significant event together determine the time of illness.

9

Fight or Flight

He has no will to live.

IF THE BREATH is our symbol of body's life, the heart is the symbol of that inner life which, for want of a better word, we may call emotional. A valentine is heart-shaped, and we give our hearts when we love. We call a brave man lionhearted and a coward chicken-hearted. Our heart is heavy or it leaps for joy. We know warm-hearted and cold-hearted people, we are touched to the heart, we wish a friend happiness with all our heart, and we speak with a full heart.

A story is told of the late Arturo Toscanini, that man of fiery temperament who put so much heart into his music. He was being examined when he was eighty, and his physician commented cheerfully, "Maestro, your heart is exceptionally strong."

"No wonder—I never use it," Toscanini replied.

We say, cynically, that no one ever died of a broken heart. But we know in our hearts that people do. "Break, heart; prithee, break," pleads the faithful Kent to Lear before Cor-

140

delia's body, praying his tragic master to find release from his woes in death.

Everyone, some time, has felt heartbroken, and at such times we imagine that the heart does actually hurt. Now the belief is growing that, under certain circumstances, people may die of a "broken heart." It is not surprising that science often confirms a popular belief. A great deal of folk wisdom may be nonsense, but a great deal of it is rooted in experience. The doctor observes a patient for a short, concentrated period, but the lore of the people is the sum of observations handed down through the generations of man.

Dr. Franz M. Groedel, the founder of the American College of Cardiology, pointed out: "The close correlation between psyche and body . . . is nowhere as evident as in the circulatory apparatus. Under agreeable emotions the heart becomes accelerated; disagreeable emotions, even dislike, slow the pulse rate. The heart beat is influenced by music, accommodates to the rhythm."

If the heart is responsive to such mild experiences as like and dislike, no wonder that it may become the target of stronger, potentially destructive emotions.

A case comes to mind, a widow of sixty-nine, a remarkable old woman. She lived alone above the small factory which was her pride. She had built the factory with her own earnings years before in order to set up her five sons in business.

When she first came to see me she thought she had suffered a heart attack, but there were no organic signs of an attack. Still, she did not feel well. She was weak, dizzy, depressed, had stomach pain and indigestion. Her blood pressure was high.

She was fighting the city, she told me, which had condemned the neighborhood in order to build a highway. She would have to move. Worse than that, the factory was going to be torn down.

Two years later I was called again to see her. She "felt like dying," she said, weeping. Her heart ached so that she could not breathe, could not sleep. The factory was gone, her boys could not find another location, and meanwhile one of her sons had died of a heart attack. "It's God's will—but as a mother my heart hurts," she said. Her heart was in fact greatly enlarged, and her blood pressure had gone up alarmingly.

Sometimes we can stave off the destructive process and gain a little time. In this case timely medical aid supported the woman's sturdy will to live. Three weeks later she was well enough to come to the office for a check-up. Her blood pressure had gone down to normal.

Since then her sons have built a new factory, and again she lives above the shop. She has around her the physical symbols of continuity with the past, and they have given her the incentive to take up her active way of life again.

Love and the Superego

A first heart attack is often reported after an emotional shock, a sudden death in the family (especially if the death is from a heart attack), a fright, or an experience of physical overexertion. But these are the immediate precipitating causes. We usually do not know what emotional conditions may have prepared the heart beforehand for an attack, or, in other words, what long-continued emotional stress had already brought the heart to the point of "breaking."

A night call summoned me to a man whom I had known for some time, a healthy man who in his fifty-three years had suffered nothing worse than a cold. He was in intense pain, breathing with difficulty, perspiring. There was every sign of a severe coronary thrombosis. From what he told me it was apparent that he had had a first attack two days before, which he had dismissed as indigestion, something which had only lately begun to trouble him. The present attack had begun during the afternoon, when he had gone to play golf. He had delayed calling a doctor until the pain was unbearable.

He was a most rebellious patient, and the next two days were an unremitting struggle to keep him from killing himself outright by disobedience to orders. He wanted to be moved to a hospital, though a move involved some risk. He insisted upon getting up to go to the bathroom, though he had been expressly ordered to remain in bed, and a nurse was present to care for his needs. He refused to accept the diagnosis by a leading cardiologist, though the case proceeded through the several stages with text book precision; he telephoned his friends, not physicians, to reinforce his stubborn belief that he had nothing more than indigestion and that doctors very often mistake indigestion for a heart attack.

Most of all he wanted to be moved out of this apartment, if not to the hospital, then at least to a hotel. If a man had the money, he insisted, he should be allowed to spend it. The apartment, he swore, was a stinking hole.

Fortunately I knew this man and understood the reason for his rebellious behavior. Normally friendly, jovial, and cooperative, he was at the moment a man in a state of blind, overpowering rage.

He was a successful business man, unmarried, who had fallen in love three years before with a beautiful woman much younger than himself and wanted to marry her, but had refrained from doing so out of love and respect for his elder brother, who did not wholly approve. In the three years that had passed, the man had twice tried to give up the girl of his choice, only to fall into a deep depression each time. He was literally love-sick. On the other hand, he had come with her to my office on two occasions for blood tests preliminary to marrying, both times when his brother was vacationing out of the city. In this man's inner judgment, his elder brother apparently represented that stern parental conscience which we call the superego.

What brought the patient's rage against me, himself, and fate to the boiling point was that he had gone to this young woman's apartment at the first attack of pain that afternoon. That was where I had found him, and now that I proposed to keep him there for four or five weeks, that would be where his brother would find him.

During the two periods of his separation from the young woman, this man had looked aged and unhappy. Yet he had been unable to take the decisive step of marriage in the face of what he understood to be his brother's disapproval. Now, when I rebuked him for his bad behavior, he told me that he "didn't care" whether he lived or died. It was clear that, having twice tried to defy his superego and marry the girl, and twice tried to get on without her, he had reached the point where he could find no way out of his dilemma.

From time immemorial, a physician has said to himself at a patient's bedside, "He has no will to live." In this case I would have gone a step farther and said, "He has a violent wish to die." So in desperation I telephoned the elder brother, described the situation, and told him that he could do more than the physicians.

When I visited the patient that evening there was a marvelous—and clinically unexplainable—change for the better. The man had lost his harassed look. He was serene, cooperative, glad to be in "this nice apartment" instead of in a hospital. His brother had visited him for a long time that afternoon.

Four weeks later, a marriage was performed in the sick room. A number of years have gone by and it has been a most successful marriage. Our patient attends to his business, goes fishing, plays golf, has not had another heart attack and insists he has never been ill in his life.

On the surface this was an average case. The man was a typical heart sufferer, successful, healthy, the type who does not complain, disregards warnings, refuses to accept the physician's diagnosis that he is actually suffering a heart attack.

But, significantly, not one of the factors generally offered as the cause of coronary thrombosis was present here. There was no evidence of arteriosclerosis; the patient's blood pressure was low rather than high. There was no history of rheumatic fever, the second most important cause of heart disease. Nor was there obesity, diabetes, myxedema, or syphilis, which were then listed in that order as causes by clinical medicine.

Nor could the high pressure of life in our times be blamed

in this case. The man was under no particular pressure. He was successful to the point where he could virtually neglect his business if he chose. If anything, he suffered not from pressure but from boredom.

The Man in His Fifties

We talked in a previous chapter about dangerous periods in life. The age of fifty is one of them, widely recognized in women because of the physical manifestations of menopause, but more obscure in men since male menopause, or climacteric, as some call it, is rather a chronological term, with no physiological changes as far as we know. We have said that at fifty a man feels he should have reached his peak of achievement, and if he has not, he begins to despair that he ever will.

But so many heart sufferers in their early fifties are men who have achieved success by any standard, often as a result of their own efforts, starting at the bottom. What shall we say of them?

Consider a man of fifty, who has achieved his material success, has sowed his wild oats, has enjoyed fully the venturesomeness of youth. All that is now past. What has he to look forward to?

His life has been one of action, not introspection. He is by inclination neither scholar nor philosopher. For most such men, there is nothing left but to grow old, and they have not taken time in the course of an active life to develop the reposeful arts, those which contribute toward growing old gracefully.

Fundamentally such a man would rather end life at its peak, while he is still in full possession of his powers. He wants to die with his boots on.

I have suggested that the man who suffers a heart attack is likely to be struggling not with business or money troubles but with, as the French put it, an affair of the heart. So often we find a man in his fifties falling in love with a young girl. We say that there is no fool like an old fool, that no good can come of such a bootless effort to recapture our lost youth. If such a

man suffers a heart attack we say that he is killing himself trying to keep up with a young wife.

In its unsympathetic way this verdict can be the truth. To a
man in his September years, love for a much younger woman
is filled with anxiety. He cannot relax for fear that he will lose
her, or be unable to content her. He is continuously mobilized
to fight for her love.

Then there are the ones who are tempted but recoil from
such an involvement because of position, public opinion, or conscience. This is not the same as a graceful acceptance of approaching age. For many men the fifties are a time of stormy
emotional conflict.

Yet I have known cases in which not love for a young wife
is involved, but sexual rejection by the woman to whom the patient has been married for many years, with the consequent
damaging effects of stress. A business tycoon who came to me
for a minor ailment confessed that he had an unhappy reaction in his sexual relations with his wife. A few months later he
succumbed to a fatal coronary. In another case a wife came to
me in tears after her husband's sudden death of a heart attack, and confessed that she had rejected his sexual advances,
less than an hour before he was stricken.

A rejection in love can happen at twenty or twenty-five
without fatal consequences. Youth is resilient, we explain. By
this we mean that the heart muscle is physically strong and the
arteries young and elastic, and therefore can stand punishment. But we may also mean that to a young man life still lies
ahead and there are more fish in the sea. In his fifties, a man
may feel that he is losing his last chance for love. Without
love he may not want to live.

In a way, each of these men was paying the price of his wife's
menopause, or of an outworn attitude toward it. In the past
menopause was looked upon as the end not only of child-bearing but of a woman's sexual life. This is not so: women go on
being desirable, and desiring. But for a frigid or discontented
wife who has submitted as a marital duty, menopause may
offer at last a legitimate excuse. This is not only a form of self-

destruction in the wife but is also destructive to her husband.

There are of course other known causes for heart attacks among men in their middle years. But women do have a responsibility to understand the importance of sexual adjustment for the prolongation of life.

Attack Without Warning?

We are repeatedly told that a heart attack comes without warning. It may be true that the patient has not complained about his heart. But so often we find that the victim of a "sudden" heart attack has been consulting his lawyer about his will, or has recently taken out a new life insurance policy.

True, we all experience premonitions of sudden illness, of death. We say this is because we will carry within us the fear of death.

Shall we say that a premonition of death means that we are in fact going to die? Not at all. But it indicates that deep within us, at that moment, a dialogue is going on. We think of making a will, of taking out more life insurance, because we are concerned for those whom we may leave behind. We are concerned with our responsibilities. Is it not possible that we feel, at such times, burdened by these same responsibilities, actually tempted by a momentary desire to escape from them?

Like Columbus' crew we all wish now and then that we could turn back. We all have our moments of weariness, of dwindling hope or courage. For example, one day a man walked into my office in perfect health, medically speaking, and remarked, "At this moment I am worth more dead than alive." A few months later he was dead.

A woman in her fifties, in good health and with no record of heart disease, called on her lawyer one afternoon in order to change her will, which involved the disposal of a considerable fortune. Although it meant keeping members of the office staff after hours, this usually considerate client was insistent on signing the new will that same afternoon. She was planning a trip, but her lawyer said afterward, "She was a lady given to

intuitions. She felt something unhappy was about to happen."
She signed the will, and that same night she died of a heart
attack.

By the same token, the unconscious debate can reach an af-
firmative conclusion. A new patient, an oil man from South
America, came to my office several years ago; he had high
blood pressure and heart symptoms and had been told he
should not fly, a serious restriction for a South American business man. After thorough examination and tests I was able to
assure him that he had no heart ailment and could safely fly.
Thus one anxiety was removed.

His blood pressure remained high. On his next North American visit he confided that he was very much upset: without
his wife's knowledge he had several children by his mistress.
If anything happened to him these children—his children!—
would be unprovided for.

The next year he came again, relaxed and jubilant. After
unburdening himself of his guilty secret on his previous visit,
he had gone home and changed his will to provide for his il-
legitimate children. Now he had no worries. "My wife—will
she be mad! But then I am dead!" he exclaimed. From then
on he no longer had any trouble with his heart.

Between those who unconsciously decide for life, and those
who give up, the difference seems to be one of purpose. The
typical heart victim apparently lacks a continuing purpose
which would carry him safely through a time of crisis.

Heart and blood vessel disorders, the cardio-vascular group
of diseases which we placed on the competitive-aggressive side
of the emotional scale, rank first by far in the list of man's afflictions today. They are responsible for more deaths in the
United States right now than the next five most common causes
put together.

Curiously, up to the age of five, diseases of the heart and
blood vessels are present in four times as many girls as boys.
But the proportion soon begins to swing to the other side,
and by the age of thirty to thirty-four, men are five times as
subject to heart and arterial diseases as women. From then on

the greater susceptibility of men to heart afflictions increases steadily, reaching its peak in the age group of fifty to fifty-nine, principally with coronary thrombosis.

Why are men more subject to heart disease than women? Medicine has no clear answer. Perhaps an explanation can be found in the different roles men and women plan in our culture. The man is typically the bread winner while the woman tends the home. True, more and more women are engaged in competitive activities in the business and professional world. But a man must still prove his manhood by his achievement while a woman has always the open door of retreat behind her, the fact that she is after all a woman.

No matter what new attitudes we profess, no matter how far education may cease to differentiate between men and women, no matter how aggressively individual women may assert their equality and individual men accept it, the difference exists as a profound principle of our society. It is learned almost simultaneously with the knowledge of whether one is a boy or a girl.

We begin to understand the reasons why a man may take this path of self-destruction as soon as we begin to penetrate the protective armor of his noncommittal outward appearance.

The world demands of a man that he deal with it in an aggressive manner. He meets competition, aggression, hostility, and he responds in kind. When the going becomes too hard, or when he reaches a point where the game seems not worth the candle, he seeks a way out.

Such a man's habitual pattern of aggressive behavior can then take a morbid, destructive direction, and the organs which are active in this emotional pattern are the ones which come under attack. Of the group of diseases to which the aggressive pattern leads, an individual's choice of one rather than another depends upon his individual patterns of response, both physical and emotional. Individual differences lead to individual responses. One may develop diabetes, another a stroke, a third a heart attack.

Arteriosclerosis is the leading cause of heart disease. Its

bodily origins are not clear. The majority of physicians believe that high cholesterol in the blood serum leads to hardening of the arteries and thus to possible coronary thrombosis. This theory has been questioned by some researchers.

Rheumatic fever, the second most frequent cause of heart disease, is even more of a mystery to the clinicians. When American medicine introduced the theory of focal infections some two decades ago, the explanation seemed especially applicable to rheumatic fever. Weiss and English suggest that it was because "medicine felt so helpless in dealing with this disease (rheumatism) and because there was often so much obvious indication of infection, that the concept of focal infection was eagerly grasped. European medicine never paid so much attention to the idea. Consequently Europe did not sacrifice quite so many teeth or tonsils on the altar of this concept."

Dr. George Draper in his work on constitution pointed out a relationship between physical and psychic factors. In rheumatic fever sufferers he found physical asymmetry, such as one eye higher in the face than the other, or one breast smaller than the other. He also found a striking disproportion between the mature size and development of the body and the "expression and gestures of extreme childishness."

Medicine has in the past been so desperate for a physiological explanation of what causes heart disease that it has grasped at almost any physical straw. As a young doctor-to-be I was taking my State Board examinations, and one of the cases I was given to diagnose was a heart disorder. I was presented to the patient and left there, to get the case history and all pertinent information. In this case there seemed nothing at all to account for the condition. The patient—a woman in her forties—had good teeth, good tonsils, no history that would give a clue. I was baffled, and frightened too, since so much depended on my working up a good case.

The woman smiled at me. "You're a nice young man—I'll tell you something I haven't told any of the doctors." What she wouldn't tell the doctors was that she had been smoking; she couldn't tell, because at that time it was not considered nice for a woman to smoke. Nor was it nice for a woman to buy cigarettes, so she had not bought them. She had taken the stubs of her husband's cigars, shredded the tobacco and rolled her own cigarettes. She had been doing this for ten or twelve years!

This was a very acceptable cause for a heart ailment, and I received an invisible pat on the shoulder for a good case.

Nicotine, fatty foods, caffeine and obesity are the clinician's favorite villains in explaining a heart attack. But shouldn't we look beneath the surface, and examine the tensions behind these excessive appetites for food, for coffee, for cigarettes?

Confronted with the Number One killer of our time, we doctors no longer have the privilege of saying, "We don't know." Today we have the evidence of the endocrinologists and the psychologists, and serious students of psychosomatic medicine are constantly offering us new indications that heart disease cannot be laid to physical agents alone.

We are not likely to conquer this disease until we understand that the man who strikes at his heart is the victim of a struggle of which he is not conscious. He is in a state of mobilization for a battle which is never actually fought to a finish. He is wrestling with a situation which he can neither adjust himself to, nor withdraw from—except by death. A man of action, accustomed to sharp, quick decisions, may choose the sharpest, quickest decision to end his torture: a heart attack.

Concealed Hostility

"Whether a person falls ill somatically (physically) or socially (mentally) seems to depend on the quantity of guilt, anxiety, and hostility in his personality," write Doctors Edward Weiss and O. Spurgeon English. These two members of the Temple University faculty, whom we have already mentioned in connection with rheumatic fever and focal infection, have produced in their valuable study, *Psychosomatic Medicine*, one of the first collaborative publications by a psychiatrist and a medical man.

Hostility is an emotion which all of us experience. We pass a man in the street talking to himself, arguing furiously, with gestures and contorted facial expressions. We see a man behind the wheel of his car, angrily honking his horn when he is trapped in a traffic snarl. We suffer bruised ribs from a man or woman who pushes into a crowded subway or bus by the elbow method. Another person steps on our toes—and glares at us accusingly. These are obvious expressions of hostility that are uncontrolled and often unknown to the individual himself.

Many people bury their hostility so deeply that everyone else is as unaware of it as they are. Though it is a normal response to life situations, hostility is destructive. When we do not deal with it, it turns against ourselves.

We have been talking about the pattern of infantile dependency, of what happens to a child who has never had enough love and who grows into adulthood still hungry for love and for the parental protection which it implies. A more vigorous personality reacts not only with a need for love. He is also likely to build a pattern of suppressed hostility.

Such a person is a potential danger to himself and to everyone around him, even to society if he reaches a position of power.

The child learns early that open hostility is not acceptable. If he strikes his father or mother, if he breaks windows or otherwise damages property, even if he breaks his own toys, he is likely to be punished. And so he learns, in sheer self-protection, to mask his hostile feelings.

The jolly fellow who slaps your back, the hearty hand-shaker who crushes your bones, the sugar-sweet hostess who makes you uncomfortable by her extreme efforts to make you comfortable, all are expressing masked hostility. The seething hatred within them, so strictly censored that they will honestly deny its existence with their last breath, is completely disguised by surface friendliness, and the only clue to its presence may lie in the excessive quality of the friendliness. The innocent victim is baffled to explain the vague discomfort he feels in his relationship with such people.

A doctor brought me a letter from one of his patients, which had upset him. He himself was suffering from that recently fashionable ailment, a herniated vertebral disc, for which he had to wear a brace.

"This," his patient wrote him, "is how you show your overwhelming hostility toward your patients." There followed an acute description of the many little persecutions this man visited on his patients: how he kept them waiting long past the time of their appointments; how he stopped in the middle of treatment to tell lengthy stories, or to make telephone calls which presumably could not wait until he was free, how whenever a patient remarked that he had an engagement and must be out at a certain time, the doctor, though making apparently heroic efforts to be swift, always managed to be extra long about his tasks.

So many of these small tortures were administered under the guise of giving extra service to the patient, of showing extra concern. He would rush breathless to his first appointment, mentioning that he had skipped breakfast to be on time, but neglecting to mention that he had delayed getting up until the last moment. He would groan, bending over a patient, "Today I had to wear my *heavy* brace."

"What a wonderful fellow!" the patient was supposed to think, meanwhile suffused with guilt at forcing this suffering martyr to take care of him.

How did the doctor himself react to this sharp and uncannily just accusation? He reacted in a very characteristic fashion. "How bad people are," he sighed, "how lacking in consideration and understanding!"

Whether a man who suffers a rheumatic twinge in his arm actually wanted to strike his mother-in-law, the psychoanalysts might be able to say. But we know the effect that emotional stress has on the body, and we can be sure that blocked hostile impulses have had something to do with the case.

Mothers and Sons

We have seen how the impulse to fight mobilizes the body, and how, when the fight fails to take place, the tensions in artery and muscle remain. We can understand how hostility, the frustrated or repressed impulse to fight, may strike damagingly at a coronary artery, a muscle, or a joint.

Domination and dependence, and their consequent hostility, fear and guilt, are clearly the background of illness in the following story of a mother and her son.

Robert G. was tall, good looking, quick and fluent of speech, with graceful manners. He was in every way a charming young man, and he earned his living as a comedian. He had been troubled for some years with pain in his back and legs, and he gave his history in a normal, routine manner, an intelligent patient telling his troubles.

Yet it seemed to me that he stressed only the physical and medical side of his story, taking pains to avoid any reference to his personal life, to events, emotions or individuals in relation to his physical complaint.

A patient seeing a doctor for the first time is likely to be reserved about his personal affairs. But a reference to a marriage or a divorce or the birth of a child, a death in the family or a business reverse, almost inevitably slips out, if only as a jog to the memory in an effort to fix the time of an illness.

This young man made no such slips. Doctors are familiar with these patients, who talk about their illness in a determinedly matter-of-fact way. They love the use of medical terms. They censor all personal information from their speech, as though they had something to hide. They are recognized as persons suffering from insecurity or from guilty fears. Sometimes the resistance to giving information is an expression of hostility, the wish not to oblige.

In an effort to break through the young man's reserve, I asked him to write down his history with whatever background of events he remembered. The neatly typewritten page and a half which he brought me on his next visit was a detailed account of his symptoms with precise medical explanations and the treatments he had undergone, but with his personal life still rigidly excluded.

He wrote that his illness began while doing hospital shows overseas, "which required several hours of standing on stage two or three days a week." X-rays showed "a wedge-shaped fourth lumbar and calcification of several vertebrae and both hip joints. Heat and manipulation plus the canvas support slowly caused relief of the pressure on the nerve issuing from the area of the affected spinal segment"—this is the patient writing, not a physician—"and cessation of pain. Treatment and canvas brace were discontinued after two years."

Some two years later, the account continued, "accidental tripping over an exposed tree root while walking in the woods caused an extreme twisting of the spine and severe impingement on the nerve—" and so on. This siege required perhaps a year and a half for recovery

"It is my opinion," the patient suggested in conclusion, "that gentle exercise and the use of a hard mattress plus . . . a quarter-inch lift in the heel of the right shoe gave nature a chance to rebuild protective cartilage which insulated the damaged fouth lumbar thus prohibiting pressure on the nerve and providing complete relief. That and the determination not to be an invalid for life."

Yet a year later the pain returned and he again took to his brace. A year after that he fell ill with an acute stomach ulcer with hemorrhage and his life was narrowly saved by numerous blood transfusions.

Here is the background which the patient censored:

He had lived with his mother, a widow, until he married and established a home of his own. He was successful in his profession, but he refused to accept weekend engagements, which were the highest paid, because he needed the time to "rest up." He was making an apparent attempt to free himself from maternal dependency, but in fact he was only thrashing about in helpless rebellion. He rejected routine work and fixed hours. He refused to get up in the morning. He gave up most of his engagements, which he described as "immature and unsuitable for a grown man." He tried to earn a living in business but he had no success.

Let us go back to the beginning of his spine trouble. The "several hours of standing on stage two or three days a week" which he blamed for his trouble adds up to perhaps a day and a half of work a week. Compare this with a salesman's job which requires standing on his feet some six or seven hours a day five days a week. What happened at that time, after a year of unsuccessful, because unrealistic, effort, was that his marriage came to an unhappy end, and he admitted defeat in his aspirations toward independence and went back to his professional work.

The day on which he tripped over a tree root was the day when he learned that his mother had a malignancy. The pain in his back returned after his sister had come across the country to see him, and died in an accident. His ulcer was the climax of mounting guilt and resentment, first over his mother's death, then over his sister's.

His mother was an able woman who had carried on her own business for years to support herself and her son. Like so many competent women left alone to bring up a family, she was over-protective and dominating. She herself eventually realized this. About seven years before this history began, she quit her business, as she explained, "to give Robert some sense of responsibility for himself."

Robert professed to approve of her retirement. But several times when he talked of feeling overburdened by his own problems, the mask slipped and he said, "She could have kept on—it was a fine business."

The mother's own history makes us wonder how accidental an accident actually is. Thirty years ago she fell and broke her right arm. Six years later, in an accident, she injured her right knee. Six months after that, she tripped and injured the same knee. A few years later she tripped and again injured the same knee. Finally she developed a suspicious lump on her right thigh, which she dismissed as a bruise resulting from a fall. The growth was removed and a biopsy confirmed the suspicion that it was a malignant tumor. Despite all efforts the malignancy spread and a year later she was dead.

We have already learned that accident and coincidence need not be pure chance. Like a slip of the tongue, a slip of the foot may give a momentary glimpse into the vast and largely unexplored continent of the unconscious.

In her own words this mother revealed an emotional clue to her son's illness and her own. "He is a man, and should stand on his own feet. I am tired of his standing on mine."

And later: "I thought he was a genius. He was always talking in millions. One day I realized it was all dreaming, not reality." And she added, in despair and defeat, "I have not helped him."

This man, haunted by guilt, torn between his need for the protection his mother too long provided and his pride which demands that he make his own way, cannot deal with these powerful forces beyond his understanding, without professional assistance. But when psychiatric help was suggested, he reacted as to an insult: "I'm not crazy!" He is making some effort at adjustment, but to seek medical attention is to him a sign of weakness and, unaided, his progress is slow.

A great deal of suffering of this mother and son might have been avoided with a better understanding of the emotional pitfalls which life presented to them. Over-protection in childhood, domination by a parent, and particularly the situation of a woman left to bring up a son single-handed, may cause misery in later years.

"So many laws argue so many sins," wrote Milton in *Paradise Lost*. We might paraphrase the line today and say, so many ills argue so many sins—of parents and educators.

_____ SUMMING UP_____

When we feel threatened, the healthy body mobilizes for fight or flight.

❊   ❊   ❊

When the impulse to fight or to flee is frustrated, the tensions in arteries, muscles, and vital organs remain.

❊   ❊   ❊

Hostility is the frustrated or repressed impulse to fight or to flee.

❊   ❊   ❊

Long-continued stress can bring a heart to the point of "breaking."

❊   ❊   ❊

When a situation involves wife and husband, parents and children, brothers and sisters, we must be on guard against reacting in adulthood as we would in childhood, whatever the apparent justification may be.

❊   ❊   ❊

We must strive to use adult judgment for ourselves as we are usually able to do with ease for a friend or neighbor.

❊   ❊   ❊

Thales, one of the seven wise men of ancient Greece, was asked what was difficult. He answered, "to know oneself." When asked what was easy he replied, "to advise another."

10

Escape into Illness

*If illness is shock therapy, convalescence is
a time for taking stock, making decisions,
laying out a new course.*

THERE are times in the lives of most of us when we
need to be ill.

There are times when we need illness as a respite from struggle to regroup our forces, or to gain new perspective, or to
mature a little. At such times illness is not a defeat, and the
destructive drive, destructive though it is, becomes an ally to
the will to live.

We must not think of the creative and destructive forces
as antagonists always locked in battle with each other. In
health they work together to achieve the best of which we
are capable. At such times all our energies are united and
channeled toward a single goal.

But when we meet opposition—either from without or from
within—which we cannot master, the state of ease changes to
dis-ease. Now we become ill to avert disaster.

There is the face-saving illness without which diplomacy or
government could barely function. A minister resigns be-

cause of ill health; a conference is delayed because of the in-
disposition of one of the conferees. Behind the protecting façade of illness a new minister comes to the helm, a new policy
is formulated, and the wheels are again set in motion in a
new direction.

In its constant task of acting for the individual in his relationship with the world, the ego, the conscious part of the
self, comes now and again upon an apparently insoluble problem. It encounters an inability to bring external conditions into
harmony with inner need or desire. Or it meets a stubborn inner resistance to the adjustment necessary toward an external
situation. The ego as secretary of state has negotiated a treaty
abroad, but congress—the home government, the inner self—
refuses to ratify it. Hence the face-saving illness.

We get ourselves into these situations. Suppose we have acted
on impulse or with poor judgment. We have not explored the
full consequences of what we have committed ourselves to do.
Or we were not clear about what motivated our action. Suddenly we are trapped into doing something against our interest, or against our deeper wishes, or in violation of some standard of our integrity. And we see no exit.

For the moment our creative energies are blocked. Now the
destructive drive becomes an aid to survival. "Reason is not
the foe of the instincts, and illness not a curse," wrote the philosopher George Santayanna.

A distinguished actress was rehearsing in a new play in London, when she collapsed with a sudden acute appendicitis.
She was at the peak of her career; the play in which she had
made her London debut had just concluded its run in an aura
of brilliant success, with tributes from the press and a reception by members of the royal family. Now as the actress was
hurried to the hospital for an urgent operation, colleagues and
admirers deluged her with sympathy. What a pity that her
new play had to be canceled, that her ride on the crest of success was brought to an abrupt halt. Her friends might have
been surprised to learn that instead of mourning her lost
laurels, she lay in her hospital bed in a mood of relief despite

her pain. She alone knew that an appendectomy did not blight her career; it saved it.

During rehearsals of the new play she had become increasingly uneasy. The part, she felt, was wrong; instead of enhancing her first success, the play might jeopardize or even destroy it. Her conviction grew, and she became desperate. To go on in the play would be disastrous; to withdraw during rehearsals, even more damaging to her reputation.

Walking the London streets she thought, "If I fell in front of a car . . . ?" But no—she might be killed, or maimed for life. To fall into the Thames? And be pulled out dripping—oh, no! Only in the theater could drowned heroines look glamorous, like Ophelia. And there was also the chance that she might really drown.

The opening was only a few days off when one night she woke in frightful abdominal pain. Hysteria, she told herself firmly, and tried to ignore it. But as the hours passed she grew frightened, and at last called a doctor.

There was no question about the appendix: the royal surgeon himself performed the operation. The appendix was not only inflamed but ruptured, and there were consequent complications. But the actress sailed through the physical suffering, happy to sacrifice her appendix for her career. Eventually a new play with a satisfactory role was found, and her next opening confirmed the success of her debut.

Theater folk often live dramatic personal lives. We may think that only an actress could present such a clear demonstration of the interplay between mind and body. But everyday people have such experiences too, though the circumstances and also the resolution may be less theatrical.

A young woman in her thirties, a private secretary, was subpoenaed as a witness in a trial against a man to whom she was secretly engaged. As the date drew nearer she became nervous and harassed. Suddenly she developed a pain in her lower abdomen. She welcomed the diagnosis, made at a leading medical center, that she had to have a hysterectomy. The selection of her illness in itself was significant.

She was recovering from a successful operation when news reached her that the trial had been postponed. "Then the operation was all for nothing!" she wailed, inadvertently putting her finger on the true connection between the trial and her illness. But the destructive drive came to her rescue again. As she was about to be discharged, she developed a complication which required her to stay in the hospital several weeks longer. When she came out, the trial was in session. But since she was convalescing from a serious operation, the court excused her from appearing.

Illness in Self-Defense

An individual driven by an ambition which he does not really accept sometimes saves himself by unconscious measures. A son exerting himself to gratify his parents or a husband striving to meet his wife's standards of success may need illness in self-defense. I have as a patient a boy of sixteen whose mother is very proud of his mental capacity and constantly goading him to new efforts. Before every important examination he falls ill with an acute infection of some sort. He comes out a top student anyway, but still he approaches each test of his ability in a state of anxiety lest he fail to measure up to his mother's aspirations for him.

A store manager, whom I have known for some time, was strongly dominated by his ambitious wife. He liked his modest work but he kept doggedly trying to better himself out of fear that he might lose her respect. One Friday night he called me in great urgency. He was in excruciating pain from a sudden sciatica, so extreme that he cried out when I gently moved his leg or even touched the skin. He told me that he had to be well by Monday. He had a crucial interview for an important business opening.

The drugs which are usually effective in such cases produced no results. He was slightly better Sunday but worse again on Monday, and of course he could not keep the appointment. At the end of the week he dressed, moaning with pain, and went to the store.

A few days later the opportunity he had sought was awarded to a competitor. He had definitely and conclusively missed his chance. The following day he came to my office. He did not limp; his pain was completely gone. All he wanted was a sleeping pill so he could get a good night's rest.

Emotional Blackmail

We come now to a curious love story with the self-destructive force as a somewhat dubious ally. The story began quietly enough when an attractive young widow sent me a friend for examination, to determine whether he had actually suffered a heart attack some three weeks before.

I knew this friend who had been driving the widow to and from my office during her own course of treatments, and who had made good-natured jokes about his unsuccessful courtship. He was a big, hearty man of thirty, rather a slow-moving companion for the dynamic little Mrs. L who had successfully carried on her husband's business since his death from a heart attack about a year before.

The young man's supposed heart attack had occurred when he was driving his car, and the symptoms were the standard ones: pain in the left side of the chest, numbness in the left arm, shortness of breath. At the hospital to which he was rushed, he responded in the normal way to the traditional treatment for heart attack. The hospital diagnosis was "possible coronary thrombosis." All clinical examinations were negative, including X-rays and several electrocardiograms. At the time of my examination, three weeks later, he had no complaints except that he felt very tired. He confessed to smoking about fifty cigarettes a day.

I found no pertinent symptoms, especially no sign of arteriosclerosis which is concomitant to a coronary thrombosis. The cardiologist confirmed the fact that there had been no organic damage to the heart, and suggested nicotine poisoning, or "an allergic reaction to a considerable secretion caused by a chronic sinus condition."

Up to this point the case is in no way unusual. Medically we would make nicotine and perhaps the stress of big-city life the villains. In spite of the absence of organic confirmation, we would consider the attack a serious warning and would advise the young man to take it easy.

Then the charming young widow attempted suicide, and the whole strange story came out. I discovered that she had been secretly married to the young man before she had sent him to me for examination. It was she who had wanted to know whether his "heart attack" had been real.

We must remember that her previous husband had died of a heart attack; and that marriage, she had told me more than once, had been a very happy one. She had resisted this suitor until he suffered a heart attack, and then she married him.

If I had been able to tell her positively that he had suffered a heart attack, would she have attempted suicide, or would she have repented of her marriage in more subtle ways? No one can tell. As it was, she found herself committed to a man she did not love. Unquestionably, whether consciously or not, she felt she had been blackmailed into the marriage. A year later she was able to admit that she could not forgive him for the device by which he persuaded her to marry him.

Did the young man have a heart attack? He was not capable of consciously simulating a coronary thrombosis; he was not the actor for such a performance. He would have had to deceive an experienced hospital staff, both in the original attack and in his physical reaction to the drugs and stimulants which they administered to him.

Consciously he could not have known that a heart attack was the one way to break down the resistance of the woman he loved. He could have had no understanding of her guilt feelings toward her dead husband, of her fear that she might be responsible for another death of the same kind if she did not marry him.

And he was certainly under stress, such severe stress as to create a picture of illness. In an individual whose arteries had already suffered damage—for example, an older man—there might have been a real heart attack. This was not conscious, deliberate blackmail.

Yet it was emotional blackmail, though unconscious. Freud half a century ago pointed out that disturbances of the heart function could be brought on by anxiety. There is no need for the conscious mind to know and enact the symptoms of a disease. There is no necessity for the conscious mind to understand that a heart attack would succeed with the desirable widow where all other efforts had failed. One unconscious mind understands another.

Little children know how to penetrate the defenses of grownups and get what they want. Why shouldn't the child within the man have the same skill? And if the need is great enough, the unconscious mind will find destructive forces to work upon the organs of the body and accomplish the desired purpose.

The Shock Therapy of Illness

Doctors have observed that people who have gone through grave illness in their youth are likely to live long and in good health. I had a friend, a respected writer, who in his seventies was in excellent health and mentally as keen as a far younger man. He had been a premature baby, always delicate, painfully aware of the contrast between himself and a robust older brother who was an officer in the army. As a child his chances of living even to middle age were considered poor. Yet at seventy he was in sturdier health than any of his contemporaries.

It is a familiar pattern, the sickly child who grows up to be a vigorous man or woman. There are biological explanations, such as the development of immunity. But there is also another possible explanation. Such an individual often makes a strong effort to overcome his bad start in life. The prospect of inferiority, of perhaps an early death, seems to galvanize the will to live in many small but significant ways. Such an in-

dividual takes better care of himself, conserving his strength for
the things he wants to accomplish. He strives creatively to
make his days meaningful since he may enjoy fewer of them
than the average man. In time by these efforts he does in fact
overcome his weakness, and he goes on to a life of normal
length and better than average health and achievement.

Illness, itself a response to stress, may also have the therapeu-
tic effect of shock. As a matter of fact I have observed over
the years that either sudden, dramatic illness or accident has
the effect of shock therapy, not unlike the insulin and electric
shock which are recognized therapy in psychiatry.

A.C. is a gifted fashion designer widely recognized in her
field. There was a period in her life when she was involved in a
relationship with a brilliant but difficult man. The relationship
was unsatisfactory. She was unable to attend to her work, her
business ran down, and more than once she said to me, "I deserve to be hit on the head."

One day I was summoned to the hospital. She had tripped
in the street and struck her head against the curb. I found her
with a dangerous fracture of the skull.

During her convalescence I told her, half in jest, that she
had given herself perfect shock therapy, but of too dangerous
a kind to be self-administered. The injury had missed by a
millimeter a vital sector of the brain. She made a remarkable
recovery and returned to face her problems as though her
accident had awakened her from a daze in which she had
been drifting. She broke off her relationship with the man and
took up her life again with vigor and effectiveness.

Taking Stock

If illness is shock therapy, convalescence is a time for taking
stock, making decisions, laying out a new course. Despite the
weakness of the body, the patient who has resolved in convalescence the conflict which precipitated his illness may return to normal life able to embark with great resolution toward
a new goal. A woman patient married to a hopeless drunkard

could not break with him until after she had suffered a serious physical collapse. She has since remarried and had a child, and her new life is a very happy one.

I was called at three o'clock one morning to the bedside of a man I did not know. He lay moaning in pain, struggling for breath. His wife, a handsome blond woman, stood in the doorway with her arms crossed.

"There's nothing the matter with him—just tell him not to eat like a pig," she said harshly. I shut her out of the room and made my examination. The man was in critical condition, with every sign that he had an occlusion of a coronary artery. The tense home atmosphere prompted me to advise the patient's immediate removal to a hospital.

His wife refused to let him go. Early the next morning an older man, the sick man's father-in-law, was waiting in my office. Quite overwrought, he at once began to argue that doctors are often mistaken, diagnosing simple indigestion as heart attacks. By repeating that I could not be responsible for the man's life if he were left at home, I finally succeeded in getting the patient to the hospital.

The sick man spent four weeks in the hospital and then went away for a long convalescence to a quiet resort. He returned, got a divorce, and later married for the second time. That was ten years ago. He has not had another heart attack.

More remarkable was a call I had one day from a woman, whom I had never treated. "Please take me to the hospital for a few nights—*I don't want to break down,*" she said on the telephone. There was nothing physically wrong, but she was in an extremely tense emotional condition. I gathered that she faced a critical situation in her marriage, for which she needed a little time, a little perspective.

After four days, calm, confident, she told me she was ready to go home, and I discharged her. I am certain she resolved her situation, whatever it was. A woman with the wisdom to run away and consider her problem *before* she became ill more than likely learned how to deal with it.

Dependent Children

The struggle for emotional independence begins early in life, and for many it continues long into adulthood. For some, indeed, it is a lifelong battle which is never really won. American mothers have been attacked for their supposed tendency to hold fast to their children. "Momism" has been regarded as a serious factor in the American way of life. Yet in other societies, perhaps, it was the authoritarian father who had an equivalent influence on the child.

But we must agree that, whatever may be the pattern in other times and other cultures, in this country today we find a very large proportion of both men and women who either accept passively the bond of the silver cord, or else struggle far into their adult years, and at great emotional cost, to sever it.

A parallel observation is the great number of grown men and women who suffer from one of the dependency group diseases.

The pattern of infant dependence is the harder to dissolve because it is unconsciously maintained by both parties to it, the parent needing to dominate and the child seeking protection. We think of the tie as existing chiefly between mother and son. It is hardly less prevalent between mother and daughter.

I remember a family of five. At the outbreak of World War II the father, a European diplomat, had sent his American-born wife and three daughters to the United States to protect them against the hazards of the war. He himself eventually lost his life in an air raid attack in London.

First to come to my office was Annabelle, the oldest daughter. She was then thirty-two, tall, slender, with a colorful, dynamic personality which however gleamed only occasionally throughout the first interview. She talked about herself through a glaze of cautious uncertainty.

She was tired, jittery; her hands shook perceptibly. Her natural slenderness was marred by a thickening of the hips and especially of the legs. Her ankles were swollen and puffy. She complained of feelings of weakness, weariness; of palpitations, prickling sensations in her arms and heaviness in her legs. She remarked that these sensations left her only when she went to the country.

Medically her most marked symptoms were a hyperthyroid and a chronic gall bladder disturbance causing dizziness, nausea, and other related distress. The thickening of hips and thighs in women has been interpreted as resulting from a lessened glandular function, in this case probably a consequence of emotional stress.

Annabelle had just been divorced. She claimed her husband was "a mental case who led me a fiendish life . . . I was constantly ill until I left him." With one child, she had gone back to her mother. She was torn between her duties toward her mother, her own child, and a desire to find a happier relationship with another man.

At the moment, Annabelle was perturbed and depressed. She was being pursued by a social lion and was tormented by her inability either to accept or reject him.

During her visits Annabelle talked of wanting to get away from home. She hinted delicately that living with her mother in a twenty-room house fully staffed with servants was less than perfect happiness. She longed, she said, for a simpler life. And after several months when she felt much better physically, she went with my consent to England, whence she continued to report faithfully by mail.

Her letters, covering a period of nearly four years, are a record of growing strength and maturity. At first she was helplessly dependent on her hormone injections, administered by her English doctor according to my prescription. But she wrote: "I would use any excuse not to come back." A year later she said: "I have definitely put [her suitor] out of my life. I feel contented and years younger, a different person

. . . Have been losing weight." Again, after three months: "I
am happier than I have been since I was eighteen . . . feel an
urge to do things which I haven't felt in years."

Two years after her departure Annabelle came home, but cut
short her visit. "My symptoms," she laughed, "are all raising
their ugly heads—I must hurry back!" Her beauty, her charm
had blossomed in the two-year interval. She struck me as a
woman who was now at last coming into the full realization
of her capacities. She stayed only three weeks and hastened
back to England.

Another year passed. "No medicine so far . . . feel marvelous." Six months later: "I am bursting with spirits . . . have
fallen seriously in love."

Annabelle is still abroad. Her latest letter discussed the danger of war in Europe and the question of whether she ought to
come home. "Things will probably be bad everywhere so I may
as well stay here!" she concluded cheerfully.

The Second Sister

Ariane came to my office a year after Annabelle's first visit,
as a result of the elder sister's airmail persuasions. She was
thirty, more classically beautiful but less dynamic than Annabelle, a rather passive personality, in her present condition almost lethargic.

She had recently recovered from a duodenal ulcer but still
suffered the symptoms and feared a relapse. Her nails were
brittle, she had frequent rashes and swelling about the body
and face, and when she forced herself to entertain or go out socially she collapsed afterward. She was fatigued, "in a terrible
state of nerves—I constantly feel like screaming." Lately she
had noticed her hips getting heavy, her ankles swelling, spoil-
ing her looks.

As a child, she told me, she was kept in bed by her mother
for long periods because she ran temperatures easily, "probably all due to nerves." Between the ages of eleven and thirteen

she refused to eat and her weight dropped to forty pounds. She was not conscious of any resentment against her mother; her only spoken comment was that her mother had over-protected her as a child.

She complained of getting upset over the most trivial problems. Medically she was in fact near a state of collapse, with a blood sugar of fifty-nine; the normal range is between eighty and one hundred twenty. She had a mild gall bladder disturbance and her blood sedimentation rate was high, indicating that destruction of tissue was going on somewhere in the body and suggesting that she still had some ulceration of the stomach. We will recall that peptic ulcer is grouped with other digestive disturbances as emerging from the definite infantile dependency pattern of emotional stress.

Besides medical treatment, Ariane welcomed guidance toward an understanding of her involved emotional situation. Two months later she groped for words to describe "a feeling of inner strength, a new feeling of self-confidence." She was better able to endure the difficulties of daily life. As time passed she talked less of her troubles and more of her child. She had hitherto left the boy almost entirely to a governess, uncertain of her own influence, but now she was spending time with him, taking an interest in his activities: "I try to correct the mistakes of my own childhood." This implied criticism was the only reference she made to her mother in these days.

A year later Ariane was making a mock complaint about going out too much, where previously she had been too tired to go out at all.

She comes only rarely now. She has no ulcer symptoms, her legs have slimmed down, and her nerves are quiet. Her growing emotional stability has enabled her to make a better adjustment to problems that used to upset her. In regard to her mother she makes no comment. In fact, too, she has apparently reached a way of living with more serenity. Even when she does feel some of her old symptoms returning she is not frightened. She is confident she can deal with them.

The Third Sister

Audrey, the youngest sister, came to see me upon the insistence of Annabelle and Ariane. She was a soft-spoken gentle young woman, who appeared frightened and harassed. With great concern she had noticed that it was increasingly difficult to get up in the morning and get dressed, or go out and shop, or do any of the things that are natural tasks for normal people. She attributed all this to her lack of energy, about which she could do nothing.

In her appearance she had become neglectful. Indeed, her drawn face, stooped carriage, and slovenly dress made her look much older than her twenty-nine years. She came in with her hair blown, her coat flying open, breathless, disorganized, seemingly on the verge of exhaustion and as though she had just made it to the office.

She complained of feeling low and being depressed. Her metabolism, which on the record was always low, was now minus thirty and one-half. She suffered intestinal irregularity to a troublesome degree. She had had an infection in her sinus which had persisted for nearly three years despite treatment. At first it had improved with medication, but then it had returned during a period of great emotional stress when she openly rebelled against her mother's domination. Audrey had recently put on considerable weight.

Her bitterness against her mother was intense. She said she had been driven to the point of choosing between killing herself and breaking with her mother. The specific issue in dispute was her proposed marriage to a decent man making a decent living, but one whose social status was scorned by her mother. Her first marriage had been to a man approved by her mother; it had ended in divorce. She had a child by that marriage. It was a difficult delivery in which high forceps were used and which was followed by a series of other complications. The child died a few days later.

Audrey, like her sisters, was quick to see the relationship be-

tween her emotional and her physical suffering. Like them she
made a conscious attack on her emotional difficulties while co-
operating in medical treatment. Her physical symptoms began
to diminish. Her weight came down gradually without strenuous dieting or radical medical treatment for obesity itself.

She went with her husband to the country for the summer,
and when she returned I scarcely recognized her. She had become a beautiful young woman; Botticelli might have used her
as a model. In five months she had lost sixteen pounds. She still
suffers spells of fatigue but she traces them to emotional involvement, and finds that when she deals with her problem
directly her fatigue disappears. Audrey, like Annabelle, is on
the way to realizing her full potentialities as a mature woman.

The Mother

When Mrs. T herself became my patient I knew a good deal
about Annabelle, little about Ariane and nothing whatever of
Audrey except what I gathered from the remarks of her older
sisters. Of the relationship between the mother and her daughters I knew nothing beyond Annabelle's reserved suggestion
that she herself was happier away from home. What I learned of
the mother's destructive grip on these three grown women, I
learned from her own lips.

She was in her fifties, tall, thin, well-groomed, with a reddish
complexion and protruding eyes. She complained of frequent
headaches, a dull pain in her shoulders and neck, an occasional choking sensation, and dizzy spells. Most of these symptoms were due to her high blood pressure.

Her specific complaint was an increasing pain in the joints of
her left arm, which impaired free movement of that limb. She
found it difficult to get dressed or to comb her hair or even to
eat without help. She was afraid of becoming totally crippled.

The examination revealed mild arthritic changes, for which
a favorable prediction could be given.

Her troubles she blamed on her daughters with a violent
feeling. They hated her, she said. They wished her dead so

they could inherit her money. She swore that Annabelle was a fool and Audrey was a disgrace to the family, running around with low people. Mrs. T's language was excessive in talking of Audrey.

The only one to whom she granted any sense was Ariane, who had made a "decent" marriage. But she complained that even Ariane was selfish. And as she talked about unkind hearts, she philosophized about how her children would treat her if she were poor.

Gradually Mrs. T emerged as a woman full of hostility, all of whose actions were dictated by this drive, thinly covered by conventional motherly expressions. Living alone in her Fifth Avenue home with a butler, cook, and maids, she had trouble keeping even these paid servants.

That she was insecure and unhappy was obvious. She relied on money and position. She was unable to appreciate human values or maintain human relationships. Her only satisfaction seemed to be in contemplating her costly possessions. There are many reasons why she cannot help being the way she is.

Of her three daughters, Annabelle has freed herself by running away, Audrey has cut herself off and taken refuge in her husband and child, and Ariane, though failing to gain complete independence, has made a tolerable adjustment.

Dependent Parent

Another mother of three daughters is Mrs. S, at almost the other extreme of the social and economic scale. She was a widow of sixty-seven, living alone in a small walk-up flat where she was supported by her daughters. Before she first came to me she had been going to a clinic for her heart.

"I can't expect you to do much for me at my age—all I ask is some relief for the few months I still may have to live," she said appealingly.

She complained of palpitations, dizziness, pressure and occasional pain around the heart. She was restless and did not sleep well. Examination revealed high blood pressure, some enlargement of the heart, and occasional missed heart beats. Medically one might well agree with her that she probably had not many years to live.

All three daughters became my patients, and eventually the family picture became clear. The eldest daughter had quickly freed herself of financial responsibility for the mother, claiming economic difficulties and her obligations to her own daughter. The widow's other two daughters were living in anxiety and guilt. When they visited their mother they were distressed by her loneliness. When they left her they were anxious about her health. I discovered that whenever one of them failed to visit her for a few days, my elderly patient's palpitations and shortness of breath increased and her pains returned.

Mrs. S had been my patient for several years when her daughters decided that it was not safe for her to live alone, and the eldest daughter took the mother to live with her. After a few months Mrs. S was carried to the hospital in a serious condition with uremic poisoning, followed by lobar pneumonia. She recovered and went to live with her youngest daughter.

After not very long, the old lady found it increasingly difficult to get along with her third daughter's husband. The situation became intolerable and Mrs. S went to live in her middle daughter's home. But after a few months there, the friction with her second son-in-law became so acute that she returned to her youngest daughter.

This sort of thing has been going on for fourteen years. Mrs. S is now past eighty, and still talks of having "maybe another month to live." Her second and third daughters, for whose sake, as she continually reminds me, she never remarried, are losing years of personal happiness. Both are childless; both live in constant tension with their husbands. Both suffer the repetitious, nagging illness of a life lived in unrelieved emotional conflict.

Unconsciously this mother seems to be driven to injure her children. Whether it is the children who are unwholesomely dependent on parents, as in the case of Mrs. T and her daughters, or the parent who leans on the children as does Mrs. S, the powerful emotions involved make the interdependence of parent and child a situation of serious stress. A breakdown into illness of one kind or another is almost inevitable.

Illness involves, of course, more complex processes than a mere desire to flee from a difficult situation, like the daughters of Mrs. T. Also it is more than a purposeful punishment of others, in the way that Mrs. S seems to be punishing her daughters.

Illness comes as a result of continued stress with no prospect of relief. These people who seem to flee into illness become ill because they live in continued stress, and they live in stress because they are unable to resolve a situation fraught with emotion. The illness takes a form characteristic of the individual's emotional pattern; with Annabelle and her sisters, the dependency pattern, and in Mrs. S's case one of unaware hostility.

In many families, parents' inability to maintain a satisfactory relationship with each other makes it impossible for them to develop a healthy relationship with their children. This is why Mrs. S appears to be using her illness as a weapon against her daughters.

_____ SUMMING UP _____

Illness may come as a needed respite from problems we feel unable to solve, perhaps unable to face.

❖ ❖ ❖

Illness may be an unconscious device to change a situation by influencing another's attitude or behavior toward us.

❖ ❖ ❖

Illness may be a way to give vent to hostility that we cannot accept within ourselves and so must suppress.

❖ ❖ ❖

Illness may be acute, a way of getting out of a temporarily difficult situation.

✻   ✻   ✻

Or it may become chronic, if the situation continues to be unresolved.

✻   ✻   ✻

But a detour into illness, however long or short and for whatever reasons, is costly to ourselves and those close to us.

✻   ✻   ✻

Understanding of the deeper reasons promises a better way to deal with life situations, and also to safeguard our health.

III

The Road Back
to Health

*—To take arms against a
sea of troubles,
And by opposing, end them.*
                    SHAKESPEARE

11

Allies Against Illness

We must first balance the books.

ONE of my professors used to tell his students: "I may have erred many a time in my diagnosis, but never in my therapy."

He was not merely making a joke. Medical therapy or treatment, has of necessity been mainly directed at symptoms. We have given digitalis for the heart, quinine for malaria, salicylic acid (aspirin) for rheumatic fever. Of the thousand drugs in the pharmacopoeia, these and a few more have been considered specific for certain diseases. The rest are for alleviating symptoms: something to bring down fever, something to relieve pain.

With vaccines we first began to stir up the body to build its own immunity against a specific infection. With a few earlier drugs, and now more successfully with antibiotics, we come closer to the cause of disease: we kill germs. Still we have not attacked the condition which made the patient susceptible to the germ in the first place.

With hormones like insulin, thyroid, the cortisone preparations, we come still closer, restoring a weak link in the body's defense system against stress. In other words, with the endocrinologist's findings, we are able to treat an earlier stage in the chain reaction of illness.

But have we attacked illness at its source?

The fight against illness cannot be made by the doctor alone. The fight must be a collaboration of both doctor and patient, a working together in the fullest sense of the word. The sufferer who has roused himself to go to the doctor at last has only begun his job. He cannot passively hand himself over to the doctor and say, "Here I am. Cure me." With such an attitude the spirit—a force that we know can move mountains—is left totally inert, inactive, a powerful resource not put to use. To find what blocks this current of power he needs to retrace the path which has led to illness.

He cannot be expected to do this all at once, nor to do it alone. Distressed, in pain, suffering not only from his sick body but from the fears and resentments which illness itself sets up, he must first have all the help which medical science can give him. He must be comforted in body and mind before he can be asked to take up arms in his own defense against illness.

The fight against illness has to be an alliance if it is to succeed. But the doctor, the strong ally, with his objectivity and experience with his arsenal of scientific weapons, fights the first battle.

The Vicious Circle of Illness

Mrs. M, a woman approaching forty, came to me with complaints of colitis, fatigue, and migraine.

She was trim, chic, looking perhaps thirty. An alert intelligence shone in her face. She seemed a model American woman, eternally young, quick, and vital, capable both at home and in the business or professional world.

It is hard to believe that such women ever need the services of a doctor except to deliver their children. They seem equal to any situation, and it is difficult to imagine them ill.

But perhaps for the very reason that they are so capable on so many fronts, that they must meet so many kinds of demands both intellectual and emotional, intelligent modern women lead lives of considerable conflict and struggle, and they form a large part of the population in the doctors' offices. They do fall ill, and they do need help. This one did.

She had suffered first from a hyperthyroid disturbance for which she underwent an operation. Her first marriage ended subsequently in divorce, and she embarked on a career. Then she married again.

Now her pattern of illness took a different turn. From the overstimulated thyroid, a symptom of frustration of the aggressive pattern, she reverted this time to the regressive side with colitis and fatigue, signs that she craved love and protection, and relief from responsibility. But she also suffered from migraine, frequently a symptom of suppressed rage, on the aggressive side of the scale.

It is characteristic of many modern women that they undertake, whether by choice or of necessity, rather more responsibility than one person should carry. A not infrequent consequence is that they rebel against the burden while conscientiously continuing to discharge their obligations. All of Mrs. M's ailments are symptomatic of this conflict.

Also, like many such women, she resented her illness. She had no time to be sick, she said. She had too many important things to do. She considered illness no escape from responsibility, only an unwarranted disruption of her busy schedule. Moreover it was the cause of still more guilt piled on top of the burden she already carried.

This is the vicious circle of illness, from conflict to illness and back again to a sharpening of conflict because of the new problems set up by illness itself.

Breaking the Circle

It is the doctor's first task to break through this vicious circle both by word and by deed. Only when anxiety is quieted, resentment allayed, and the pain of illness abated, can the patient take up his share of the real work of combating illness.

The first step is, of course, the obvious one of thorough physical investigation, both of the specific symptoms and of the patient's general condition. In this case, as in many others, the patient could honestly be assured that there was no organic illness.

Like most patients when they are relieved of their primary anxiety, she relaxed and began to talk. If there was nothing wrong, why was she sick?

"Don't tell me," she said, "that it's just nerves. I've heard that one too often."

She really wanted to know why she was sick. When a patient honestly wants to know, the first obstacle, that of resistance, is already hurdled. We talked about functional disturbances, and their origin in the emotions.

We set up a diet to relieve her colitis, which was a medical problem no matter what its origin. We worked out medication to restore functional balance, and enable the patient to meet her difficulties with greater physical stability. This is the second step in the doctor's effort to free the patient from the vicious circle of illness.

In every relationship between doctor and patient there comes a moment when the doctor sits with all his charts, tests, and diagnostic findings before him, and the patient waits for the verdict. The patient is mute, anxious to know what is wrong with him, and thinking also, "Now he knows more about me than I know about myself."

But the doctor can say truthfully, "Now I know everything about the illness of your body which modern medicine can discover. But about the cause of your illness, you alone know, and you alone can reveal it. Medicine can help you in your search, but yours is the task of seeking, and yours the gratification of its discovery—and the conquest of your illness."

In pursuit of the cause, I asked the patient for one more thing: a record of her symptoms, when they recurred, with what intensity, and what was the background of events or of her emotional reactions to events.

The Psychiatrist as a Specialist

The question arises, if the origin of illness is emotional, that is, "mental," why do we not go to a psychiatrist? The answer is, we do. A medical man does not undertake to diagnose or to treat psychiatrically a patient suffering from severe personality disorder, and the psychiatrist is one of the specialists upon whom he calls, just as he calls upon the cardiologist, the neurologist, the gynecologist.

At one end of the scale there are the acute cases of organic illness which require perhaps the quick action of the surgeon. At the other end of the scale are patients whose emotional conflict is such that it may best be helped by the psychiatrist. But between the two is the large mass of men and women, those who properly come within the province of the medical doctor, all the people who are struggling with the ordinary problems of living and who have reached a point where the weaknesses in their emotional constitution and the weaknesses in their physical constitution have together brought them to the point of illness.

In my experience, these people can be helped to understand the cause of illness within themselves, and when they understand it, many can deal with it. It has been estimated that eighty per cent of people walking around this country are in a neurotic condition and need psychiatric help. This does not mean that they cannot help themselves, nor that their own doctor cannot help them. He does not need to throw half-understood psychiatric terms and explanations at their heads. With most sick people, he needs only to take the same interest in the patient's personality as in his illness. He needs to listen as a human being to another human being in trouble.

Most patients can deal with their difficulties enough to get back on the right track. The cure may not be perfect. In a crisis they may again fall into the old emotional pattern and feel again the familiar symptoms of the suffering organ. But neither has psychoanalysis or psychotherapy a perfect score of permanent cures. In times of stress many patients come back again to the psychiatrist for help over the rough spot.

Mrs. M was typical of this great mass of people who, once they know why they suffer, are able and eager to work toward the emotional health which safeguards their physical health. At first the medication showed only moderate results. Her symptoms abated but did not disappear, and with every new situation which produced emotional stress, she suffered intense recurrences.

As she faithfully kept her record, however, she began to see a relationship between the events in her life and her sieges of colitis or headache or spells of fatigue. With each visit she wanted to know more about the way emotional disturbance affects the body, about the pathways from the emotional to the physical, about the effects on the organs of chronic emotional stress.

When she learned of the two groups of diseases and their relationship to the two basic emotional patterns, the aggressive and the regressive, her reaction was like that of Balboa discovering the Pacific. She went away very thoughtful.

Hard to Face the Inner Self

It is most difficult for each of us to face his inner self. We need time and patience to trace the path from emotion to illness. To understand with the mind is comparatively easy. To understand with the emotions—that is, to recognize and accept the necessity for changing one's emotional patterns—is much harder. We all react like Pavlov's conditioned dogs. But he changed their reflex responses by new conditioning, and we can do much the same thing for ourselves.

We have the power: that positive force within us, the will to live. This is the powerful ally of those whose profound wish is to be well. In response to their rational, conscious effort, the will to live rises to their aid in a thousand big and little ways.

It is hard for a woman like Mrs. M, for all the Mrs. M's, so competent, so self-reliant, to realize that she needs love and is sick for the lack of it. It is hard for her to face her hostility toward her work—which interests her—and toward her husband, even toward her children. It is hard for her to accept the fact that all of us show two sides to those we love best, that we are both loving and hostile in some degree.

But women, I have found, are inclined to be more realistic about themselves than men. They are not dogged by the "sissy" complex which demands of men that they be manly at all costs. There is nothing shameful to a woman, even to a very modern woman, about wanting to be loved.

After Mrs. M had been my patient for some time, her husband telephoned. He was outspokenly dissatisfied with his wife's treatments. "If she is sick she should go to a hospital and be operated on, like everybody else," he said.

Mrs. M submitted to her husband's demand and went to a physician of his choice who gave her mild sedation. But she would not submit to an operation. Instead she took a trip to Europe.

A year later she was back in my office. All in one week, her daughter had gone away to college; her stepson, of whom she was very fond, had gone into the army, and her sister had moved to another city. Her colitis had come back, and she felt her old state of fatigue. But she had no headache. She had observed that her husband was also shaken by this series of separations, and she felt only sympathy for him, no hostility. All she wanted was a little help over this spell of trouble.

"Now I know why I'm sick," she said.

Her next appointment was unnecessary. When she called to say that she felt fine and did not need to come to my office, she added: "I'd like a chart of those two groups of diseases. I want to hang it over my bed, to remind me."

Patient on the Defensive

The doctor's first task, that of breaking through the vicious circle of illness, is not often as easy as it was with Mrs. M.

An ulcer patient who has been to many doctors comes in
with resistance bristling under his good manners. He waits for
the doctor to say, "Barium test." He has made up his mind he
is not going through that again, for the sixth or tenth time. He
waits for the doctor to say, "It's all in the mind." But his pain is
in his stomach, and the pain is real.

He has been through all the tests and submitted to all the
traditional treatments. He has gone to a reputable psychiatrist,
and has rejected the deep probing into his personality; it made
his pain worse. He has come to still another doctor now because
he is suffering and unable to function at his work. But he has
begun to look upon doctors, all kinds, as strangers who make
tyrannical disposition of his mind, his body, and his bank account.

But the wise doctor does none of the things the patient is
waiting for him to do. He does not scoff at the pain as being
"all in the mind." He does not dismiss tension and anxiety with
the useless advice, "stop worrying—take it easy," since these are
precisely the things such a patient is unable to do, or he would
not have an ulcer in the first place. Nor does he ship the man,
in pain, off to a round of tests and X-rays.

He gives the patient a pill. Precisely what the pill is does not
matter. Some doctors use one, some another; it is designed to
relax the stomach spasm which causes the pain. With the pill
goes an explanation.

This pill, says the doctor, will not cure your ulcer. Your ulcer
is the end result of a great number of things, both emotional
and physical. You cannot tackle all that now. First we must
give you a breathing spell, a release from pain. Then we'll see.

The doctor, aware of all the physical and possibly dangerous
connotations of the patient's condition, badly wants his tests
done. He wants to eliminate any organic disease. But he must
weigh the risk of waiting. Such a patient has an ulcer for the
very reason that he is fighting his own need for dependence,
for someone in authority to take care of him. He does not want
to be pushed. He wants to make up his own mind. He is dis-
armed when the doctor does not even offer to make an appoint-

ment for the next visit. The patient goes away knowing that the decision to tackle the larger problem of his illness is still in his own hands.

Usually this patient calls for his next appointment in a very different frame of mind. The pill has relieved his pain and the explanation has relieved his hostility. "For the first time, I can think," he says. "What do we do now?" From then on—not always easily, not without setbacks—this patient is able to be a cooperative, intelligent partner in the larger task of changing the physical and emotional patterns which brought about his illness.

The Hostile Patient

A more pervasive hostility is found in the kind of patient who is suffering, for example, from high blood pressure. His wife telephones for an appointment for him.

"Frighten him a little, doctor," she says. "Get him worried about his heart, so he won't smoke so much." It is obvious she has bullied her husband into going to the doctor, and expects to bully him back to health with the doctor as her accomplice. She does not realize that by such an approach she is reducing a grown man to the stature of a child. She is the wife-mother, dominating him "for his own good."

It is not surprising that he rebels, and, suppressing the rebellion, he suffers one of the chronic effects of hostility, an elevated blood pressure. We may assume that this pattern of suppressed rebellion and hostility was laid down long before his marriage. In his adult life he was responding to his wife as he had responded in childhood to a dominating parent. Now emotional stress of continually repressing these feelings has had its effect at last on his arteries, and this is a medical problem.

But with such an introduction from his wife, the doctor may expect his patient to be hostile not only to the wife who badgered him into coming for an examination, and to others in his life situation; the man is bound to be hostile to the doctor as well, and to any diagnosis or treatment he may suggest.

You cannot get very far with a man who is figuratively point-ing a gun at your head. You must first get him to lay the gun on the table. Then you can talk things over.

But he is not likely to lay the gun down if you ask him po-litely, or even if you command him with your authority as a physician. He may listen, but he will not hear. His hostility is unconscious; unconsciously it has dominated his behavior for years. Persuasion must be of a more subtle variety.

So we offer him a choice. We can give him temporary super-ficial relief with conventional medication. Or we can take the next step, and determine what functional disturbances have developed in response to the stress of living. We tell him that we have ways of restoring balance, regardless of the origin of his hypertension. Then, when he is freed of his physical dis-comfort, he will be better able to deal with whatever is at the source of his illness.

He is a business man, and he knows that a business cannot run at a deficit. He understands that we must first balance the books.

The mind governs the body, but the condition of the body also affects the mind. There is no need to prove this out of the multitude of studies of people suffering from starvation or other physical conditions. We see it in our everyday life. A clever wife does not ask her husband for a new hat until after he has enjoyed a good dinner.

So with the bristling patient in the doctor's office. We do not cure his hostility. But by restoring functional balance we check the effects of stress on his system. By relieving some of his physical tensions, we soften the inner climate in which he must do his thinking. We persuade him, for the moment, to lay the gun on the table. Then we can proceed to enlist his conscious aid in the attack on his illness.

The Fearful Patient

Fear is another obstacle which the doctor must remove be-fore the patient can become his ally. In medical practice, an acute illness is recognized as an emergency which demands prompt action. Fear can also be an emergency.

We have mentioned earlier that fear is often ignored in medical practice. Out of sheer humanity a doctor may give an obviously frightened patient a reassuring word. But the patient who by great effort masks his fear behind a controlled exterior does not ask for kindness, and frequently he does not get it.

Yet fear is an emergency. Fear turns discomfort into pain, and turns severe pain into unbearable pain. Fear, built up over days, weeks, even months, has become acute by the time the patient has nerved himself to go to the doctor, and must be dealt with promptly.

The fear that we are harboring a fatal disease is very common. Many people delay going to the doctor, unable to face the moment when their fear will be confirmed. This in itself is a self-destructive act. If there is a disease, the delay has wasted time during which the disease may be arrested or perhaps cured. If there is no disease, the continued fear is a needless torture; we know that a chronic state of fear can harm the body.

Terror can hide behind a calm, composed face. The doctor assembling his diagnostic findings, must stop to deal with it, because the sooner he can dispel fear with knowledge, the sooner he has the patient as his ally against illness. The man with his inner eye fixed on the specter he fears is diverting most of his energies to controlling his terror and displaying a calm exterior to the world.

Take for example one of my patients, a man in his fifties, a successful business executive with a high reputation and no financial worries. The exaggerated calm of his manner, his pallor, and a certain tense look revealed that he was in the grip of fear. For a month he had felt a soreness in his throat, not like a cold but like something stuck there which he could not swallow but which caused a constant tickling sensation. During the past week he had been increasingly tired and low in energy. He should have come before, he said apologetically.

Now, he murmured almost inaudibly, it was "probably too
late."

There was no need to mention what he feared. Naturally his
mind dwelt on cancer of the throat. Scientific procedure demands a thorough objective investigation should come first, no
matter how long it might take, and that the patient's fear is of
secondary importance. Since he had taken his time to come for
examination, a few more days could scarcely matter.

But in such a situation, a delay of a few days, even a few
hours is an added hardship. If possible, such a patient is not
sent home to suffer additional nights of self-torture before the
diagnostic round of tests and X-rays can be completed.

So within the hour this patient was in the radiologist's office being X-rayed. The films showed that there was no growth.
The more detailed tests took longer, but at the first reassurance his fear receded, and he could talk.

He was smoking some sixty cigarettes a day. In addition, we
discovered that an overconscientious housekeeper was spraying the closets at home with DDT, and one such closet was beside the head of his bed so that he was probably breathing the
irritating fumes at night.

The spraying was stopped. Then after we discussed smoking,
especially to such excess, as a self-destructive act, the patient
gave up his cigarettes. In a few days all his physical symptoms
disappeared. This did not mean that he had solved all his difficulties, only that the storm of intense anxiety had subsided.

This patient returns every so often, but not with his throat
symptoms or his fear. He is smoking again, though not so
heavily, and he engages in bouts of intensive work which result in fatigue. He understands that his way of life is in some
respects self-destructive but like most of us, he likes his way of
life and sees no pressing need to change it. He is active and
creative enough, apparently, to counterbalance his mildly destructive habits. According to his medical record to date, he is
maintaining himself in very good health.

_____ SUMMING UP _____

To tap the powerful resources of the will to live the patient has to become an active ally of the doctor.

❉ ❉ ❉

Often the patient has feelings of hostility, fear, and defensive obstinacy toward the doctor.

❉ ❉ ❉

Recognizing these feelings enables the patient to cooperate with the doctor.

12

Incurable?

Illness of the body can be looked upon as a sign of the struggle to make an adjustment to living.

INCURABLE" is a fateful word. It has the finality of a slammed door. Yet doctors are driven to use it in many cases of chronic illness. When, on the record, every method known to scientific medicine for a specific ailment has been tried without success, it often seems to a doctor more wholesome to tell the patient that he must learn to live with his trouble, than to send him out again on the costly disheartening search for a cure which apparently does not exist.

But how many incurables are really incurable?

A woman of fifty visited my office with an "incurable" arthritis. Almost before she sat down she announced that she had determined never to go to another doctor, and had come only because a friend had nagged her into it.

She had had rheumatism since childhood. For the past four months she had had a sharp pain in her back and down her leg. She was full of bitterness against an osteopath, whose treatment she blamed for a new pain in her neck. It became clear that she was willing to submit to examination mostly in the hope of discovering some damage the osteopath had done so that she could sue him.

Her manner was witty and charming, but the camouflage was thin and any observant listener could hear hostility in every word she uttered. Her face, which showed remnants of youthful prettiness, also revealed hostility. Her features were sharpened and her mouth was compressed into a straight, hard line.

Five years before, she had been in an automobile accident with her husband, who had never before had an accident while driving. She dated the onset of her arthritis from this event. Of course she was not conscious of it, but she plainly nursed a grudge against her husband.

The patient slept poorly and was depressed. On this day, for example, she told me she had had no sleep at all the night before, was in pain from her shoulders to her toes, and felt "like jumping off the bridge." A doctor friend had told her it was all nerves and she must snap out of it.

To begin with, we used high doses of vitamins and other medication which had shown good results in arthritis. The patient submitted only half-heartedly to physical treatment and resisted in other ways. As the weeks went by and her pains disappeared from her neck, her back, her legs, she concentrated on the shoulder pain which she still felt, complaining that it was excruciating, and she also complained of splitting headaches. Although her improvement was obvious, her need to resist did not allow her to admit it.

The following winter, some nine months after the patient had first begun her visits, we instituted treatments with a cortisone preparation. Her improvement then became very marked. Even her face changed, softening noticeably.

After four treatments the patient interrupted this course for a trip out of town. Several months later she returned, with a mild recurrence of her old symptoms, some new symptoms, and an out-spoken resistance to a cortisone preparation although it had helped her.

Many times a patient resists a treatment that has helped him, with some rationalization that conceals his real reason: he is unwilling to get well, although he may not know it, because his illness serves some unhealthy emotional need of which he is unaware. In this case the patient was obviously clinging to her arthritis.

Is the disease incurable? The patient may unknowingly resist treatment that could cure him. Such a self-destructive course may explain many failures both in medical treatment and in psychotherapy. As Karen Horney says, "If there is no sufficient will to live, a person will go to pieces anyhow, analysis or no analysis."

History of a Headache

With young people the word "incurable" must be used with the utmost care. To saddle a child with a conviction that he or she is permanently handicapped may cause incalculable damage to the personality, far more serious, indeed, than the physical handicap.

In some cases, of course, it cannot be avoided. There are conditions of actual destruction of nerve and muscle tissue, as in paralysis resulting from polio, which we may ameliorate but may not be able to eliminate altogether. It is better for both the child and his parents to concentrate their efforts on developing the capacities which remain, rather than in the hopeless attempt to restore the damaged limbs.

But where tissue damage is not apparent, we have no right to condemn a young person to an incurable disease. We have youth on our side, with its resilience of both body and mind, its willingness to learn, to change, to grow. In youth the patterns are not likely to be rigidly set, either emotionally or physically. When we close the door to hope with the word "incurable," we may be making a costly mistake.

With youth we have still one more valuable advantage in our attack on illness: the emotional pattern behind a young person's suffering is often dramatically clear. We also often have the parents still alive and very much on the parental job. The sharp edges of an unsatisfactory parent-child relationship usually show up in some way, and it is usually this relationship which is at the bottom of the child's illness.

One day a father brought in his son, a university student, who had been suffering from nausea and stomach pains for the past eight months. He had a history of frequent disabling headaches dating back to the age of seven, when he was struck with a golf club and received a severe skull fracture and concussion. A skull operation was performed at the time to remove blood clots; the extensive scar was a visible reminder.

The boy had had regular check-ups for his headaches, and had been told repeatedly by various doctors that they were a consequence of his accident, that there was no remedy for them, and that he must learn to accept this permanent handicap which would limit his capacity throughout his life. The youth admitted that he was depressed. He also had a bad acne, and he was somewhat overweight. He had the fatty thighs and lower abdomen which signify incomplete masculine development.

After a reassurance that the headaches would probably respond to treatment, the father took over the interview, mainly to talk about himself. He told with a complacent smile of how he had worked his way through college, had acquired three academic degrees, and had built a successful business. Every boastful word was a gloved blow at his son's inadequacy.

I remarked that something ought to be done to relieve the boy's feeling of inferiority, so greatly intensified by the medical verdict that he was permanently handicapped.

The father corrected me. "You don't understand—he is quite the opposite. He is full of superiority feelings—he's arrogant, difficult and demanding." To the suggestion that there was such a thing as overcompensating to cover one's real feelings, the father did not respond. But behind his parent's back the boy winked at me.

Silent and hostile until that moment, from then on the young man relaxed, and when we were alone he confessed that he felt

himself different from the other fellows, that he was belligerent
and did not get along well with his fraternity brothers.

At my request the boy kept a record of his headaches, their
frequency and intensity. He brought in an admirably worked-
out chart, with symbols devised by himself in a scientific manner. The chart revealed that his headaches were periodic, in a
cycle suggesting the female menstrual cycle. This and other
evidence indicated a decreased functioning of the sex glands.

We began treatments, using among other medications an
anterior pituitary hormone stimulating the sex glands. We
timed them to precede the intense phase of his headaches.

At an early visit he confided that he was secretly engaged
and was certain his father would interfere with the engagement
if he knew of it. After this confidence he confessed to feeling
much relieved, and his stomach upsets quickly subsided, finally
disappearing entirely.

After three months the young man reported that he had enjoyed forty-two consecutive days without headaches. Later he
had two separate attacks, one following the death of a friend
and the other when the family was moving. Four months after
treatments were discontinued he had had only one headache,
when he stayed up through the night "cramming" for an exam.
It was, he reported happily, "different from those headaches—
it was the kind of headache the other fellows get."

Five months later, his acne had vanished, and he felt more
energetic. His thighs had thinned and assumed a more masculine contour.

Shortly following graduation he married the girl to whom
he had been engaged. He has since had a child and has made
a happy adjustment to adult life. His headaches are definitely a
thing of the past.

"Nervous" Disease

How far can we go with medical methods toward curing a
so-called "nervous" disease?

The classification of some diseases as "nervous" may seem

artificial, if we consider that all diseases may have an emotional origin and all proceed by way of the nervous and glandular systems. But there are unquestionably some purely functional symptoms which arise from an immediate emotional problem.

Such a symptom is nervous vomiting. Food and the act of eating are here used symbolically as they are in so many digestive disturbances. Psychoanalysts explain the spasm as an effort to reject or make restitution of something which one has taken. Guilt may be one of the reasons.

An intelligent woman of thirty-nine, a divorcee, had been suffering from this distressing symptom for five years. She experienced it usually at the end of the day, often during the day, but almost never in the early morning. The vomiting was accompanied by considerable pain in the upper abdomen and a burning sensation in the throat. After the attack she felt better. She had been told the cause was a chronic appendicitis. Her appetite was poor and she was losing weight. Examination revealed no organic explanation of the symptoms.

We tried to discover whether it was in relation to her work that she was suffering the disturbance. She was the director of a private school, and according to her own belief she was happy and effective in her work with the children. She was, however, often upset by her interviews with difficult and disturbed mothers. Furthermore she was constantly coping with financial problems.

From the fact that hers was a digestive disorder, we could infer that this woman was in need of love and a release from her responsibilities, that she wanted someone to care for her. The reason for the failure of her first marriage, as well as the origin of the guilt feelings by which the psychiatrist would probably explain her vomiting, could not be discovered except by a psychiatric approach. She claimed, however, that she was not ready for psychoanalysis, and that in any case she could not afford it.

After her fourth visit her vomiting stopped, and she felt only occasional pain. At the end of five more visits all her discomfort was gone. There has been no recurrence.

This therapy of a condition which had gone on for five years was completed in seven weeks. What accomplished the cure?

First the patient was reassured that there was no organic illness. This reassurance was based on thorough examination and testing.

Second, we treated the symptoms medically.

Third—and most important if a real cure is to be achieved instead of merely an alleviation of symptoms—came an understanding of what makes illness.

If a patient can understand what makes illness—if he can follow the causal pathway leading from emotional stress to physical tensions, and from physical tensions to physical illness—then, most often improvement begins.

Psychological Antibodies

When the physical system is exposed to germs, it forms antibodies. What happens in the patient who understands that his emotional disturbance is making him ill seems to be a mental process very like the physical one. I have come to call the process the development of psychological antibodies.

When we inject diphtheria bacilli into the body, the body forms specific antigenes against the bacilli, thus building a state of immunization. In the same way a patient who still has the will to live and who comes to realize that a specific emotional reaction to a situation in his life is at the basis of his illness, seems to develop specific antigenes to that emotional reaction.

This wholesome response can be looked upon as part of the individual's natural process of adaptation of both body and mind to a situation. I have seen a man refuse to get upset by his mother-in-law or landlord or business partner. He does it by recognizing first of all that to get upset emotionally means bringing on his physical suffering. He then builds his defenses —develops his psychological antibodies—against that situation and his emotional response to it.

Two conditions must be met before he is able to do this for himself, and in both he may need help.

First he must be assured that he is not born with a weakness which dooms him to illness, or that he is physically damaged so that illness must be accepted. In some patients this is a fear; in some it is a comforting delusion into which they escape.

Second, he must accept the truth that illness is not a visitation of evil fate, but that he himself brings about illness and he himself can avoid it. He must come to understand and to accept the connection between his emotional responses and his illness. He must see that by the way he responds to his problems he is inviting illness.

Changing Our Response

Most people are aware of their living problems, on the one hand, and of their physical symptoms on the other. They are likely also to be aware, in many instances, that the problem and the symptoms are related.

We say, "He makes me sick," of a boss or a colleague, and often we mean it quite literally. We are conscious of the rising nausea or the stab of gas pain, or of the throbbing which forecasts a headache. What comes as a surprise to most patients is that not the boss or the coworker, but our own emotional response to him is the cause of the indigestion or migraine, and that *we can learn to change this response.* The physical pain is the body's response to the emotional stimulus, as real as laughter when we are amused or tears when we are sad. If we can adjust ourselves to a situation so that the emotional stimulus does not arise, then the physical reaction will not follow.

Usually we sit and wait for the outside situation to change. But in order to get well, we ourselves must change.

It is not easy, nor is it an overnight cure. The patient must work hard, first to understand, and then to revise his emotional pattern.

There are some, of course, who cannot accomplish this re-education of the emotions without intensive help. These are the sufferers who must have psychiatric treatment.

Illness of the body can be looked upon as a sign of the struggle to make an adjustment to living. Psychotics, as Menninger and others have observed, are likely to be physically healthy specimens, and psychotics are those who have withdrawn from reality and thus escaped the need to adjust themselves to it. Therefore we have reason to say that the sick man or woman is one who is struggling to make an adjustment.

Most human beings are struggling with the common problems of living. While in our times the great majority show neurotic reactions to some of these problems at some time during their lives, they are not therefore incapable of dealing with them. It is not always necessary, and often it is not desirable, that an entire personality be revised, or that the original emotional foundations laid down in childhood be explored. With understanding and a knowledge of how mind and body function together many people can themselves deal with the problems which are making them ill.

_____ SUMMING UP _____

"Incurable" often means that the patient, not the disease, is resisting cure.

❊   ❊   ❊

A chronic illness may be serving some unhealthy emotional need of which the sufferer himself is unaware.

❊   ❊   ❊

In chronic illness the disease is actually part of the adjustment to life, though a faulty and a costly one.

❊   ❊   ❊

A person may be able to part with his chronic symptoms once he is aware that behind there lies a chronic emotional response.

* * *

In the same way that we develop physical antibodies to infection, we can develop psychological antibodies to familiar situations that bring on familiar symptoms.

13

In Deep Waters

I wanted to die.

ILLNESS is a kind of adaptation to the difficulties of living, though a costly one. We have seen how illness can have the effect of a temporary retreat from a difficulty, an opportunity to consider and regroup one's forces. It is an old observation of physicians that a man may come out of an illness wiser than he went in.

One may come out wiser, that is, if illness is understood, if the opportunity is used for considering our difficulty and setting a rational course toward resolving it. That it often is so, perhaps unconsciously, we have many examples to prove. "The whole experience has been tremendously maturing," one patient wrote me, looking back understandingly at his illness.

Acute illness in particular often have this salutary effect. I saw a sample of this in a refreshing incident, the case of a girl of fourteen.

I had examined the child a few months before, when she had come home from camp. An alert, attractive, very popular and successful young girl, she stood high in her studies and got along well with her friends, both girls and boys. After the summer in question, however, her mother thought she seemed languid and apathetic. I found a strong bile reaction in one of the tests, and wondered what situation could call forth in this friendly, outgoing child the little sign of disturbance. She was in good physical condition, and I so assured her mother.

During the winter she had an attack of flu, and afterward I was called with great urgency. The child was well, but she refused to get up and resume her normal activities. She lay in bed, staring at the ceiling, rejecting any attempt by her mother to find out what was the matter. A member of the family who was a physician insisted that the child was in need of immediate psychiatric attention.

The anxiety in the household was acute, and the girl could not help being aware of it, but she was coldly unresponsive to her mother's hovering concern. When the mother left the room, the girl burst out bitterly, "Why don't they leave me alone?"

Examination showed that she was physically well and able to get up. But it was apparent that she needed to remain withdrawn from her active pursuits. She was evidently going through some effort at adjustment in which she must not be interrupted. My advice to her worried parents was to let her alone for a few days; the mother especially was to restrain her impulse to hover anxiously about the sickroom, and she was not to ask questions. A trusted maid, who had been in the household almost since the child was born, could look after the girl's needs.

Two weeks later the girl was back at school and behaving perfectly like her old self. Once or twice that spring her mother telephoned in anxiety to say that the child wanted to stay home from school again; I advised the mother to let her stay home and make no fuss about it. The little girl made up her school work without difficulty, passed with her usual high grades, and went abroad that summer with an adult friend.

I afterward learned that the girl had in fact suffered a setback of a social nature during her summer at camp, a trivial defeat but her first one in a short and successful life. As is often true with acute illness, her attack of flu gave her the opportunity for meditation and resolution.

She had to resolve the discrepancy between her sovereign position as a beloved child at home, and her first significant experience outside the home as one of many girls and boys, subject to rules and regulations like everyone else. She had not quite figured things out to her satisfaction when the doctor pronounced her recovered from the flu and well enough to go back to school. A strong little personality, she insisted on taking all the time she needed to adjust herself to her first experience of defeat on her own without her parents' reassuring presence and to prepare for whatever new experiences must come as part of the intense growing-up years of adolescence.

Encounter with the Death Wish

Acute illness, though it can be a maturing experience, usually begins as an outspoken wish to escape, sometimes to escape even into death.

What a person may feel, on the brink of death during an acute illness, was once described to me as a conscious experience by a young woman of an adventurous temperament, an amateur aviatrix. Actually she was not ill when she had this curious experience, but perfectly well. She was alone in the cockpit of her plane, flying over the ocean at night.

What she experienced was a species of reverie, in which a friend and fellow flier, who had been shot down during the war, stood beside her and took her hand. "Come with me," he said. He—or her own thoughts—pictured the beautiful infinite world of space which went on and on forever, without cares, without fears, where all is quiet and soft as clouds.

"I must go now—are you coming with me?" he urged. She sat transfixed, while her plane roared on and out over the sea, away from land and away from reality.

Suddenly she came to herself. "If I hadn't turned back quickly," she said, "it would have been one of those flying accidents, a plane lost, down in the ocean. What's the difference whether you run out of gas or die of a fever?" she asked.

The analogy is apt. What this calm, poised young woman experienced during a moment of despair in the cockpit of her plane is not unlike what a patient experiences during the high fever of an acute and dangerous illness. When we hover in that unreal world between earth and sky, when everything that binds us to life, the faces of those we love, even our own limbs, waver and become unreal through the glaze of fever, then the mind confronts the death wish unmasked.

Returning from such an experience, a patient often says, "I was almost gone, wasn't I?" not in fear, but rather in wonder. And often, in that unguarded first moment of returning consciousness, comes the admission, "I wanted to die."

A young wife, just twenty, was having her first baby. Pregnant, she was radiantly beautiful. Her glowing skin, her lovely young features held such happiness that people stopped to look at her for sheer pleasure, and to watch her proud walk. She was an answer to the question of why the classic painters choose for their models young women in the early months of pregnancy.

When she came to the hospital for delivery, her pains developed normally at first from mild to medium strong, and then they diminished. The obstetrician became concerned and mentioned that he might have to use high forceps. Present at the husband's request, I observed the patient's face rigid with fear, and I begged for time to bring her out of her state of anxiety. The obstetrician feared the umbilical cord was strangling the infant, and decided to go ahead with the instrument delivery.

The delivery was difficult. Even under anesthesia the young mother's muscles were rigidly contracted. She was delivered of a normal baby boy, but she suffered a dangerous hemorrhage from a broken blood vessel. By the next day her temperature was soaring. She had developed bronchial pneumonia. The day after, the bronchial pneumonia seemed to be checked.

But very early the following morning I was desperately summoned by her husband. The hospital had informed him that his wife was dying.

Almost Too Far

The young mother had sunk into a coma and was in fact next door to death. She had developed an embolism in the lung. Her temperature was 105.5, her pulse was scarcely perceptible, and her breathing was shallow even in the oxygen tent.

The whole arsenal of medicine was now thrown into the battle to save her life. She had penicillin, streptomycin and aureomycin around the clock, intravenous heart stimulants, and another blood transfusion.

Toward evening she became semiconscious. "You have a boy!" I shouted into her ear.

"I don't care," she murmured, and fell back into unconsciousness. The fight went on.

Two days later the first trace of color came back to her bloodless lips. By that time we knew we would probably save her. She wanted to talk.

She had heard the supervisor saying, "Call the priest," and a nurse answering, "She won't last until you come back on duty tonight." She had heard the wings of great birds beating above her, higher and higher, and had come back to hear the nurse say cheerily, "Well, dear, I thought by now you'd be pushing up daisies!"

She could not remember the delivery, but she remembered her terror of the high forceps, and of anesthesia. She remembered one thing more; during the nervous last days of waiting for labor pains to begin, her husband had become very jittery, and she had insisted that he go off for a day in the country.

"He needed to go," she said, justifying her urging and his going—but she had wanted him to stay. "How could I know he loved me?"

She had gone into labor not sure she was loved, not sure

she was ready for the tremendous responsibility of motherhood that was now imminent. Fear added its deadly measure to the balance. Her pains, which had begun normally, stopped, and the rest followed almost inevitably, the death wish growing steadily more irresistible as the body succumbed to one dangerous development after another and the will to live grew weaker with the body's weakness. Or the body grew weaker with the fading will to live.

Something of this girl's history may explain the extreme measure she was driven to, because she was not sure of being loved and because she was in fear. She was still a child, barely twenty. She had never known the security of love. She had been brought up by nurses and governesses, had been sent to a convent for her schooling, and had seen her mother once a month.

Her marriage brought with it the first home she had ever known, and the first relationship of love with another human being. How permanent, how dependable that love might be, she could not be sure. In her immaturity, and without knowing that she was testing that love, she had urged her husband to go away for a day. The fact that he had innocently taken her at her word and left her, though only for a day, was enough to shake her confidence in his love.

This she admitted with great difficulty, and in far fewer words than I have put down here. But even if she had not been so young, even if she had not had such a loveless childhood, she might have swum out into dangerous waters in that delivery, because of fear.

Once she had talked a little about her encounter with the death wish, this young mother gained strength. She had two more embolisms, and was not out of danger for some days, but she recovered. Her unconscious wish to destroy herself had not had time to damage her youthful resistance. She swam out almost too far, almost into the deep waters, but we were able, with her own young strength and the help of modern medicine, to bring her back.

After the Storm

And after we bring them back, what then? If you jump into
the water to save a drowning child, do you leave him shiver-
ing alone on the shore? No, you see that he gets safely home.

In order to develop its present scientific weapons against
illness, medicine had to free itself from such imponderables
as the patient's personality, and the doctor's personality, from
the inexact, elastic approach to healing as an art. But surely it
is time to remember once more that the patient is a human
being, and that after we have cured the illness, the human being still remains. It is still our responsibility to see that he gets
safely home after his dangerous bout with the destructive drive.

It is not enough to cure the ulcer or the asthma, not enough
to save the patient from death by pneumonia or a heart attack. If the inner drive which has led to illness is not understood, it will break out again in the same or in another, possibly more perilous form. Physician and patient must together
attack the inner force which has driven the sufferer toward
disaster once and may conceivably do so again. Only then
can we grasp the full possibilities of therapy, a word which
means "to care for, to nurse, to serve."

────────────── SUMMING UP──────────────

*Dangerous passages in life, perhaps even a brush with
death, cannot always be avoided.*

❋   ❋   ❋

Living fully means taking emergencies into account.

❋   ❋   ❋

*Crisis demands action; it is not a time to ask, "How did
I get here?" but a time to struggle and fight one's way out.*

❋   ❋   ❋

Once safe ashore, those who wish to live can learn to recognize the dark forces that drew them into dangerous waters.

✿   ✿   ✿

To fight one's way back from such a brush with death leaves the thoughtful a trifle wiser, and may reveal to them a strength they never knew they had until they called upon it.

14

A Regimen for Stress

The will to live can be strengthened, nourished, cultivated—and this we can do consciously.

IN THE foregoing chapters we have talked of what makes illness. We have shown how necessary is the alliance of doctor and patient, and how it can cope with illness.

For most of us, illness for which we need a doctor is not an everyday occurrence and when it comes it may be a crisis in our lives. The artist Heinrich Zille once said that people devote the first half of their lives to making money, so they can spend it in the second half of their lives getting back their health. The gibe has the sharp but partial truth of most gibes. It would be more accurate to say that we spend a good part of our lives trying to work things out for ourselves, alternating between successes and defeats, between greater and less happiness, between better and poorer health.

It is to the many people who are not sick, and who want to be able to go through the stresses of life without becoming sick, that this chapter is addressed. It is also addressed to those who have illness in the family, and who would like to guard themselves from breaking down under the stress which illness brings to all those whose lives it touches.

Most of us try to meet our responsibilities, but rarely do we achieve the best of which we are capable. In some way, conscious or unconscious, we acknowledge this. We may strive toward a goal or we may be content just to "get by." Whichever way we choose, we are generally traveling blind. We function, but often at too great a price, because we lack understanding.

Even while we are well we pay a price for ignorance; we work hard for things that may not be so important as they seem at the time, and we forget when and how to let go.

We permit pride, guilt, vanity, jealousy to devour vast—often our best—energies. Not even aware of their destructive presence, we enjoy less happiness than we might. And because we are not conscious of the source of our wants, we pursue illusory goals with the uncontrolled compulsiveness of children.

Thus we exhaust ourselves needlessly. And there is always the threat that one day the struggle may become too much for us, and we will be sick. Since none can escape times of stress, this possibility is always present.

How then can we manage better? How shall we live to achieve the best in us, and to safeguard ourselves against stress?

The answer is that we must learn to cultivate the will to live.

The will to live is so powerful a force that we may think it can very well take care of itself. Yet we have noted throughout this book—and we can see in our own lives and those around us—how we ourselves lay hidden traps for this valuable life force. We have seen that in everyone's life there are periods of danger, situations of danger, and directions which lead to danger.

The will to live can be weakened; it can be destroyed. Otherwise we would not have the spectacle of people falling ill and dying before their time, or of living at half capacity, or of killing themselves outright.

The will to live is not a will, in the sense of that conscious or "free will" by which we like to distinguish man from the animal kingdom. It is a biological and psychological force. It is the product of many factors. Like an iceberg which is seven-eighths under water, the greater part of the will to live is sub-merged below the surface of our consciousness. We can uncon-sciously weaken and destroy it.

But though the will to live is mostly unconscious, it can be strengthened, nourished, cultivated—and this we can do con-sciously.

Each of us is the sum of what he was born with and every-thing that has happened to him up to this moment. He is the product of his inheritance, environment, cultural background, the personality of his parents, school influences, religious in-fluences, the customs and morals of the society in which he lives. On the other hand some psychologists are telling us today that we can throw all these big words out of the window—if our mother loved us.

Most of what has made us what we are, including our mother's love or the lack of it, was beyond our control. We re-alize this, not to weep over it, but also not to let it pursue us throughout our life. We cannot rewrite the past. But we can modify the present. And we can reshape the future.

We can do this in two ways. First we must know how to sup-port the will to live in times of stress, so that we may come through the inevitable crises in life with the least damage, and with the most momentum for proceeding on our route. Second is the long-range program, the cultivation of the will to live in all possible ways in order to make our lives as rich and happy as they can be made.

Recognizing Stress

How do we know that we are laboring under stress? All too often we are not even aware of it.

When we feel well we hardly know that we possess a stom-ach, a heart, a pulse beat; but under stress we are likely to be-come disagreeably conscious of some part of our body: the stomach feels distended or the heart pounds, or a muscle twitches that we never knew we had.

We are easily irritated: the bus goes too slow or too fast; people seem rude and inconsiderate. We become sensitive to things that do not ordinarily bother us: the children's noise, the smell of someone's cigar or a car's exhaust. One catches himself smoking above his normal quota, gaining weight or losing it, or losing his taste for ordinary enjoyments and people he used to like.

Signs like these come and go in all our lives. When they persist, they are signs that we are under stress.

What is stress and what does it do? The word seems self-explanatory, but biological scientists are now using it with a specific meaning. It is the effect on the body of disturbance, either external or internal or both.

A conflict with a business partner or a marriage partner, sexual dissatisfaction, illness or injury to somebody close to us, the threat of unemployment or the reality of it, a death in the family, a disaster that threatens or befalls a child, all these and many more produce stress.

Stress may be produced by our inner reaction to an external situation. We fear a challenge or an obstacle, or doubt our ability to meet it. Or we cannot make up our minds on the best way to meet it. Or we suffer a setback in dealing with it and cannot accept the defeat. As we have seen in earlier chapters, stress may also be produced entirely within ourselves, as a result not of any specific external situation, but by our own anxieties, resentments, and conflicts.

If the stress is temporary—if we can fight the battle or run away from it—then the body relaxes and no harm is done. This is what the body is built for.

But prolonged stress, either external or internal, gives the body no chance to regenerate, refuel, regroup its forces— what we mean when we say "relax." In prolonged stress the body is maintained in a constant state of mobilization. Reserves of energy are constantly being poured out, tensions are merci-

lessly sustained, and organs like the heart and those involved
in complex chemical processes are driven to their utmost capacity without pause.

In prolonged stress we are racing a high-powered motor at
top speed—but with one foot on the gas and the other on the
brake. We are burning up fuel. We are wearing out parts. But
we are not going anywhere. This is the destructive effect of prolonged stress.

We might say, let's avoid stress. We can certainly say, avoid
unnecessary stress. But it takes the wisdom of experience and
also some courage, to decide in advance what stress is unnecessary. We can learn to distinguish. But not all stress can or
should be avoided. We cannot live under glass. To avoid stress
altogether means to avoid living, because stress is an inescapable part of living. So we must find a way of meeting stress.

Emergency Measures

Stress mainly does two things: it sustains tension, and it
spends energy. We must therefore answer it with two kinds of
measures. We must find ways to release and to break tension.
We must learn how to conserve and replenish energy.

If you have ever been very angry you know how much
you have longed to tell someone off. But suppose the someone
is your boss? Or your wife or husband whom you love and do
not want to hurt? A device that has helped many is to sit down
and write a letter, furious, seething, uninhibited—and never
send it! Just to write the letter releases their tensions. Calm
judgment returns, and usually they can go on to deal sensibly
with the situation.

Sometimes the state of affairs is more complicated than a
letter can cover. Write the story of it; let all the stirred-up
emotions pour out on the paper. No matter whether it turns out
to be a short story, a drama, a case history, or simply a record
to look back on. Once you turn from chaotic feelings to organ-
ized thinking in words, sentences, order of events, you have
made the transition from a destructive to a creative process.

Intuitively we seek ways of breaking tension. You call up a favorite relative or have lunch with a trusted friend. You pay a call in a serene home where for an hour or so you draw reassurance from another family's tranquil flow of life. Some flee to the movies; others take a hot bath. Some people take a walk and some take a nap. Some actresses and ballet dancers lie down with the feet higher than the head. People who can keep going for long stretches at a time generally have a talent for the short nap, in a train or plane or car. Napoleon is said to have napped sitting on his horse.

Breaking tension is an art at which many men who bear weighty responsibility learn to become most skillful. During the terrible tensions of the war Churchill would undress completely and go to bed for ten minutes, if ten minutes was all the time he had. Roosevelt joked with his circle of experts, or withdrew for a quiet time with his stamp collection.

These men were coping with the most desperate problems on a world scale. They were daily called upon to make decisions on which the fate of nations and of continents might hang. But their problems were external. The art which they mastered was the art of putting aside the problem for a few minutes, to take a deep breath, to stretch the muscles, and then to return refreshed to the task in hand.

This is not to say that the leaders of nations do not suffer illness under stress. Quite otherwise. General Marshall described some of his difficulties while he was Secretary of State.

"Ulcers have had a strange effect upon the history of our times," General Marshall said. "In Washington I had to contend with, among other things, the ulcers of Bedell Smith in Moscow and the ulcers of Bob Lovett and Dean Acheson in Washington."

The general himself underwent a serious operation. President Eisenhower, Secretaries Hull, Stettinius, Byrnes, Sumner Welles, and a long line of American statesmen and military leaders past and present have been on the serious sick list during the stressful times of their public service.

Nor are the European leaders immune. Attlee's ulcer and eczema, Bevin's tired heart which finally gave out, significantly, after he had retired on his seventieth birthday; the French statesmen Queuille and Schuman with their stomach ailments; the Italian de Gasperi's arthritis and siege of gastric trouble; Vishinsky's ulcer, Molotov's insomnia, and Gromyko's visible aging all testify that the human body's reaction to stress is no respecter of national or idealogical differences.

At the French government's banquet to the Paris conferees in the fall of 1948, the Big Four delegates scarcely touched their plates. One was off coffee; another couldn't smoke; pills took the place of cocktails; and always there was the chorus, "nothing fried."

Because our problems are on a less heroic scale, limited to one person, one family, one business or professional crisis, this does not make them less important to each of us, nor does it lessen the stress which they impose on us. We struggle as hard with our problems as leaders of nations do with theirs. The winning of a first case may be as important to a young lawyer as the winning of a war to a president or a prime minister. And perhaps the young lawyer suffers more in his struggle. His is a lonely struggle while a leader of peoples has his advisers, and he is carried by the trust and faith of millions. A private individual must carry his burden almost alone. Sometimes those closest to him do not help but only increase his difficulty.

We add our inner conflicts to our external problems. The more personal the problem, the less perspective we are able to bring to it. This is why most of the ways of breaking tension which the average person chooses are not good ones. Most of them are not so much relaxation as *evasion*.

A man may run to a bar, or the races, or sit up all night in a card game. A woman may go shopping, or redecorate her bedroom, or flee to an afternoon visit. There is nothing wrong with these occupations, or any occupations which may suit a particular individual's taste. The question is, do they refresh the body and mind? Can the man who sat up at an all-night poker game, or the woman who returns from an exhausting shopping expedition, truthfully claim that he or she returns to the stressful situation refreshed and better able to deal with it? Haven't such devices served as an escape from facing the problem, rather than a genuine breaking of tension in order to cope with it?

This does not mean that we must grimly stare the problem in the face every waking minute. There are times when it is better to put the problem aside and engage in some other activity. But it must be an activity which truly refreshes, not one—like shopping or gambling—which is accompanied by more tension.

Sexual activity serves many people as a means of relieving tension, except in those situations where, perhaps because of guilt or underlying hostility, the sexual relationship is in itself stress-producing.

We may put our problems out of mind for a romp with our young child or a game of ball with an older one. We may undertake a pleasant gardening task or household chore. Many a housewife relieves her tensions by cleaning out closets, or attacking a task that has hung over her for a long time and getting it done at last.

We may go out to bask in the sun for a while, or take a solitary walk. If it is inadvisable to go outdoors, even looking out of the window may remind you of the world beyond the four walls which hem you in with your difficulty, and thus help you to gain a little perspective.

Lunch hour can be a real break in the day's tensions, but not the way many people take their lunch. I heard one of my patients say, "I run down to a counter and grab a sandwich, and when I run back I don't feel so well." The pattern is so familiar that even the words scarcely differ from patient to patient.

I told this patient, who was taking his lunch on the run, to run straight on to a gymnasium near his office and spend an hour there. He was horrified. He asked, "How can I take the time for that?"

When we are under stress, that is just when we must take

time for exercise, for games, for hobbies that release our tensions and refresh us with healthy enjoyment.

One man who complained of indigestion after lunch protested that he did take a walk before he went back to his desk, but his troubles walked right with him. The man was habitually stooped as though he carried the world on his shoulders, and his troubled face was bent always toward the ground.

"You take a walk," I told him, "and report to me how many pigeons you see flying along Fifth Avenue."

He looked blank at first, and then he saw the point. "I'll try it," he agreed.

I did not see him again for six years, and then he came in with a minor ailment. "I'm still counting pigeons," he reported with a smile.

A woman may walk two miles from store to store and counter to counter, but this is no relaxer of tensions. A walk should be undertaken for exercise and relaxation, not simply to get somewhere.

A "change of wallpaper" is the prescription an old-fashioned doctor used to give his patients. A trip or a visit away from the physical setting of your problem does not solve the problem, but it may give perspective, time to think, time to consider.

These are ways of breaking tension. They are also ways of conserving energy during a period when energy is being used up at a rapid rate under stress. Any devices which suit your situation and your inclination are good, provided they fill these two requirements: they must break the tension of stress, and they must conserve the energy which is being used up under stress. Any device is good to include in your stress regime if it does either, and better still if it does both.

To ignore these needs of body and mind for refreshment under stress is to be a traitor to your will to live. If under stress you go without sleep, eat carelessly or irregularly, ignore the symptoms of strain and fatigue, then you are courting disaster. You are aiding and abetting the self-destructive forces.

To let yourself get run down because you are under stress is no excuse. What you are indulging in is a self-destructive act.

This is the most baffling facet of self-destruction. As you seek relief from its oppression, it creates new harmful appetites— another drink, another cigarette, another box of chocolates, another sleeping pill. The curse of evil is that it creates more evil.

But once you know that the drink or the cigarette or the sleeping pill is not a solution, but only a temporary crutch, then you can safeguard yourself. Once you glimpse what is going on inside you, you can take steps to answer these appetites in sensible ways. This is what is meant by supporting and strengthening the will to live under stress.

What Stress Does to Digestion

We know from laboratory experiment a good deal about what happens in the digestive organs under stress. We can thus work out ways of eating which will replenish the energy being squandered in the stressful situation, and at the same time put the least extra strain on organs already being strained to function under difficult conditions.

Some people stop eating altogether under stress. Others eat too much. Still others choose the wrong things to eat. All three are destructive reactions, and all can lead to trouble.

The self-starver is likely to suffer from depletion, since he is spending energy and not replenishing it. Fatigue, irritability, and loss of efficiency are obvious prices which he must pay almost at once, and serious illness may result. Certainly, not to eat is a self-destructive act.

The nervous appetite of which many of us are conscious under stress is a more logical expression of the body's need, since there is a demand for more and more fuel when so much of it is being used up. We must eat. But how shall we eat?

Stress makes heavy demands on our metabolism. We are asked to keep a war machine constantly supplied. Our fuel storage depots in the liver and other parts of the body are being emptied into the blood stream to feed the heart, muscles and brain. At the same time our digestive organs are likely to

be either inhibited or over-stimulated. We must make it easy
for them to deliver what is required. We must give them food
which they can digest under these difficult conditions.

For example, a group of laboratory dogs were shown a cat.
Immediately the constant flow of bile from the liver through
the biliary duct into the gall bladder either slowed or stopped
entirely for twenty minutes. Then the dripping of bile began
again, slowly, and in one and one-half hours the normal flow
was restored. Of all the dogs observed during several experiments, only one dog remained unperturbed by the cat, as revealed in the uninterrupted flow of bile.

One individual, like one laboratory animal, may retain the
privilege of reacting differently. But for most of us the average
reaction is the one which we may expect. Bile is ejected from
the gall bladder into the upper part of the small intestines in
the digestion of fats. Without bile, fats cannot be digested. If,
under stress, bile is in short supply, then the logical conclusion is that under stress we should not eat fatty foods.

The fact that we do eat fatty foods and that we should not
is given ample and uncomfortable testimony by the millions
of sufferers from gall bladder disturbances throughout the
country. Twenty per cent of all male patients and twenty-five
per cent of all female patients in the United States have gall
bladder disorders, and this does not include the many who do
not go to the doctor.

The disturbance of the biliary tract is only one aspect of
what happens in the digestive system under stress. The entire
system is similarly disturbed. The factory is working short
handed, with diminished power, with machinery at half efficiency or less.

The man or woman who gets acid indigestion under stress, or
who reacts with diarrhea or constipation, is now understood
to be showing an unconscious need for protection and ap-
preciation. We have seen how in the infant the need for love
becomes associated with food. This association persists in the
unconscious. When in a stressful situation we long for someone to protect us from our difficulty, or to solve for us a prob-

lem which we feel unable to solve for ourselves, this longing is expressed by a stimulation of the digestive organs as though we were about to receive food.

Thus we have the oversecretion of digestive juices in the stomach under stress, causing indigestion and setting up conditions for possible peptic ulcer. We have the overactivity of the intestines causing diarrhea, or the reverse, a rigid spasm causing constipation, or an alternation between the two.

A Diet for Stress

The stress diet must therefore be designed to counteract the overactivity of the digestive system, and to avoid causing further stimulation. This is what we mean by the familiar "bland diet" with which almost any stomach sufferer who has ever been to a doctor is acquainted.

We choose protective and nonstimulating foods according to three principles; chemical, mechanical, and thermal. Chemically, the foods must tend to the alkaline side so as to counteract the hyperacidity, and they must not be rich, heavy, or spicy dishes which stimulate the stomach to still more work. Mechanically the foods must have a minimum of roughage, to avoid further irritation and further stimulation. Finally they must not be excessively hot or excessively cold.

Meat protein is one of the complex foods which demand extra digestive effort, and so are fats, not only meat fats but cream and butter as well. (Small amounts of uncooked butter are well tolerated.) Spices, as any cook knows, are used with the specific purpose of stimulating the digestive juices. Sugar in large quantities, especially cooked sugar, can cause fermentation. A large amount of food at one time puts an extra strain on the already overstrained digestive organs.

Besides this, the stomach which is secreting gastric juices at an excessive rate needs to have those juices used at frequent intervals. The sheer accumulation of them causes distress.

Under stress, therefore, we should eat little, but often. Instead of three substantial meals, we should divide the day's requirements into five or six small meals. An individual whose stomach reacts to stress with oversecretion of the gastric juices should eat something every two hours; a few crackers of zwieback, a small glass of milk, a piece of fruit if the accompanying irritation is not severe—and it is better to peel the apple or pear. Citrus fruits are effective in neutralizing acid.

People who cannot leave their work every two hours to eat might try keeping a jar of honey in the desk. A spoonful of this simple natural sugar is soothing to the overactive stomach, and to some of us its quick energy is as stimulating as a shot of whiskey is to others.

Where diarrhea is the tendency, the same regimen of frequent light meals is good, with particular avoidance of roughage, sugar, milk, and fatty foods. Scraped raw apple, which we give to infants, is a specific for diarrhea. Apples have a high content of pectin, the natural jelly-forming substance in fruit. If you haven't time to fuss with a knife, gnaw on the apple; your teeth are a good scraper.

For constipation, the remedies are legion, but prevention is better. The continued use of cathartics actually encourages the continuation of constipation. A patient of mine embarked on a trip to Europe and after the ship had left the dock discovered to his dismay that he had forgotten the little pills without which, as he thought, he could not survive. After a few days on shipboard he forgot he had ever needed them, and he never used a cathartic again.

Part of the reason for his liberation was, of course, the relaxed atmosphere of an ocean voyage. He was free of the situations which caused his tensions. We can achieve the same liberation, even under stress. Precaution can be as good as a pill. When the tensions mount, take a breather. Get a drink of water. Go out for a walk even if you have to invent a small errand.

The important thing is not to let tension pile up. A tense day may bring a tense night. You know this, but under stress you tend to forget it; perhaps this forgetfulness is another instance of the ever-ready self-destructive force. Lean back at your desk and consider whether the problem which is making you tense is really worth all the discomfort you are likely to suffer later. If you will remember the connection between this moment's stress and tonight's or tomorrow's physical distress, you will find ways to break the tension before it gets hold of you.

People who overeat and gain weight under stress often torture themselves by going on starvation diets. It is not enough to curb the appetite by an effort of will. One must also be considerate of the emotional tension which causes the appetite, and work out an acceptable diet that does not put on weight.

A low-calorie diet is meant to yield less energy so that the body fat will be used to fill out the needed supply. Such a diet is therefore low in fat and carbohydrate and high in protein. To fill the stomach comfortably such a diet also contains salads and leafy vegetables, and fruits with low sugar content.

Quick Energy

The patient suffering from high blood pressure is put on a rice diet. We can explain this now: continually geared for a battle which is continually postponed, he is in constant need of quick energy. Rice is an ideal quick-energy food, high in easily digested carbohydrate, low in protein, and without fat. When his body is quickly supplied with the energy it needs, that part of his tension which results from the depletion of his energy supply is relieved. He is calmed; his blood pressure subsides.

Nietzsche remarked that rice makes for Buddhism, and beer —another source of quick energy—for German metaphysics. Certainly the peoples who live on rice are less combative and more meditative than the meat-and-fat eaters.

Alcohol is an even quicker energy source than rice. When after a tussle with unpleasantness a man says, "I need a drink," he is obeying a specific demand of his body at that moment. He can use a drink. Alcohol is a stimulant with quick food value besides. To take a drink for relaxation is healthy. But a dependence on alcohol to dull the senses and evade the problems of living is obviously self-destructive.

The elements of the stress diet now emerge: simple starch or sugar, no fat, a low amount of protein. The protein should not be eggs, which have a high fat and cholesterol content, nor meat. Milk and milk products such as the fresh cheeses, and vegetable proteins, are the proteins the body can handle best under stress. And no rich desserts, no creams, custards, or pastries which are full of fat. Coffee has a certain amount of fatty acids; tea is comforting and less irritating.

What's wrong with a good steak, you would like to know. Nothing at all, if you pick the right time to eat it. After a real battle or a siege of hard work, you can take on a steak—because the stress is over. The jungle animal first fights, and then eats. It is safe to assume that the tiger does not suffer indigestion on his regime. But no animal eats under stress, except man.

Still, you can have that steak even under stress, if you take your time about it, both before and after. It is mere common sense that you don't come straight from the tense business conference and sit down to your steak. You take something first, a cup of hot broth or a glass of juice and a cracker—for some, a drink—and wait half an hour or longer. Then you can enjoy your dinner.

And give yourself an hour or so afterward to digest it. Take a tip from the tiger, who goes to sleep after dinner.

Eating a good meal is like building a fire in the fireplace: first you must have the energy to build the fire. The digestive organs are the first to be robbed of energy by the alarm reaction of stress. You must give them something to work on before you can ask them to digest a heavy meal. Hostesses invented snacks and canapés to meet this need.

We are sometimes so disturbed, or so tired, that we cannot eat. To force yourself to eat because you know you need energy is not necessary. You do not have to be a slave to the clock and eat a heavy meal because it is mealtime. No one ever died from missing dinner! Those who cannot bear the thought of going to bed with an empty stomach can comfort themselves with a glass of milk or some hot chocolate. For situations of severe stress I have recommended strained, lightly salted oatmeal gruel such as we give to infants. A cup or two washes down old mucus and bile in the digestive system, and gives quick energy at the same time. Half an hour or an hour later you are hungry and can eat.

If you think that all the tempting things are left out of our stress diet, here is a surprise for you. A perfect stress diet is: caviar and champagne. Caviar is very compact in food value, and champagne, besides its quickly useful alcohol content, is also a stimulant for the circulation.

One of my professors, a very elegant gentleman, advised us that for patients with certain circulatory disorders we should prescribe caviar. "It will make a hit with them—and so will you." So order up the caviar and champagne—unless another stressful situation will arrive with the bill. In that case, you better have oatmeal gruel.

How to Get a Good Night's Sleep

A problem looks much less formidable in the light of morning than at night, as we all know. It dwindles still more if the night has been restful.

But when we are under stress, a good night's sleep seems the most elusive of luxuries. The more troubled we are, the more cunningly sleep escapes us. Yet there are ways to invite sleep, both common-sense ways and scientific ones.

Sleep is good even if it is occasionally induced by a drink, a tranquilizer, or a sleep-inducing pill. We have liquor, we have pills, and they are for use in an emergency. Sleeping pills are habit-forming. Especially when we are under stress, we must guard against becoming dependent on them. Such dependence is, of course, an overt evidence of a dangerous self-destructive trend. But to take a sleeping pill for one night's needed sleep, or in order to break a pattern of insomnia, comes under the heading of protection of the body under stress, and is an aid to the will to live.

Our grandmothers, and their grandmothers before them, had many homely devices for inducing a good night's sleep, and some of them are sound. They were on the right track when in chilly weather they tucked the would-be sleeper into a warm bed with bed socks or a hot-water bottle for his feet.

Quiet, a comfortable room temperature, absence of light, and security from disturbance are the combination which invites sleep. Of course some of us prefer other combinations. The mother of a patient of mine always asked the hotel clerk which was his noisiest room. "Oh, but madame, I won't give you that room," he would protest, and her answer was, "But that's just the room I want!"

The amount of sleep we need varies enormously with the individual. Some of us get along well on five or six hours, others need eight or nine, and some feel worse the more sleep they get. It is the height of unwisdom to argue with anyone who insists that he has not slept a wink. A woman (or a man) says, "I tossed all night," and her husband (or his wife) retorts, "You were snoring all night!" and then the battle is on. Rest is a subjective matter. It makes no difference how many hours we sleep. What is important is the quality of sleep and whether we wake refreshed.

Chronic Insomnia

There is a distinction between acute and chronic insomnia. Acute insomnia—a night or a few nights without sleep—is a common experience. Its cause may be a specific problem, or nothing more than a strange bed, different noises, or no noise at all, such as a city dweller's first night in the country. Chronic insomnia has its cause in anxiety, and this requires looking into. The sufferer from chronic insomnia also needs careful preparation for sleep.

A bear shuts himself in the depths of a quiet, dark cave to hibernate. The anxious seeker after sleep should go to bed with the same cozy confidence that he will not be disturbed. If he does not have to get up at a certain time, he should make sure beforehand that no one is going to awaken him. But if he is obliged to be up, someone else—or an alarm clock—should take over the responsibility of getting him up on time so that he can dismiss that worry from his sleep.

Sometimes the alarm clock itself becomes a source of worry. The sleeper wakes in anxiety that it will not go off on time, or that is has not been set, or, contrarily, he dreads the shattering sound which will wake him. In such a case another member of the family should, if possible, take over both the alarm clock and the waking-up job.

Sleeplessness is commonly intensified by anxiety about losing sleep. This is often instilled in us in childhood. A mother, trying to get a child to bed on time, urges, "You'd better go to bed or you'll be tired tomorrow." It is a fact that lack of sleep is not fatal. We would wake up fresh enough after a night of little sleep, if we were not convinced that we ought to feel tired.

One who has been fitful and tense during the day is likely to be the same at night. This is why it is important to "let go" during the day. It is a mistake to go to bed tense. Prepare for sleep by relaxing first.

To eat or drink before going to bed is a common-sense counsel. We observe that in nature animals sleep after eating; it follows pragmatically that a person suffering from insomnia might do well to eat a snack before sleeping. Physiologically, when the digestive system is engaged, the rest of the body tends to be dormant. The parasympathetic mechanism is in control. Brain and muscles, heart and circulatory activity are quieted by a diminished blood supply and a minimum of glandular stimulation.

This is why we get drowsy after a heavy meal. But this does not mean that to eat a heavy meal will bring on restful sleep. Quite the opposite; when the body is under stress, eating the wrong food or too much food is like taking a bomb to bed with you. All your careful plans for rest will fly up in splinters.

Yet against all good sense, men who have been wrestling with problems in a late evening conference will adjourn to a restaurant and put away heavy meat sandwiches or egg and meat dishes, and then top this off with rich pastry and a second cup of coffee with cream.

Those for whom the conference was successful may be able to sleep on such a midnight meal. But if the evening's problems were unsolved, or if some of the conferees suffered personal defeat or disappointment, there are miserable nights ahead for some of the group at the table.

The bedtime snack must follow the rules for a stress diet. It should be light, easily digested, carbohydrate, with low protein content, little meat, and no fat. If it is warm rather than cold it helps the warming of the body which encourages sleep. A milk or chocolate drink is generally a safe sleep-encourager.

Much of what we are suggesting here may sound naïve and obvious. Yet these are the little snags on which people get caught. Whether your favorite relaxation is reading or soft music, a drink or a cup of milk or a dish of breakfast cereal, the important thing to remember is that the accumulation of tension is the cause of your sleeplessness.

A colleague of mine found that reading a book on botany was better for him than any sleeping pill. During college he always fell asleep over his botany text book, and it has never failed him since. No real lesson is learned in a day, and no method of inviting sleep should be discarded after one unsuccessful try. You must practice your lesson in relaxation.

A Walk Before Bed

A suggestion which often shocks the weary seeker after sleep is that he should take a vigorous walk, a really long one of a couple of miles, before he goes to bed. Exhausted as he is, how can he go out and tramp through the dark? Surely he will drop in his tracks.

We have heard and talked a good deal about the power of mind over body. Such a walk will reveal to him the power of body over mind. But he must perform the experiment correctly. He can not let his depressed spirits do his walking for him, with reluctant lagging stride. He must step out strongly with a long and rhythmic pace, body swinging, head and chest up, lungs filling with deep breaths. It is obvious that he must be dressed properly for a good walk, with appropriate clothes, comfortable shoes (this for the ladies especially), and no encumbrances.

Such a walk has more than one useful purpose. First of all it draws blood away from the brain into the muscles, thus quieting the spinning mind. The movement and the full regular breathing stir the circulation which has become sluggish in the limbs, and the body is warmed and nourished throughout. Nervous tensions are gradually relaxed with the rhythmic muscular movement and the relaxation of mental activity. Soldiers have been known to fall asleep on the march, while continuing to trudge along.

As the body begins to enjoy greater comfort, so does the mind, since the two are one. The inner climate changes. Even the very problem which has been whirling unresolved may emerge with greater clarity as the smoke of inner battle clears. The sleeping pill simply puts the problem away until morning. But the long walk may bring the problem closer to solution, if only because it has been seen more clearly, or been placed in better perspective by a sky full of stars.

Back home, after a hot bath and a drink of something warming, you climb into bed in a quiet and well-ventilated room. Your body is tired, but your mind is quiet. You have left the problem outside your door, like a pair of shoes to be shined and picked up again in the morning. You have every reason to count on a good night's sleep.

------------------ **SUMMING UP** ------------------

Stress is a part of living and it is necessary to deal with it.

*   *   *

Measures to meet stress aim to release and break tension, and to conserve and replenish energy.

* * *

*Since stress affects every aspect of daily living, food,
social activities, recreation, sleep, all have to be adjusted
to the needs of the stressful period.*

* * *

*A regime for stress is different for each individual and
each situation, but the goals are the same: to reduce tension and keep up energy.*

* * *

*To allow oneself to become run-down under stress is self-
destructive.*

15

Amateurs in the Art of Living

The fault is often not the book's but the reader's.

$\mathbb{T}$HE BOOKSHOP counters are laden with books that tell us how we can live longer, eat better, be happier, richer, and more beautiful, and find inner peace. Many of these books appear for months at a time on the best-seller lists. According to their sales figures, we ought all to be young, beautiful, healthy, happy, long-lived and rich.

That we all yearn for these good things is no surprise, nor is it surprising that many of us wishfully believe we can buy long life, inner peace, etc., for $3.95, more or less.

Generally these books offer very good advice. Time and again someone will say to you that he has just finished reading such and such a book and "it made sense." Yet you will observe no perceptible difference in his life, and a week or a month or a year, later he can scarcely tell you what the book said that made such good sense.

The fault is often not the book's but the reader's. We buy books as we take pills, or trips, or go to the doctor or psychoanalyst, looking for an easy answer to our problems. We seek endlessly for some magic which will banish trouble and make life fall into a more comfortable pattern, like the woman who asked me once, "Can't you give me a hormone which will sweeten my disposition?"

The doctor, like the book, gives us very good advice. He says, "Relax," and surely that makes sense.

The hitch is that making sense is not enough. We must go deeper than the make-sense level. The reassurance which you can get from a book, even this book, is momentary. You feel for the moment that someone understands, that you are not alone in the world with troubles like yours, and that there are ways out. But when you close the book the reassurance fades in the light of reality. Your problems still haunt you—until you realize that you are not imprisoned. There is a door through which you can walk out to freedom. But this step needs to be prepared for and adjusted to.

A long-range program is exactly what the words mean: a slow, patient, brick-by-brick building of a new and sounder structure for living. Life is not made up only of great decisions and noble moments. Small acts and choices day by day prepare us to meet a challenge when it comes.

A New Year's resolution which is too hard to keep is simply not kept. All we get out of such brave beginnings on too large a scale is one more defeat, to add to those under which we already smart. If we are modest in the demands we make on ourselves, but persistent, we have a better chance of making progress. It may be slow but it is progress. You won't move the mountain, but you may climb over it, if you set your goal within reach.

A long-range program has two phases. There is the distant eventual goal, the specific form which your idea of a better way to live may take for you, whether you call it inner peace, better health, a better relationship to your work, to your family. All are related, but one aspect may appear more vital to you than another. You want to know what you are aiming for.

The other phase is the daily lesson. A pianist practices every day. A singer vocalizes every day. A boxer, a runner, a baseball player trains every day. When a doctor is away from his practice for a month he returns to find his familiar routine strange.

If you think through your day you will discover that a great part of it is daily habit. To add one more habit to your routine of tooth brushing and bathing is not too large an order. The new habit, of taking daily account, can become as much a part of your day as any other. Many people find that keeping a diary is a help. A diary shows the direction in which you are moving, like the curve on a graph.

Postponing your stocktaking from day to day is another habit, the lost-day habit, which can become as hard to break as any other habit, healthy or unhealthy.

This daily lesson is your step-by-step examination of yourself. You are your own stock; your assets and liabilities are all within yourself. In the business of living, no man can get by forever without re-evaluating himself.

The search for a better way to live begins with self-searching. Man has been granted this unique gift; he can stop and think things over. He can re-evaluate a situation in the light of new knowledge and new experience. He denies himself a precious human prerogative if he fails to make use of it.

Most people now and then spend some thought on trying to find a connection between events and their reactions to them. Doing this occasionally is like playing a musical instrument occasionally.

The man or woman who takes stock *occasionally* remains an amateur in the art of living.

Self-Appraisal

Whether you come up with the right answer in your stocktaking depends on how deep you dig for it.

A young business man said to me, "I ate shrimps for lunch and they didn't agree with me." What he left out was that whatever he eats at lunch with his boss disagrees with him. Should he therefore avoid shrimps? Or his boss?

Perhaps he is sensitive to shrimps, but he will not make much progress if he stops there; his body's reaction is only the top answer. He will have to examine his attitude toward his boss, toward his work. What fears, what resentments toward his work and the symbol of authority, his boss, does he swallow along with the food he takes at the weekly luncheon?

The closer he can come to the kernel of the difficulty within himself, the better will be his relationship to his work, his boss —and his lunch. The discovery of the something beyond shrimps which is giving him his indigestion is a long step. And incidentally he may get rid of his indigestion.

What makes self-examination a hard job is that we must penetrate behind the overt behavior, the *strategy* which each of us has adopted in our dealings with the outer world. One person wears a cloak of modesty to hide his driving ambition, and another carries an aggressive chip on his shoulder, to cover up his self-doubt. One is all sweet compliance, with a heart full of rebellion, and another says "no" to everything like a child blindly striking out for an independence he knows no other way to achieve.

Some people beat their breasts with guilt for everything that happens, whether they are guilty or not. The more usual device—one with which all of us trick ourselves on occasion— is to blame everyone except ourself, like the young woman who burst into my office one day and exclaimed, "Today everyone is fighting with me—my husband, my mother, and just now my maid! What is the matter with *people?*"

If our self-examination is to be fruitful, we must get behind our own masks. The penalty for lying to the world is severe, but the price of lying to yourself is disaster. Sooner or later the lie catches up with you. However successfully you deceive the world, you never really deceive yourself. Deep within you, in some way, you acknowledge the fiction, and the deeper it is buried, the more power it has to do you harm. We can add one more truth to Abraham Lincoln's homely wisdom: you cannot fool all the people all the time, least of all yourself.

The next step after blaming everyone else for the things that happen to you is to blame the state of civilization we live in. Certainly there are aspects or our way of life which put severe pressures on the individual. Indeed the farther we travel from the primitive state, the more complex is our struggle for adjustment.

Just to complain about world affairs, the job, or the community, is a kind of excuse for doing nothing about it. The healthy way to protest is to work for improvement. A constructive effort, in a way which seems right to you and which is within your capacity, will at once remove much of the sting of frustration and powerlessness.

How big a constructive task you undertake is less important than the doing of it. To work for one's neighborhood school may bring as much satisfaction on a personal level as a university president derives from stating his principles of education to a nation. The joy is in the creative effort, whatever the scope of the work.

Still, progress is slow, and a dramatic improvement in the world within the lifetime of one individual is unlikely. This is the world you were born into, and no matter how you may work to better it you must nevertheless learn to live in it, and live in it today.

Often people who feel that the world is bad are expressing a discontent more with themselves than with the world. They have perhaps set unrealistic standards for themselves, and their complaint against the world is in the nature of an alibi for failing to achieve those standards. They are like the boy who won't play unless he can be captain.

The Stiff Upper Lip

Learning to live in the world does not mean that we must accept without question a way of life as it is handed to us. The most commonplace rules for living can be dangerous, if only because they take no account of individual differences. Slogans can act like a lid on dynamite.

Take for example the "stiff upper lip" of the English, or the

American version, "Be a good sport about it," and the scornful
"You can't take it." On the surface this is good counsel. What
cannot be cured must be endured, and one may as well put a
good face on it.

The danger lies in what is behind the stiff upper lip, and
what is under the sportsmanlike behavior. If the good sportsmanship is nothing more than a cap on top of rebellion, if the
stiff upper lip is only a stopper on resentment, then you are
setting up perfect conditions for a volcanic explosion. "I'm
ready to burst!" we exclaim, and it is a precise definition. Few
of us break out into the open rebellion of delinquency or crime.
But the toll in self-destruction is universal.

To screw the cap of good sportsmanship on tighter is no solution. What is necessary is a genuine acceptance of this failure
or this defeat, whatever it may be. A good boxer knows how to
roll with the punches. This time you lost. Why did you lose?
What can you do better next time so that you can win? Or,
you might ask, is it important or necessary to win? Being a
good sport in terms of absorbing what happens to you, and
turning it to your realistic use, is the productive, the creative,
the healthy kind of sportsmanship.

Which Basic Reaction?

We learned in earlier chapters about the two types of basic
emotional response to difficulty, the aggressive, and the dependent. In our self-examination, we will come upon now one
and now the other response in ourselves. The average human
being has a little of both, and swings back and forth between
the aggressive effort to deal with life by fight or flight, and
the regressive tendency to seek protection like a child.

Our mixed responses may make it harder to understand ourselves. But they are one more evidence of the effort of the human being to achieve and maintain balance in what seems often
like a precarious walk on the high wire. The fact that an individual swings from one response to the other is one of his
best claims to being normal. It suggests that he is making a

positive effort to cope with his problems and manage his own life. It indicates the inner restlessness of growth toward emotional maturity.

Suppose, like many men actively engaged in the competitive business world, you are a go-getter on the surface, but underneath you have longings to be taken care of, to be protected, to be dependent. So well have you covered up your dependency needs that you may never have been aware of these longings, perhaps until you read this book, and realized that your delicate digestion was a tip-off to the inner softness which you have so long denied.

Now that you begin to penetrate the aggressive outer crust of your personality, you may realize that the woman you married is a strong individual. You may observe how you have tended to attach yourself to a strong business associate, or that you turn to your lawyer for that protective relationship which you need, or to your doctor.

You may also discern within yourself a certain hostility toward these very people from whom you crave love and care. You are perhaps sharp and dominating with your wife, argumentative with your business associate, inclined to disparage the advice your lawyer gives you or complain about his fee.

What's wrong here is not that you have a need for dependence, although that is an immaturity and you must recognize it as such. What's wrong is that you deny your dependence, cover it up, suppress it, and feel guilty about it. This is why you are combative, hostile, resentful, and it is also why you have a delicate digestion.

Suppose you were to recognize the fact that you have a need for a certain amount of love, of "mothering." Suppose you could accept, for the moment, this immaturity in your personality. So you need love. Why don't you ask for it?

In your own way you are asking for it now, but the way is not a good one. Pride prevents you from asking in a mature way. You hide your need and expect those around you—your wife, for example—to guess what you want. When she disappoints your unexpressed demand you are resentful. Perhaps you provoke a quarrel, when you really want to be loved. Perhaps you try to dominate her, to prove that you are stronger than she and to earn her respect. But respect is a poor substitute for the love you seek, and in any case you are more likely earning her hostility by your tactics. If she is a strong personality she resents your effort to dominate her.

There are good ways of asking for love. One of them, and probably the best, is to give love. How much thought have you spent during the past month on your wife's happiness and contentment? How much interest do you show in her achievements? How much do you really care about her? How do you show her that you care?

When did you last take her out to enjoy a dinner she did not have to cook? A present of flowers can mean as much to a woman as a new bracelet. More, perhaps, because it is only when the relationship has reached a state of mutual hostility that she needs to be bribed or placated by a showy, expensive tribute.

(To put the shoe on the other foot for a moment, one might say without fear of contradiction that any woman worthy of the name knows a thousand small but effective ways to show love. If she declines to practice them it is probably not out of ignorance. We are told that we forget things for unconscious reasons. Perhaps forgetting small errands and comforts for a husband can be understood as a concealed gesture of hostility.)

The go-getter with great dependency needs is ashamed, or too proud, to show his wife how he feels toward her. He is so busy keeping her from finding out he needs her that he has no time to think about her side of the life they live together. What if he were to let down the bars and admit that he needs her? Not sloppily, not childishly, but as one adult to another? If at the same time he can show her that he is genuinely interested in her, that he values her for herself apart from what he can get out of her, that he tries to be considerate of her rights and privileges and *her* needs as well as his own—then he is likely to get a heartening response. Most people need to be needed!

One thing we may be sure of: from the moment we recognize and accept our human need for love, we are on the way to a mature relationship. And that ulcer may never develop after all.

He Who Fights

Let us see what the aggressive side of the personality reveals in this self-examination. Suppose you are a man or woman who does not evade responsibility. You do not turn to someone else to take care of things for you. You are trying to deal with your problems in an adult way, that is, by your own efforts.

But often you are frustrated. It is one of the conditions of living that people do not always behave as we want them to, and situations do not resolve themselves as we have planned. When you have lunch with your boss—or dinner with your in-laws—or receive an unsatisfactory telephone call or letter or come out at the wrong end of an interview, you may not get indigestion, but by the end of the day you have a splitting headache.

What is wrong? You have tried to deal with a person or a situation in an adult manner, and all you have got out of it is a headache. But not quite all. Behind the headache lie rebellion and resentment against the way things have turned out, a feeling of helplessness, a suppressed rage. The headache is what you are aware of. The other feelings are buried because they are not acceptable. It is not *right* to be angry with your family. It is not *safe* to fight with your boss. Fear has kept you from fighting back. Fear of the consequences may even have kept you from fighting for what you wanted in the most effective way, with careful preparation, with a minimum left to chance. You yourself may thus be responsible for the frustration which now irks you.

A patient of mine came in one afternoon in a state of jubilation. "I feel marvelous—I feel as though I had had a workout in the gym—I feel the way I felt when I was twenty, after a hard game of tennis," he said.

What had happened was nothing unusual in the course of business. A colleague had offered unexpected opposition to his favorite project. But this time, unlike many previous times, he had first looked into himself before confronting the colleague. He had considered the consequences of opposing the other man. He had decided that he could afford to accept the consequences. Having first looked his own anxieties in the face and found them not realistic, he was freed to fight for his project.

Two discoveries astonished him. First he discovered that once he had consulted his own fears, he was able to tap reserves of courage and energy he did not know he possessed. He went into his conference with the confidence that he could win his point. There is no doubt that the strength and conviction with which he entered the fight were important factors in his victory.

His second discovery was his feeling of *physical* well being after the fight was over. His body felt limber, young, resilient, as after healthy athletic exertion.

There is an important moral to be drawn from such an experience. We can say with positiveness that in most of the difficulties which we must face in life, it is not the external situation which trips us up, but those inner forces within ourselves *which we have not consulted*. It is because we have disregarded them that they hamper us. It is because we have ignored or suppressed them that they block our way.

Those inner voices rise up to torture us afterward. We turn a situation over and over, when it is too late. The French have a phrase: *esprit d'escalier*, the wit that comes to us on the stairs after the interview or conference is over, the answer we should have given, the way we should have acted. We have a bad night, or many bad nights, with our *esprit d'escalier*. We are annoyed with ourselves, and often with the world as well.

We say of someone, "He is his own worst enemy." The same is potentially true, to a greater or less degree, for every one of us. If we will take time to recognize those inner forces, if we will pay them the respect which is their due and confer with them before we confront the outer world, then we are in a fair way to achieve inner unity. We may in time turn to the world an integrated personality.

And He Who Runs Away

Sometimes, after consulting with ourselves, we do not come out fighting. A realistic evaluation of our position points to defeat if we fight. Flight is the wiser course.

Here is a common source of confusion. It is considered "sissy" to run away. It is considered weak and cowardly to decline the challenge of a stronger opponent. We applaud the little man who tackles the big bully, even though the little man takes a fearful beating.

It is true that the little man, for all his inadequacy of size, may be moved by such strong indignation that he wants to fight, he must fight, and even though he is beaten he is satisfied at having fought. But more often we fight because we are ashamed not to fight. We go into battle already defeated, and come out with only the small comfort that we were right in expecting defeat.

The animal in the jungle feels no obligation to be that kind of hero. Confronted with a known enemy, he acts according to whether he is likely to win or lose a battle. A stag will fight another stag for a doe, but he will probably not attack a leopard if he has a chance to flee. He is not ashamed to run from a natural enemy stronger than himself.

I was once briefly lost in the Burma jungle, and came suddenly face to face with a panther. He gathered himself to spring, but he did not spring. He waited, glaring at me, and I waited, not daring to breathe. Then he turned and glided away. I went away too, at a run, grateful that the powerful cat had more sense than to charge an enemy whose strength, fortunately for me, he overestimated.

Flight from a situation is not cowardice. We ought to get as much satisfaction from successfully escaping a situation as from successfully fighting it, because either course is healthy depending on the circumstances. The reason most of us do not

is that we have been brought up to identify fight with cowardice, and a reasonable estimation of defeat with a want of
manhood.

Let us look at the difference between flight and escape.
Flight is the act resulting from a realistic evaluation of a given
situation. We run away to avoid getting hurt. But we may pick
up this same challenge another time when we are better prepared. He who fights and runs away lives to fight another
day!

Escape also looks like running away, but it has a different
motivation. Escape is avoiding involvement with the expectation that someone else will take care of the trouble for us. This
is a negative action, an avoidance of responsibility—the behavior of an immature personality.

How shall we flee from a situation which we cannot fight?
A woman patient, after considerable self-searching, realized
that her visits to her mother-in-law's home were the occasions
for her headaches and backaches. The older woman was fighting for possession of her only son, and behind a deceptively
loving exterior she took every opportunity to undermine her
son's attachment to his wife. Our patient was the innocent victim of this struggle between mother and son, the one for possession and the other for independence.

The young wife saw that she could neither fight her mother-
in-law nor stay away without endangering her marriage. Either
course might force her husband into making a choice between
his mother and his wife.

She was not yet mature enough to remain free from a hostile
response to her mother-in-law, and from the inevitable quarrel with her husband afterward. So she avoided the impact of
the situation. She carried a sedative in her handbag; when she
felt the tension rising, she excused herself from the room and
popped a pill into her mouth. With its help she was calmer during the visit.

She became more confident of her husband's love, now that
she did not put upon it the added strain of competition with
his mother. In time she understood, even pitied her, especially

when she saw her mother-in-law suffering from chronic attacks of an irritating skin rash, evidence that the older woman too was under the stress of emotional conflict. It followed that with her growing inner strength the wife became a source of strength to her husband, and the bond between them deepened into one which the relationship with his mother could no longer threaten.

_____ SUMMING UP _____

Living is an art at which everyone begins as an amateur.

❖   ❖   ❖

The experiences of others, a brave façade, or escape into fantasy and wishful thinking are make-believe living and not living itself.

❖   ❖   ❖

Active participation in life has no substitute.

16

The Child Within the Man

The rebel who is only running away from something and never toward something is wasting himself.

WEISS and English speak of man as having four ages: chronological, physical, intellectual, and emotional. It is not unusual to encounter a man who is forty years old according to his birthday, but who may have the physical vigor of thirty, the intellectual development of fifty, and the emotional age of ten.

Our chronological age is automatically decided for us, but our three other ages are more or less subject to ourselves. We can make rational efforts to maintain the body in a state of youthful vigor. We can reach out for intellectual growth through study, reading, and the companionship of well-developed intellects.

Of the three ages beyond the chronological, the hardest to develop is the emotional. The groundwork for our emotional growth is laid down in early childhood, when we have nothing to say about it. Whether we know it or not, we are the people our childhood made us.

So it should not surprise us that, in the course of our self-examination, we may find clinging to us traces of the child we once were. Growth is by nature an uneven process. We leap suddenly ahead, and then for a time we seem to stand still or even to slip backward. Educators are aware of "plateaus of learning." A child learns in spurts, alternating with level periods in which no progress or very little is apparent.

Since growth is so uneven, and may take place on different levels of the personality at different periods, we must be prepared to find that some aspects of our growth are slower, and some may be definitely held back. Freud was the first to point out that an emotional shock in childhood may arrest an individual's emotional growth at that point. *Fixation* was his explanation of many nervous illnesses which had puzzled medicine, for which there was no apparent organic cause, such as paralysis, blindness, deafness, vomiting, tremors, compulsions and phobias. Behind them, Freud found arrested emotional development.

All of us are familiar with certain kinds of childishness in adults. Sometimes it shows through plainly. The individual who habitually reacts with screaming, desk-pounding, uncontrollable rage is the child given to temper tantrums, only in a man's body and very often in a man's position of responsibility. He may even be your boss.

The man who is "just like a baby when he has a little pain" is in fact a baby asking for a mother's care, though he is a grown man. The woman who spends forty dollars for a new hat and then finds she cannot pay her butcher is the same little girl who ate all her party candy at once and then cried because the other children still had some to enjoy later on.

More often we cover up our childishness, as much from ourselves as from others. Our devices for hiding our immaturities are cunning, and it is hard for us to discover them.

Yet we must not be discouraged in our search for them. An emotional immaturity is a weakness in structure, and under stress the weaknesses show. Even without extraordinary stress, our immaturities may exact a constant price from us in happiness and achievement.

On the other hand, we are rewarded for the toil of achieving maturity. In proportion to the effort we make, we feel ourselves freed of the dragging burden of our childishness. It is as though we can put down at last the heavy baby we have carried, as though the childish hand which has clung to ours has loosed its grip, and the childish footsteps which have slowed our pace have ceased at last to follow us.

Some Common Immaturities:
The Eager-to-Please

The more the students of childhood tell us about children, the better able we are to penetrate the immaturities which persist into adulthood. Some childish patterns are so commonly found in adult behavior that we can label them immediately— in other people. We are naturally slower to recognize them in ourselves, and some of us refuse to recognize them at all.

A powerful motive in children is the need for approval, especially the approval of adults. In a child this is readily understandable. He is dependent on the good will of grownups for his continued care and protection. He is constantly confronted with the necessity of meeting adult standards. His behavior is good if it pleases his parents. His school work is good if it satisfies his teachers.

As he grows to maturity, this need for outside approval should diminish in proportion as he develops his own standards. The desire for approval cannot disappear entirely, since we are human and gregarious. Each of us needs to be accepted in some community, whether it be the family, the office or factory, the congregation or neighborhood.

The mature adult achieves a balance between his own standards and those of his community. The immature adult, however, continues to live for the approval of others, even at the sacrifice of his own needs and wishes. He is thus thrown into conflict with himself. The needs which he buries are in conflict with his outer behavior, which is designed to satisfy others, not himself.

We know about people who "grow away from each other." At the end of the war many young wives and husbands who had been separated came together to discover that they were not the same as they had been. Sometimes a separation has the effect of freeing one or the other partner from having to live up to the other's expectations of him. A separation plus a profound experience such as war service—or, equally, the wife's experience of carrying on alone at home—may be genuinely maturing.

If the two young people can accept each other's new status as more mature individuals, then their marriage will flower in ways which were unlikely before. If one or the other cannot make the adjustment to the new relationship, then the partnership founders, and indeed many such marriages did.

The question you must ask yourself is not whether you need to be liked and approved by one person or many in your life, because you have a right to this need. The question is, how much do you depend on this approval? How much of yourself will you sacrifice to win it? How much are your decisions and your behavior governed by the desire to please others, not yourself?

Child psychologists tell us that the child who is too obedient is often in greater difficulties than the one who expresses his rebellion by antisocial behavior. In adults this can be equally true. The adult who conforms too docilely to the standards of his class or group or parents, who never dares to express his individuality, is also likely to be in difficulties. His way to maturity is to learn to understand and respect his own needs as an individual, and to overcome his fear of expressing them.

If this seems difficult—and for the cautious conformist, the Mr. Milquetoast, it really is difficult—then he should remember that he can begin in little ways. The smallest assertion of himself will give him courage to attempt the next one. If he makes his small self-assertions pleasantly, not as an attack on the other person involved but genuinely for his own positive reasons—

and in a spirit of being willing to take part and do his share—
then he is likely to find himself not less popular, but more respected in consequences.

Sometimes an individual will go through his whole adult life
unconsciously trying to earn the approval of a parent, or to
prove that parent wrong. I know a woman who is beautiful and
very successful in her social aspirations. She has been courted
by men of world importance, has become wealthy through
marriage and is accepted in the most exclusive circles of international society. She has made one socially acceptable marriage after another, but has been unable to find happiness in
any.

This woman was born in an obscure middle-class family in
a small American town. She has achieved the success she
sought solely by her own efforts. Her tragedy is that she does
not believe in her achievement and cannot enjoy it. When as a
girl she dreamed of such a life as she now leads, her mother
warned her, "You will never make anything of yourself." It
seems that she has spent her whole life trying to prove her
mother wrong. The constant need to assert her self-importance
above any man with whom she begins a relationship soon defeats the relationship.

Unhappily it is true that standards are often set for us in
childhood which we can never meet. Must we let this poison
our whole life? Can we not try, by self-searching, to exorcise
this need to prove ourselves worthy to a father or mother
whom we should long ago have outgrown?

Rebel for Rebellion's Sake

Peer Gynt sailed the seven seas, vainly searching for happiness, unable to accept the necessity for conforming to any society. He is the symbol of perpetual adolescent rebellion as
Peter Pan is the symbol of refusing to grow up. A young patient of mine set out to find happiness by crossing the country
on horseback. This was his second great idea. His first great

idea was to write a new philosophy which would replace all previous philosophies. He accomplished neither.

There are slippery corners in all our lives, points at which a wholesome drive may be deflected into unproductive channels. The need to rebel against authority and find our own way is a good and healthy one, just as the need to work and earn our own living is a good and healthy one. But the boy who sets out to earn his living may turn into the man who wants money for money's sake, or for the power that money may bring. Just so, the child who rebels in order to reach his own full development may turn into a rebel for rebellion's sake, without cause and without direction.

The rebel who channels his efforts toward a goal may become a great reformer, a leader, a breaker of new trails in man's struggle to improve himself. Menninger's clinic reports that those who were rebellious children make good psychiatrists. But the rebel who is only running *away from something* and never *toward something* is wasting himself. His sturdy spirit is arrested at an immature stage, with the result that his potentiality for effective achievement in the world is thrown away.

Most of us do not run away. Most of us remain in the home, the job, or the marriage to which we are committed, and nourish our rebellion in secret. This is a real danger point. Unacknowledged rebellion is, as we have seen, the beginning of many an illness. It is a free grant of power to the destructive drive to turn against the self. It is a constant whittling away at the very sources of the will to live.

Attention-Getters

One of the French poets, it is said, dyed his hair green, in the latter part of the nineteenth century when green hair was only one of the milder efforts to shock the complacency of a Victorian world.

Some individuals will go to any length to attract attention.

I read a story from the London *Times* of a century ago, describing the performance of a criminal at his own execution.

He had dressed with great care for the occasion. His proud, graceful walk to the gallows was made to the accompaniment of vociferous admiration from the crowd. At the foot of the gallows he bowed with great dignity, received a torrent of applause and cheers, and climbed grandly to his death as the fitting climax of the greatest moment of his life.

Hangings are no longer public, but opportunities for attention-getting are far from lacking. Recently a dowager was pictured on front pages across the country when she put her feet on a table at a Metropolitan Opera première. A jealous rival for attention stood on his head for the photographers outside the opera house. In another city a woman was photographed carrying a basket of ripe tomatoes with which she planned to assault a concert artist who had declined her invitation to dinner.

Fortunately for the dignity of mankind, not many of us take such extreme measures in the effort to achieve distinction. But some of the subtler ways we take are far more damaging to ourselves. There are people, both men and women, who devote most of their adult lives to being seen with celebrities and claiming to know famous persons by their first names. I know at least one woman who will drive her husband and herself to exhaustion and perhaps bankruptcy in order to live like her wealthy friends, with a large expensive home staffed with cook, butler, and maid. She does no useful work herself, because the women by whom she craves to be accepted do not work.

The need to be noticed by association with the rich or famous betrays a sad lack of faith in our own worth. The need to attract attention by being different is a confession of profound self-doubt, just as taking refuge in perfect conventionality betrays a lack of self-confidence.

I can think of one example of an attention-getter who was nevertheless true to himself. When I was a boy in school a new youngster joined our class. Tall for his fourteen years and thin as a lath, he wore a pince-nez with a little chain, and English knickers though they were not yet in fashion. The fact that his father was a well-known novelist did not impress his classmates. But this boy found a way to impress us.

An ordinary boy would toss a nickel or a dime in the air. Left severely alone during recess in the school yard, this boy tossed a twenty-dollar gold piece. When it fell and rolled away he did not leap for it, but nonchalantly walked to the spot, kicked the dirt away, and stooped with languid indifference to recover the coin. It did not take long for him to be accepted as one of the leaders in our group. But once accepted, he proved himself a worthy member, no sissy but as able to take the rough-and-tumble as any of us. He has since become a successful film producer.

The Poor in Love

Love is said to be a cure for everything, but many adults are not capable of love. They confuse love with possessiveness, clutching at the loved one and giving little in return. They treat love like securities, to be kept in a vault but never used.

Some are afraid to give love, as though it were money and if you gave it away you would have no more. Or they are afraid of rejection, of ridicule of hurt, or of a foreign invasion. Or they express a contempt for love as a weakness, like the woman patient who described her suitor as a weakling because he had not been able to resist falling in love with her. Is she really contemptuous of love? Or is she rather afraid, seeing in his expression of love a demand for her to give love in return?

People rarely die of love like the woman in our second chapter, but many dry up for lack of it. I have been watching a patient, a young widow, for several years. She is drying up physically. Her skin is dry, her hair is dry and thinning, her fingernails are dry and brittle. Her whole personality is drying up. Even her income is drying up, because she mistrusts the people who could help her with her investments.

She says, "I haven't had my share of happiness. Someone will come along." But she has not gone out to find that someone.

Instead she withdraws still further. When a man shows interest in her, she at once begins to destroy the relationship by arguing, trying to prove herself his superior. She offends men by her aggressive prudery even before they make any approach to her. Her friends have warned her, but she is superior to her friends too, and gradually she is losing them. She wondered why, one day, she found in her young son's pocket a piece of stale bread. She could not understand that the boy, too, was suffering from her inability to give love, and had taken the bread with the plan of running away from home.

This woman is a deeply unhappy person who defeats herself completely, even to rejecting the medical help which might save her. Many people defeat themselves in love, though not to such a degree. They are people who did not learn in childhood how to give love.

We learn in childhood to give love if we are first loved by our parents or by those who stand in the relationship of parents to us. Well, then, perhaps you were not loved enough as a child. Unconsciously you resent your parents' lack of love for you, but unconsciously you are visiting that same lack of love on others now. If you have children, you may be failing to love them as your parents failed to love you. Must the chain of lovelessness go on unbroken from generation to generation? And must you live out your life without love, because you never had enough of it to begin with?

A child is born selfish. He is the center of his own small universe. Others, like his parents, are important only as they give to him, as they satisfy his needs. As he matures he learns to share his parents' care with his brothers and sisters, his toys with other children, his pleasures with other young people. He can do this if he is secure in his parents' love. If he is not sure of their love, he clings to the symbols of love: food, attention, toys. He clutches these to himself. He remains a selfish little animal. As a grown man he may make generous gifts to charity, but possibly this is only a cloak for his selfishness, for he has learned that to be obviously selfish is not socially acceptable.

To those closest to him, and in that coin which is least material and most valuable, he is still miserly.

How can such a person learn to give love? He can make a beginning by taking a different and more positive kind of interest in those around him. He can begin to look upon them, not for what he can get out of them, but for what will best help them to be themselves. He can turn his center of interest outward, and try to understand others—not merely some unidentified people whom he does not know and for whom it is easy to write out a check, but those whose love will really warm him if he can win it.

Until now this book has urged us to turn our eyes inward, on ourselves. But sometimes the first effort we must make in self-discovery is to turn our eyes outward, on those around us. In learning to give love, we must first learn the needs of those around us.

Johnny Appleseed strode through the country, planting the seeds of trees of which others would enjoy the fruit. He is a homely symbol of love freely and lavishly given, and he lives in the legend as not only a good man, but a happy man.

And I remember a story in a school book about a man who had the finest apple tree in his county. All year he nursed and tended his tree, but when the apples were ripe and the boys climbed the wall and stole them, he did not stop them. He wanted the boys to have not only the apples but also the fun of stealing them.

Learning to give love is like learning to use a new skill. At first we feel awkward, perhaps frightened. It is necessary to go slowly, to work in small, familiar, even trivial ways, and not to be discouraged if the response is slow in coming. We cannot change a pattern of years with a single gesture, an occasional word. But love freely given, without strings attached, without even a demand for thanks or gratitude, will sooner or later win love in return.

_____ SUMMING UP _____

Childishness is a heavy burden to carry through adult life.

✦ ✦ ✦

To indulge one's childish needs is to deprive oneself of mature gratifications.

✦ ✦ ✦

The recognition of one's particular childishness is a step in outgrowing it.

17

Cultivating the Will to Live

The enjoyment of both work and play are
symptoms of a flourishing will to live.

THE LIST of common immaturities in adults could go on and on; by now the reader may be adding his own observations of childishness in grownups he knows.

We meet immature adults in the office, store, and factory: the executive who surrounds himself with yes-men, like the willful child who must have his own way; the floater who keeps changing jobs, like the child who is always beginning projects and never finishing them; the slave to routine, like the child who is upset if things are not always done the same way.

We meet them in the home: the husband who is always reminding his family how hard he works for them, the wife who makes her housework a martyrdom. I know a woman whose husband provides her with a maid all week, but who cannot join the family outings on Sunday because that is the day she does the laundry.

We all know men who work nights as well as days. Such a man might ask himself whether his long hours of work are really necessary. Any business or profession may require occasional periods of intense work. But to drive oneself to work grimly day and night, month after month raises the question whether there is not something more behind this compulsion than the need to earn a living or the ambition to make a mark in a profession. An enslavement to work that leaves no time for leisure, family, friends, may be destructive rather than creative.

We know people who cannot make up their own minds, like the man who asks his wife which suit he should wear, or the woman who goes shopping for a dress, looks at suits, actually buys a coat—and returns it the next day because a woman friend was critical of it.

Why we are as we are is less important than whether we recognize ourselves. It is no shame to be immature in one way or another. The human being is a complex creature in a complex world, and it takes him a long time to grow up.

From time to time we may be aware of a childish trait, but it is easier to suffer an hour or so of remorse and self-criticism, and to bury the weakness out of sight again, than it is to make the effort to revise it. With the effort we waste covering up our weaknesses we could make quite a lot of progress toward working them out constructively.

What is lacking, generally, is the incentive to make the effort. We do not realize the price we pay in happiness. We do not estimate the loss we suffer in productivity. We do not face the danger we run of illness.

A buried dissatisfaction with life leads to fatigue, to irritability, to inefficiency. A failure or rejection leads to worry, fear, and tensions, which in turn lead to more failure and more rejection. We pay the price in happiness and achievement first; the body's illness is likely to follow more slowly.

Boredom and Health

Boredom can be a serious illness. Boredom is that invisible disease caused neither by germs nor toxins, nor by organic change. It is the mental counterpart of that physical state which we call fatigue. Boredom can be chronic or acute.

Acute boredom can arise from discontent with a given situation. The company or the occupation does not suit you, or there is somewhere else you would rather be, someone else you would rather be with. It may be a stage in creative work, the time before the birth of an idea, the fallow period when we are regenerating. Acute boredom is temporary boredom and not necessarily a sign of trouble.

Chronic boredom is serious. It is an evidence that the creative drive has surrendered and the will to live has handed in its resignation. Boredom is a total absence of the incentive to go on living. But whether or not we accept the fate of dying of boredom, either metaphorically or in fact, is eventually up to ourselves.

We can reverse the decision and cure ourselves of the disease of boredom, but only if we will take rational action against the symptoms and make an earnest examination for the cause.

Well-being has its symptoms too, of joy, kindness, and interest in life and people. A healthy adult, like a healthy child, has energy left over for play. A healthy adult, like a healthy child, is interested and curious and wants to learn things and do things. It is normal to enjoy your work and the rewards it brings, both the material rewards and the satisfaction of achievement and recognition. The enjoyment of both work and play are symptoms of a flourishing will to live.

It is true that our complex industrial civilization offers less and less scope for the majority to find individual creative expression. Many of us must work at routine occupations and many of us do work which we do not enjoy.

The solution to the problem is still the same: fight or flight. Either we deal with the situation aggressively and find a rational solution within it, or we get out. We do not resign ourselves to it, if resignation means, as it usually does, that we remain in the situation while secretly rebelling against it. That way is suicidal.

A young dentist complained that he was unhappy in his profession, and particularly in his work as an assistant in a large fashionable office catering to wealthy patients. His gall bladder was giving him trouble, he was subject to dizziness and spells of faintness, and it was obvious that he could not continue in work against which he was in such protest that it was making him ill. He wanted to be a writer. But he had a wife and young child to support. He received treatment for his symptoms, and in the course of his visits I suggested that he might try to find a workable solution, one which would not jeopardize his integrity.

He found his solution. He moved his family to a small town where the cost of living is considerably less than in the metropolis. His house is tiny and almost bare. He keeps limited office hours for patients, just enough to pay his living expenses, and devotes the rest of the time to writing. His first novel had a fine reception, and he is working on his second. The austerity of his life troubles him not at all. He is a happier young man, and a healthier one.

His solution combined both fight and flight. He escaped from the particular conditions of work which were unacceptable to him. At the same time he found a way of combining the professional earning of a living with the work he wanted to do.

Not many of us are so fortunate as to have another kind of interest which we are longing and able to follow. But if we must remain in work which gives us no joy, then we must make a *positive adjustment* in our lives. We must make the unsatisfactory work a part of a more satisfactory whole. We must seek ways of spending our leisure time which will give expression to those creative forces to which our work does not give scope. To ignore this need for expression, to refuse the choice of fight or flight, is self destructive.

The same is true in our attitudes toward home and family, toward parents and children, toward marriage and our marriage partner and our parents-in-law. *Resignation is not adjustment.* The only true adjustment, the one for which the human mind and body are equipped, lies in the choice between fight, which is an effort at adjustment, and flight, which is the act of getting out of an unwholesome situation.

Resignation does not end our dissatisfaction. We do not "forget it." We only stifle the open protest. We bury the conflict—and thus give our dissatisfaction the greater power to do us harm.

When we say we resent our work or our marriage because we have no success or happiness in it, we may be stating the case the wrong way 'round. We may first resent it, and therefore fail to make a success of it. We tend to wait passively for someone or something outside ourselves to change. We try to reform a husband or revise the personality of a wife. But we cannot change other people. We can change only ourselves.

Some people extricate themselves from one unsatisfactory relationship only to enter another and divorce one wrong partner only to turn to a similar one. But most of us make the effort, with more or less success, to learn from our mistakes. Critical events can change us. A serious accident or illness, sudden wealth or the loss of it, a birth or a death among those close to us—such experiences may push us with the shock of strong emotion either farther along on the path of maturity, or backward toward less capacity to deal with life. It is obvious that the better an individual understands himself, the more capably he can deal with the big and little events of living.

Each human being has his specific way of reacting to situations. The difference between the normal and the neurotic is one only of degree. The normal itself offers quite a spread. The medical normal in blood pressure, blood sugar, metabolism, height and weight, is never a single point like 98.6 on the thermometer, but a spread between two figures. To find oneself somewhat outside the normal spread occasionally is not necessarily serious. An occasional limp is not an illness.

Everyone becomes confused now and then, stuck in a dead-end road, not knowing which next step to take. To run away from ourselves at such times is to court confusion as a permanent state. Precisely in time of stress is when our personality weaknesses show. Precisely then is when we have most to gain from examining ourselves.

The difficulties we encounter in life are not insoluble. If we cannot find a solution through either fight or flight, then our thinking about the situation is faulty. A situation with no possible solution is rare in real life. Usually, we fail to discover the solution because it is one which we are unwilling to accept: that of making a positive adjustment.

Our refusal to face a solution is nourished by our own destructive drive. To resist solution is to destroy oneself.

Preparing for Later Years

As our birthdays mark the passing of youth, the will to live is apparently challenged by a failing body.

We can seriously question whether it is really the body which fails. We can ask whether we have not unconsciously crippled the will to live in our earlier years, even before we reach our prime.

A significant observation was made by one of my teachers, the physiologist Rubner, in a study of the physical symptoms of aging. Rubner found that the average man does not begin to age merely in his later years. The first signs of physical aging actually come *at the beginning of his adult life,* about the time when most people finish school and settle down to the practice of a chosen occupation.

This early aging of the body, Rubner explains, is the result of "narrowing the mental horizon, sinking into . . . purely occupational tasks, neglecting any further development of the self."

This self-limitation reveals its full destructiveness when a man retires from his business or profession. He finds that without his work he has nothing to do. He has no interests, no direction, actually no reason to continue living. It is, therefore, not surprising that so many men, vigorous until they retire, fail rapidly afterward.

"Knowledge and timber," said Oliver Wendell Holmes,

"should not be used until they are seasoned." But Dr. Holmes did not intend that we should never use them at all. By the time knowledge should have seasoned into the wisdom of maturity, most people have given up both the acquisition of knowledge and the use of it. Most adults tend to live, not by knowledge, but by the set patterns of habit.

Childhood and youth are periods of many interests and activities. A characteristic of the normal child is his eagerness to learn and explore. Youth has the privilege of rushing forth to make its own discoveries, without thought and without plan. But there is no natural law which prevents the mature man from continuing to explore and discover. Only, because he is mature, it is characteristic that he should first stop to consult with himself on the why, where, and how.

Most of us, however, shed not only the rashness of youth, but also youth's eagerness to discover. When we reach what is hopefully called the age of reason, when we finish our youthful preparation for the way in which we will earn our living, then we discard most of the activities and interests of our youth, even though they could continue to give us both pleasure and profit. We put them aside, we say, until we have more time. This is the moment at which we begin to grow fatty tissues in our muscles.

How many musical instruments, how many collections and handicraft tools, how many skis and skates, bats and balls, books, records, albums are gathering dust in your attic? How many arts and skills are withering in you, not from aging, but from neglect?

Often we throw these things aside in a gesture of rebellion. We are thumbing our noses at authority. Many a graduate hurls his books into the farthest corner vowing that he will never look at another book. I know I did.

But once the smoke of rebellion has settled, there is great satisfaction in picking up some study again, one that either enriches one's daily work or deepens the enjoyment of leisure hours. In the pages of a book we share the ripe fruits of another's work, thought, and experience.

But leisure for such joys seems an unwarranted indulgence to a young person obsessed with the demand that he make good. He has been warned many times that life is not meant to be easy.

In his anxiety to be adult he puts on the trimmings of maturity. He smokes and drinks like his elders. He represses his young hopes under cynical talk. He plays bridge instead of baseball. He carries a brief case as though this will magically make him a man of affairs. His old interests seem childish; they threaten his new dignity. He makes a clean sweep, not stopping to question which things really are childish.

Resting or Rusting?

Mountain climbing is a strenuous, perilous sport, a young man's sport. But a man who continues climbing can enjoy the exhilarating sport far into his late years. Rubner mentions the number of men who are good mountain-climbers at sixty and sixty-five. As a young man traveling in the glacial heights of Switzerland, I was myself amazed at the aged Englishmen who gathered at the mountain resorts for the season's climbing. If these men had stopped climbing in their twenties or thirties, postponing this pleasure until they had more time, they would never have climbed again.

Making up for lost time solely on vacations and weekends is not, however, the way to keep muscles young. We don't need to prove that we are still young by playing three sets of tennis in an afternoon after not playing for a year. Exertion in spurts is a dangerous risk for people in their middle years. We keep our bodies young, not by putting intermittent violent strain on them, but by using them habitually in enjoyable physical activity.

While muscles which are used do not age until late in life, a mind which is used need never age at all. The idea that learning stops with the end of the school years denies us knowledge and pleasure. It is also self-destructive. It invites old age.

The belief that only young people can learn has been thoroughly disproved by the current flowering of adult education in this country. People in their middle and late years who want to learn, and who are not ashamed to learn, have no trouble in learning. Adults who never touched a musical instrument, or who were forcibly exposed to one in childhood, are learning to play music for pleasure now that they turn to it of their own free will.

I know a man in his sixties who recently began to study philosophy. He took private tutoring and graduate courses, and has collected a library which is a pride and pleasure to him. A grandmother at the age of seventy-eight won her college degree, with her seven children and twenty grandchildren present at her commencement.

The sharpness of George Bernard Shaw's wit was not dulled even at ninety.

When we stop learning, we begin to grow old. When we stop being interested, we begin to grow old. When we stop using our bodies, we begin to grow old. There is no physiological age at which we must stop all activity. Hence there is no age at which we *must* grow old. Like Shaw, we can be fully alive until we die. We need never be old.

The interests, arts and skills which we recklessly toss away on entering adulthood may be the very tonics which could lift us over the darkest moments of our life. If we put them aside until we have leisure to pursue them, then we are inviting old age before our time. When at last we come to the advanced years, when the sharpest struggles are over and we are freed to enjoy the fruits of our life's labor, there may no longer be any fruits to enjoy. We have let them wither, long before. All our efforts to prolong life may mean that we do not live longer, but only die more slowly.

With science each year adding new length to the average life span, a new branch of medicine has been developing to preserve our health and enrich our lives during these added years. Geriatrics specializes in the diseases of old age. Gerontology is the branch of research devoted to old age. A mass of data from research and practical work with old people has already accumulated. All our knowledge points inescapably to the need for preparation during our young and middle years of interests and attitudes which will maintain us in health during these added years. Dr. Harry Benjamin in the magazine *American Medicine* pointed out that the problem is not to add years to our life, but to add life to our years.

Second Childhood

There is another aspect of aging, which is not merely emptiness or dullness but actual deterioration. It has occurred to me that those old people who have reached the second childhood of senility may have been just as childish all their lives as they reveal themselves to be in old age.

When a man must deal with the world as an adult, he is obliged to hide his immaturity behind a front of seemingly adult behavior. If he has position and prestige, if he becomes rich, the childishness he may show is tolerantly called eccentricity; he is a "character." In old age there is no longer the necessity nor the energy to maintain the front, and such a man may revert to his true childish self. He could not grow old with dignity, because he never grew up.

Otherwise how shall we explain the fact that some old people do not become senile, but maintain to their last day the dignity and wisdom which properly belong to advanced years? Oddly, we often find that these beautiful old people also retain their physical faculties. They see and hear, and their minds are not only tolerant and kind but also alert. They are rare people, and they are memorable.

Many of us cherish the image of such a grandparent or wise old family friend. We remember with gratitude having known such a person, although we may be mystified to explain the basis of his or her unique quality.

I will make bold to say that the reason is not mysterious. I believe that a man or woman who grows old beautifully is one who has achieved maturity. Such a person may have been gifted with a fortunate constitution at birth, or may have had a

nurturing environment. It is just as possible that he or she over-
came by great effort a disadvantage of birth or environment,
or a critical experience in youth. If we were to know everything
about the lives of such people, we would find, I am certain,
clues to the maturity which illuminates their old age.

I believe that to grow old in dignity and wisdom we must
first grow up. We must deal with those immaturities left in us
from childhood. We cannot merely hide them, or trust passively that years of living will do away with them. We must
consciously seek maturity by making that positive adjustment
to living which is maturity.

To live long, not only in years but in the enjoyment of them,
we must understand and control the forces which shorten
life. Both early and late, we must take time to cultivate the will
to live.

―――――――――――― SUMMING UP ――――――――――

Many grow old before they grow up.

❀   ❀   ❀

*Staying young means keeping up the active interests of
youth.*

❀   ❀   ❀

The mind, like the muscles, grows flabby with disuse.

❀   ❀   ❀

An active and interested mind never grows old.

❀   ❀   ❀

*"The measure of man's life is not the length but the well-
spending of it," said Plutarch.*

IV

The Doctor
as Teacher

*You cannot teach a man anything;
you can only help him to find it
within himself.*

GALILEO

18

Teaching the Patient to Be Well

A human being is something more than the sum of our medical specialties.

THE IDEA of medicine in people's minds is a ragout of what they hear and what they read, seasoned with childhood impressions, left-over superstition, and old wives' tales. But the solid content of what they know about medicine is learned from their doctors.

The doctor holds a unique position. Among the motives which lead him to choose his exacting profession is the idealistic wish to serve. For the layman the word "doctor" has emotional overtones. It is touched with the mystery of childhood's belief in magic and its accompanying awe. When we were children the doctor was an almighty personage called in times of anxious need and capable of performing miracles.

He was more powerful than other adults, more powerful even than parents. A mother or father could be struck down, sick and helpless in bed, but the doctor always appeared robust and hearty, with the fresh cheeks of outdoors. He went confidently about his ritual, dispelling anxiety, spreading an air of comfort. He made us feel that all would be well now that he was there.

We remember fear and anger, too, when he pressed down our tongue and stuck a needle into our flesh. To some he was a threat: "If you don't take your cod liver oil I'll call the doctor!" In other people's minds the doctor has inherited the mantle of the high priest, and some physicians are not averse to trying it on now and then.

Yet the physician is not made of material different from other human beings. He is subject to the same natural laws, the same feelings and reactions as any other man.

In his own life the physician is not spared stress. He has the same anxieties and conflicts, the same alternating hope and depression as other men. Finally, a doctor seems more disposed than the average man to die of an illness which we consider "unnatural"—that is, premature—such as a heart attack.

We know that he carries the burden of anxiety for his patients in addition to the problems all other people have. We may suppose that his profession sharpens for him the conflict experienced by conscientious men in many fields, the conflict between ideals and the practical demands of living. His economic struggle is made acute by the frequent inability of his patients to pay. Many a doctor is confronted almost daily with a choice between the need for his services, regardless of fee, and the needs of his own family. When Talleyrand said that a married man will do anything for money, he was only exaggerating a bitter truth.

Doctors too must struggle to make their adjustments to life. They hide anxiety and insecurity. We have doctors who are emotionally mature and doctors who are immature. Their immaturity does not necessarily make them bad doctors. It does however, put them under greater stress in their work. It makes a good doctor-patient relationship more difficult to achieve.

A doctor absorbs a great deal of childish behavior from his patients and sometimes he retorts in the same spirit. Many a patient limps away from the doctor's office, his ego bruised, forgetting that he himself threw the first snowball, remembering only that the answering snowball felt twice as big, with a rock inside it.

The doctor has voluntarily chosen a life of dedication. Yet not all doctors can be expected to have the strength of a Kant, who lived up to what he wrote at twenty-two, "I have already fixed upon the line which I am resolved to keep. I will enter on my course and nothing shall prevent me from pursuing it."

Patients are not inclined to see the doctor as a human being, fallible and subject to weakness. They do not want to see him in any disappointing human form. For many patients the doctor is the last substitute they can find for a father. They cling to their belief that he will look after them, will see that nothing bad happens to them. Each one likes to think that *his* doctor will take care of everything with his little pills and his magic injections.

Though they cannot expect the doctor to be superhuman, they have every right to expect him to be superior, not only in his skill and knowledge, but in his humanity. Unlike most other professions, the doctor deals almost exclusively with people in trouble. The patient and his family are frightened, confused, full of anxiety and tension. They must put their trust in the doctor; they have no other recourse. The patient's family are often more difficult for the doctor to treat than the patient himself. Nevertheless we do not allow our doctor the right to an outburst of temper, or a cold indifference.

Illness brings out the best in some people, and in others the worst. Doctors speak of good patients and bad patients. The good patient is quiet, docile, grateful, and moreover he responds well to treatment. The bad patient demands explanations, comes up continually with new complaints, takes the doctor's time, and worst of all, his symptoms are as stubborn as himself.

The doctor must be prepared to deal wisely with both types. The word "doctor" comes from the Latin word meaning "to teach, to instruct." For many years now doctors have seen no actual need to teach their patients how to be well. The doctor felt he could depend on his highly developed methods of testing and prescribing.

Ours is an age of experts, each trained in a particular part of a most complicated whole. We gratefully acknowledge the necessity of scientific research in modern medicine. But we must face the danger of getting lost in the details.

A human being is something more than the sum of our medical specialties. The physician has to see his patient as someone whose life situation may delay or prevent his recovery despite all the doctor's scientific skill.

Medicine as Service

A physician who does not feel a sympathy for individual human beings should not feel obliged to practice. There is a need for pure scientists in medicine, for research men whose intellectual gifts can make enormous contributions to the cause of health. A man who is not emotionally dedicated to medicine can achieve the rewards of his intellect in those fields. He should not subject himself to the tensions of dealing with people.

Why must the physician be dedicated above most other professions? Not so much because of the long years of training, nor even because, both waking and sleeping, he is at the mercy of his patient's needs and, sometimes, whims. He must be dedicated principally because the material of his work is not drugs nor mechanical appliances, not chemistry nor physiology, although he must use all these. The material of his work is human beings.

He cannot afford to indulge in impatience or intolerance. He cannot make moral judgments on his patients' behavior. He cannot preach. He may not approve or disapprove. He must only help.

Medicine is not a business. It is a service. Most doctors accept it as such. My professor of anatomy started his first lecture in this wise: "Gentlemen, before we begin, I want you to take serious thought. Any one of you who is guided by motives other than devotion can still withdraw from medicine. Banking is a better profession in which to make money."

Most doctors are not rich men. Most doctors enter upon

their profession without any expectation of wealth. They hope to be able to make a living. In this reasonable expectation, the doctor who is truly dedicated to his work is not likely to be disappointed.

The patient is not necessarily impressed by a fine office and showy evidence of a prosperous practice. On many patients this atmosphere has a chilling effect. They are repelled by the suggestion of mass production.

I had a young patient, the heiress of one of the country's great enterprises. When she was approaching the final months of her pregnancy she declined the services of a city obstetrician and went to a small New England village.

"I want a country doctor," she said. "I don't want a big production. I want a normal delivery, and a normal baby."

The patient cannot judge the doctor's skill and knowledge. These he must take on faith. But he can judge the doctor's attitude toward him. He can feel the doctor's interest in him as an individual.

To this interest the average patient responds. When he knows that the doctor is laboring unreservedly in his behalf, the patient will generally give his cooperation, his gratitude, and his loyalty. Even a very rebellious patient, hostile and unmanageable, is likely to return again and again to the doctor who does not answer hostility with hostility, but who continues to work in the patient's own interest.

How the patient responds to this attitude in a doctor, even during a first interview, is described by Binger in *The Doctor's Job:*

> In the course of such an interview something transpires. The patient reacts to being listened to with a certain half-perceived feeling, which he may indicate with look, gesture, or word. What does this mean? It means, I think, this: "I am in trouble. I need help. I have found someone who cares and who wants to help me."

The doctor's reward is first a security in his practice. Since, for all his ideals, he must still pay his bills, this is a matter of no small importance.

But he has a deeper reward than the economic, deeper even than the satisfaction of work well done. It is in what he gets back from his patients in depth of fellowship and breadth of human understanding. The doctor can learn medicine out of books, but the practice of medicine he learns from his patients.

The Doctor's New Job

Where must you go to find such doctors?

Most doctors are like that. The big-city specialist, separated from his patients by this very specialty, is not typical. In rural areas, in small towns and cities, in the neighborhoods and suburbs of the metropolis itself, doctors give themselves thus freely and devotedly as a matter of course.

The doctor now stands at a turning point in his profession. A century ago the emphasis in medicine changed from the art of healing to the techniques of science. Today doctors are conscious of the need to combine the scientist with the healer.

Until now, the physical and psychological sciences of medicine have seemed to be in opposition. Now they meet and fuse, and their fusion will be felt most profoundly by the general practitioner.

An impressive practical demonstration of how the general practitioner is preparing himself to meet this new demand was begun some years ago in Cincinnati, where the Department of Medicine and Psychiatry of the University's College of Medicine and the Cincinnati General Hospital joined forces in a psychosomatic clinic for medical residents and fellows.

The success of the clinic from the patients' point of view was clear from the minimum number of sign-outs; that is, of patients who voluntarily gave up coming to the clinic although they were not well enough to be discharged.

Seventy-five per cent of the patients had physical disorders such as hypertension, various types of organic heart disease, asthma, peptic ulcer, diabetes, skin diseases, migraine, epilepsy, hyperthyroidism, obesity. The remaining twenty-five per cent had primarily neurotic disorders, that is, the symptoms of which they complained showed no physical evidence.

The majority of the patients improved. About half the patients were able to return to almost normal life at home and at work.

What is most significant, however, is the reported effect on the doctors: "For the first time, the medical residents began to develop feelings of stability and security in dealing with patients who have emotional disorders." They were not upset by the behavior of patients, once they understood the cause of it. They observed how even a most difficult, belligerent patient calmed down before tolerant kindliness in the doctor.

The resident physicians found that most patients are willing to talk about many vital personal matters "if the physician not only listens but by his accepting attitude conveys the impression that such material is important and meaningful in the general medical illness from which they suffer."

In every way the relationship between doctor and patient was humanized. The patient always came to his own doctor, instead of to just any doctor who happened to be on duty and available. The interview was personal, not conducted before a group of students with the patient as a guinea pig for the purpose of instruction. Compare this with the practice of psychiatric clinics in many hospitals, where the whole spirit of psychiatry is defeated by the use of the patient for demonstration.

The necessity for "maintaining the patient's dignity, self-respect, self-esteem" was stressed. The doctor was expected, and was given the opportunity, to develop a real interest in the patient as a human being. The "basic reassurance stems from the patient's conscious and unconscious awareness of the strength, integrity, and *sincerity of purpose* of the physician," the report points out. (Italics mine.)

Out of such promising experiments the future of the general practitioner emerges as far more satisfying than it has ever been. He will find that he is doing a better medical job. His insight into the patient's personality and the background of the case will guide him in his purely medical therapy. He will attach his patients more securely to him. He may win back to medicine the lost sheep who have wandered to "healers" for understanding.

_____ SUMMING UP _____

Doctors in the past have been first healers, then scientists; the doctor of the future is both scientist and healer.

❋   ❋   ❋

The true meaning of "doctor" is "teacher"; his task is not only to cure, but to teach his patients how to be well.

19

It Is Easy to Hate,
but Healthier to Love

*There is no way to withdraw from member-
ship in the human race.*

LAPLACE is reputed to have said on his deathbed
that science was mere trifling, and nothing was real but love.

The historians who coin titles for the successive eras in man's
history may argue how to name our time. It has been called
the machine age. More recently it became the atomic age.
Man's advances until now have been materialistic for the most
part. In his quality of humanity he has made little progress.
He lives differently, dresses differently, travels differently, fights
differently. Tools and methods have changed but man himself
has remained basically the same.

Now we stand at the threshold of a new era, perhaps a crucial one. It should be named the Age of Ambivalence.

Ambivalence is a psychological term meaning the simultane-
ous existence within us of opposite emotions toward the same
object or person. We may be outwardly, consciously friendly,
and inwardly, unconsciously hostile at the same time.

Ours is the age which has discovered, by way of science,
that a man may speak with conviction of friendship and broth-

erhood, while inwardly he is moved by active antagonism. This two-sided oneness of man's strongest emotions, love and hate, was defined by Freud's contemporary, the Swiss psychiatrist Bleuler.

Today we are not content with calling the convulsive emotions of enmity, bias, bigotry, and intolerance merely "human nature." The Janus-like character of the emotions of love and hate give us the clue to man's contradictory behavior.

Ambivalence is a revelation. It explains man's darkest eras, those of persecution, of sadistic tribunals, the burning of witches, the extraction of confessions by torture, the killing of people en masse like vermin, and last, the burning of books, brain-washing, character-assassination, the destruction of individuality for the sake of submissive conformity, all in the name of progress.

With the new depths of insight given us through our understanding of the unconscious, man for the first time can examine his acts. He has now both the opportunity and the obligation to achieve real maturity. Before the judgment of history, man must henceforth willy-nilly assume responsibility for his deeds.

In the thousands of years of his childhood man could be irresponsible. He could follow his drive toward cruelty and destruction unpunished, not even understood except by a future century. Because he was a child, and knew not what he did, he could be forgiven.

Today he has no excuse. He cannot continue to be a man with the mind of a child. Emotional immaturity speaks with the voice of the beast, whatever the alleged noble cause it may put on as a garb.

It is a clear issue on which each one of us must take a stand. It is a question which none can evade. There is no way to withdraw from membership in the human race. There is no way not to participate in the common fate of man.

A sixteen-year-old who shoots three members of his family we recognize as a sick adolescent. A nineteen-year-old who stabbed seven and killed four is no longer dismissed as merely mad, a freak to be put in an asylum for the insane and forgotten.

Today we see in these desperate youths a reflection of all mankind. We understand at last that if either of them had had the intellect, the opportunity, the education, but no basic change of character, he could have achieved a position of power and wreaked his destruction on a world scale. We have seen the expression of hate and destruction on a world scale in our time. It cannot be brushed off as national insanity or national suicide.

It can happen again, as it has already happened. Man's destructive drive cannot be dealt with in terms of discipline or punishment, more policemen, more prisons, and more insane asylums. It cannot be isolated like leprosy or manacled like a criminal, because it exists to some extent in every human being. We must open our eyes to destructiveness everywhere. We must deal with it at its roots in human nature.

Those who declare that men are either good or evil are at best naïve, or else they themselves are the disciples of destruction. Those who say that there will always be wars because there have always been wars do not believe in the progress of mankind since they do not love mankind.

Human Nature Can Be Changed

Human nature can be changed. It is being changed. It has always been capable of change. Leaders have arisen in age after age, who have changed human beings into beasts, or into men. False propaganda can change friendly human nature to hatred, and truth can change enemies into friends.

Science shows us how the "human nature" of a child—self-centered, greedy, fearful, destructive, but also needing to be loved and to love, needing to be taught and to learn—is changed into a thoughtful, considerate, self-contained, mature man or woman. Science shows us also how that child can be arrested in his growth, and can carry with him into the recognized outer form of maturity the unsocialized instincts of the child. The child in a man's body, with a man's power, is the enemy which men of good will must seek out everywhere.

This realization, that man may be mature in body but in mind childish, that he may speak of creation but do destruction, gives us new measurements by which we may guide our evaluation of men and deeds, of beliefs, prejudices, and causes.

There are signs that man is growing up to the realization of his responsibilities. His ideals are no longer only the dreams of a few good men. They are the results of new and solid psychological gains.

What our new self-knowledge may do for mankind on a global scale is suggested in the report of the UNESCO Conference on World Tensions and the International Congress on Mental Health, held in London in August, 1948. The conclusions of the joint conference, as reported in the *Journal of the American Medical Association,* are based "on the premise that human emotions ('human nature') can now be scientifically studied, understood, and even changed, both for the individual and the group.

"Wars are not considered an inevitable consequence of human nature. Some needs are vital to all men. These include freedom from disease, insecurity, and fear. Men everywhere desire at the same time fellowship, respect of their fellow men, and a chance for personal growth and development."

What this conference suggests as a way to a better mental health may be broadened to include better physical health. Even the plagues which sweep men into death by the hundreds of thousands are now recognized as a concern not limited to the biologist and the sanitary engineer. There are causes behind the virulent germs, causes behind the unsanitary living conditions.

"Human history shows that [the] root [of epidemics] is not the epidemic disease but poor health," writes Dr. F. K. Meyer in *Global Strategy in Preventive Medicine.* "An epidemic of malaria in Ceylon was recorded after an economic depression, with an enormous mortality rate in a disease the cause of which is known and for which specific treatments are available . . .

Men fight not only because they are hungry, but because they want to extricate themselves from the cycle of sickness-hunger, hunger-sickness."

The influenza epidemic of 1918 followed upon four years of war and hunger in Europe. It is estimated that five hundred million people fell sick in that epidemic. Fifteen million of them died.

The World Health Organization's constitution begins: "The health of all people is fundamental to the attainment of peace and security and is dependent upon the fullest cooperation of individuals and states."

We curb the germs of epidemic disease, and the physical conditions in which such germs thrive and spread, on the same principle as we relieve the symptoms of illness in the individual, the fever and infection of the body. But simultaneously, we recognize the deeper causes. These are the causes with which it is our new responsibility to deal, tirelessly and vigorously, because now we know about them. We know how they work.

For or Against Mankind

"When men are friends," said Aristotle, "justice is unnecessary. But when men are just, friendship is still a boon."

Justice on a world scale is a present aspiration of men of good will, but justice is not enough. We will still need friendship, and understanding is the first step toward friendship. The more we understand ourselves and our neighbors, the greater is our hope of health, both as individuals and as a world. This is the new and greater task of the doctor, to teach us to know ourselves and each other.

Doctors have never shirked their responsibility. Prevention has always been the physician's hope. Preventive medicine has written an inspiring chapter in man's history. The physician wants to do more than put together bodies shattered by shellfire, bombs, and radioactive fall-out.

But the doctor cannot succeed without the patient. The fight against illness, as we have seen, is an alliance of doctor and patient. On the larger scale, the long struggle for world health, physical and mental, can be won only if we all work together toward that goal.

The issue is not of one political doctrine or another. The issue is for mankind or against it, for creation or destruction.

Voltaire said bitterly, that we all leave this world as foolish and as wicked as we found it. These words need not be forever true. As the new knowledge of man's ambivalence enables us to understand and thus work for health, it will enable us to understand and work for peace.

Peace and friendship grow from the same roots as health and happiness. As we strive for the one, we win the other. All are the flowers of a sturdy and vigorous will to live, in every man and in all men everywhere. To hate is easy, but it is healthier to love.

Index